THE VILLA OF DREAMS

LUCY COLEMAN

Boldwood

First published in Great Britain in 2020 by Boldwood Books Ltd.

A CIP catalogue record for this book is available from the British Library.

Paperback ISBN 978-1-83889-061-2

Hardback ISBN 978-1-80426-222-1

Large Print ISBN 978-1-83889-808-3

Ebook ISBN 978-1-83889-063-6

Kindle ISBN 978-1-83889-062-9

Audio CD ISBN 978-1-83889-059-9

MP3 CD ISBN 978-1-83889-805-2

Digital audio download ISBN 978-1-83889-060-5

Boldwood Books Ltd
23 Bowerdean Street
London SW6 3TN
www.boldwoodbooks.com

A heart felt 'thank you' to the wonderful people whose paths I crossed on my research trip – your generosity and kindness will stay with me forever. It's no wonder I fell in love with Lisbon...

PROLOGUE
OCTOBER

How many people are lucky – some might say foolhardy – enough to grab the chance of a fresh start? Well, I've been offered a job opportunity which is going to turn my whole life upside down. Three weeks today, I will be saying goodbye to the UK and jumping on a plane to Lisbon.

After working for my father for six years, the day that I finally decided I'd had enough and I handed him my letter of resignation, his reaction was one of disbelief.

'You're making a big mistake, Seren,' he warned me. 'Don't expect me to bail you out if things go wrong. It's a tough world out there and you've led a privileged life – you just don't appreciate that fact.'

With his words ringing in my ears, I walked out of the office feeling... free. You can't live life trying to please a man who uses a balance sheet as a measuring stick.

My father takes pride in the fact that he worked hard to build up his business, which allowed him to provide a good standard of living for his family. That makes him sound like a loving man, doesn't it? But somewhere along the way it changed him, and not for the better. In a sad twist of irony, the father I remember from my childhood was different – as a family man he was kinder, more forgiving and less driven. I can't remember when exactly he stopped appreciating the small things in life, but it's a loss I mourn.

Working for my father for the last six years has destroyed not only the relationship I have with him but has also meant stifling my own ambitions. And my poor mother is caught in the middle, her heart torn as the chasm grows between us all. My father longed for a son and instead he got a daughter. One who wanted to please him, until he side-lined me for a total stranger. Three months after Stuart Lang arrived, I resigned. He saw me as a threat and wasted a ridiculous amount of time and effort in systematically undermining every decision I made. Obviously, he wasn't quite as astute, or confident about his own abilities as my father perceived him to be. Mind you, my plans to leave were well in hand, even before his first day on the job.

It's time to pack up my things and put them in storage.

There is no looking back, only forwards from now on. It's up to me to manifest the sort of life I want to live and, yes, I'm a little scared, but it's also empowering.

PART I

JANUARY

1

KINDRED SOULS FOREVER

The sound of tinkling bells makes me snatch up my iPad and swipe right, placing it on the table next to my breakfast plate. The familiar face of my best friend, Judi, comes into view. We met on our first day at pre-school and being naturally shy and timid little souls, we gravitated towards each other. To this day, we have an unbreakable bond.

Judi had little support from her fractured family, who were all too caught up in the constant battle between warring parents and stepparents. I, on the other hand, was being moulded by a father who wanted to control every aspect of my life. We were at opposite ends of the spectrum in one respect and yet we were spiritual sisters and confidantes in another. Judi had freedom but no advantages; I had advantages but no freedom. Helping each other through the tough times made us realise that everyone's personal battles may be unique, but we all have them.

Now, here we are, about to begin the next exciting phase of our lives – nearly two-thousand miles apart.

'Well?' I say, excitedly. 'Are you ringing with good news?'

'A *good morning* would have been nice.' She gives me a little wave.

'Sorry. Good morning, Judi. How's the weather in wonderful Wales?'

The smile on her face dissolves into a grimace. 'There's a bitingly cold frost this morning, but it's supposed to warm up a little. Snow is forecast later today and well into tomorrow. If it's heavy, then I'm stuffed, because I have a meeting in Birmingham this afternoon and then I'm off to London in the morning.'

Giving her a sympathetic smile, I ignore the bed hair and the fact that she's still in her pjs. Normally she's in the shower, dressed and ready to go before most people have even opened their eyes.

'It's funny you should call right now, as I was just thinking about our little jaunt to the Loire Valley. I still smile whenever I think of our *bonne année* – it was the best Christmas and New Year ever, wasn't it?'

'Ha!' she laughs. 'Well, it was certainly a brilliant way of avoiding our families at the worst time of the year. We must make it an annual pilgrimage, as it already seems like an eternity ago. So much has happened in the last three weeks and I'm flagging already.'

She sounds maudlin and that's not like her. When we booked the gîte, this time last year, I had no idea I'd be living in Lisbon by then. But the holiday had turned out to be the perfect answer to all our problems. I had a legitimate reason not to go back to the UK to spend Christmas with my parents; Judi avoided a house crammed with people and the risk of being drawn into personal squabbles with unforgiving kin.

'Has something gone wrong? You sound a bit down.'

There's a moment of hesitation before she clears her throat. 'The promotion is mine if I want it.'

I stop nibbling on my toast and lean forward, unable to contain my delight. 'But that's brilliant news!'

Judi shrugs her shoulders nonchalantly and I'm struggling to understand why she's not punching the air.

'What's that saying? Be careful what you wish for... Well, everything comes at a price, I suppose. I should know that by now.'

I'm totally confused. Judi has been working hard towards this promotion for over two years now and she's been almost obsessive in her dedication. As the social media coordinator for a company making eco-friendly cosmetics, she never switches off because it's her dream job. Normally, she's bouncing off the walls, her head full of crazy ideas which frequently turn into 'aha!' moments.

'What do you mean *if you want it*? You didn't get the assistant campaign manager post, after all? I wasn't aware there was more than one position up for grabs.'

She gives a sigh, avoiding eye contact – which is a bad sign.

'No, that's not the problem. There's been a general restructuring. I'd be reporting to Alex Martin, as Tim is leaving next week.'

She glances directly at me, as if that should mean something, which it doesn't, and I'm at a loss for words. I continue munching in silence.

'Why did this have to happen *now*?' she continues softly, sounding like she's talking to herself, rather than to me.

I'm trying my best not to stare back at her blankly. Alex... Alex... I think that's the new guy who started a few months ago. At times like this, the UK feels like it's a million miles away and it's frustrating not being able to pop round, put the kettle on and give her a comforting hug. I had no idea she was having problems and can't believe she didn't raise the subject when we were in France. Normally, we talk everything through like sisters. In hindsight, it's obvious that with my own life in such turmoil, she was simply ensuring nothing spoiled our break away. 'Judi, did you get any sleep at all last night?'

'About an hour, in between bouts of pacing around, and drinking several cups of herbal tea to try to relax me,' she groans. 'If I can avoid Alex, I'm okay. But working in close proximity to him – can you imagine how impossible that would be?'

Impossible?

'You've mentioned his name in passing probably... twice. The only thing I can remember you telling me was that he was brought in to shake things up.'

'Yes, that just about sums it up. So, what do you think I should do?' The eye contact is intense.

'Do?' I ask, but her lips stay firmly shut. 'Well, you say *yes* and get on with it. If he has a problem with you, then take it to HR.'

'Yes, well... the problem isn't his, it's mine. Whenever Alex is around, it makes me extremely nervous, so I've been avoiding him.'

Nervous? 'Is he trying to intimidate you?' I ask, appalled.

'No, nothing like that!' Her response is firm.

'Then stand your ground. You're obviously the best candidate for the job and it's not like you to back away from people unless... you're attracted to him, aren't you?'

I groan, inwardly. Almost two years ago now, a guy named Peter transferred into her department. Even Judi will admit that she has a *type*. Given the chaotic environment in which she was brought up, it's not difficult to see why. To protect herself, she's a perfectionist and someone who values her privacy, above all else. Peter was a consummate professional: organised, focused and discreet. Not only was he her *type*, he was an A+, but, to Judi's horror, her worst fear was realised when they had a row at work. The thought of everyone suddenly knowing her business mortified her. Worse still, when an opportunity for promotion came up and they were both interviewed for the same post, she was passed over and Peter got the job. Judi was angry with herself, as not only did she have seniority in the department, but everyone thought it was a foregone conclusion that she'd get the position. So, then she had the added indignity of her female colleagues commiserating with her and inferring she should challenge the decision. She told me at the time that it was like living a nightmare, but she held her head high and kept working through it. It was ironic that less than six months' later Peter was headhunted by another company but, by then, Judi had changed jobs. As they say, everything happens for a reason and she was much happier, but her pride had taken a serious knock and for a while her confidence had dipped. It was a big price to pay.

The pained expression on her face now tells me that just when the memories of the past had begun to fade, this is raking it all up again.

'There's something about him that's different,' she explains.

The pause is ominous.

'He's the first guy to catch my attention in ages and you know that's true, Seren.'

A part of me wonders if what's really behind this is a growing sense of loneliness. Judi and I spent a lot of time together and now there's a gap in her life. I just wish this wasn't her potential future boss she was talking about.

'It's unfortunate, given the timing, Judi, but is it possible that you're panicking a little unnecessarily? Just don't jump into anything and see how it pans out,' I reply, my voice full of compassion while trying to reassure her.

'I can't seem to help myself. I've worked damned hard to get to this point and I can't risk making myself look foolish a second time around.'

Judi and I made a pact before I left... get ourselves in a position where we can afford to have the freedom to do what we want to do. Our dreams for the future might differ, but more responsibility means a better salary and being able to set money aside to turn a dream into a reality. If this developed into another Peter scenario it could be disastrous. The sooner Judi addresses the situation, the better.

'Okay. Let's put this into perspective. He's just a man, like any other. It's been a while since you met anyone you really fancied and, heck, we all get that urge from time to time. Just get your emotions back under control and let that business head of yours rule. You can't pass up an opportunity like this because you'd end up regretting it when this little flurry of emotion turns out to be a passing thing.'

Her forehead puckers up as she digests my words. 'I know that. But this is weird, Seren, because I just can't seem to get him out of my head and, goodness knows, I've tried. I'm only too aware that I don't need this sort of distraction right now, as this is my time to step up and demonstrate what I can do. That's why I haven't been able to talk about it. I thought I could rationalise it and move on.'

She sounds wistful and it saddens me. We both decided to step off the dating treadmill for a while. All that time spent getting to know someone new is exhausting. Then by date number three, it's a case of 'where's the exit?' when you realise why no one has snapped them up. We've often laughed together, over a glass of wine or two, wondering if we were just too fussy. Neither of us are pushovers though, and reject out of hand the sort of guys who spout the usual, inane dating drivel. We decided that if we are meant to find true love then it will probably happen when we least expect it and our energies are better spent manifesting the life we want. I think there's an element of self-sabotage wrapped up in this and Judi's insecurities are in play.

'Hit the problem head-on. Just ask him out and see what happens. A couple of dates and you'll probably be done, just keep it friendly and everything will be fine.'

'Now you sound jaded.'

'I do, don't I?' I reflect.

'It's not that easy, Seren, and I don't know what to do about it. What I do know is that the moment we first met, I looked at Alex, he looked at me and there was something. I mean, *something* there between us. Like we'd met before. There was a *connection*.'

'Can you hear yourself, Judi? It's called instant attraction and it usually doesn't last very long.'

'But what if that isn't the case and he's the one?'

She has a point, but how on earth would I know?

'Well, it's time to woman-up. Take a deep breath, calm yourself down and then accept the job offer. It's not as if you'll be with him every minute of the working day, is it?'

She pauses for thought, raising an eyebrow as if she's weighing it up very carefully. 'No.'

'To begin with you'll be a little cautious around each other, but everyone – him included – will assume it's because you're settling into a new role, with a new boss. Your back is covered as long as you hold it together.'

'But what if I can't hide how I feel?'

I roll my eyes. 'You'll soon get to see his flaws and start looking at him in a different light. No one is perfect, trust me. And when it comes to work, once you're sitting at your new desk, there will be no stopping you and he's going to be impressed. He won't want to risk losing your skills if he's trying to make his mark.'

'Thanks. I guess you're right. It's difficult not having you around. I needed that little pep talk as I've been stressing over this big time. Anyway, how about you? Have you been in touch with your parents since you've been back?'

'I've been emailing Mum, but there's not a lot to say right now.'

'Seren, emailing her, really?' Judi makes it sound like an accusation, but I ignore it. 'And how is Lisbon?'

'It beautiful, vibrant and busy. My new life is everything I hoped it would be. Coming back after Christmas made me realise that I am beginning to feel at home here. I love this little place I'm renting. My neighbour, Maria Santos, is a delight. Her English is much better than my Portuguese, thankfully. Her daughter-in-law, who was born in Surrey, and her grandson live with her, and they are both bilingual. She doesn't mention her son, but I get the impression that he died. I do miss... well, I miss my bestie and meeting up with friends to hang out.'

'Oh, me, too. It was a brave decision to make, and I don't know if I would have had the guts to face the upheaval. It takes time to get to know people, longer when you come from a totally different culture. Is there anyone you've managed to become friendly with, I mean, outside of work?'

I can hear concern in her voice.

'I've been working closely with the gallery's publicity manager, Carolina. We have quite a bit in common. She's single and ambitious, too, and she's about our age – thirty-two, I think. She also lives in Almada, about a ten-minute walk from where I'm renting, and we often travel into work together.'

'Well, that's a good start. I can't even imagine what it's like for you now. Sometimes it still doesn't feel real, you know, that you have this whole new life going on.'

'When you fly over for your first visit, think of the fun we'll have. By then I'll know my way around properly and I'll be able to give you the tour like a local. You will utterly and completely fall in love with Lisbon, I promise.'

'Please do not mention the L word.' She sighs. 'And the job is going well?'

I feel an immense sense of satisfaction wash over me as I realise that this is the happiest I've felt in a very long time. Admittedly, I do have moments when loneliness creeps up on me without warning, but I think it's more akin to homesickness. The one thing I do know for sure, is that I have no yearning to go back to my old life and no regrets. 'In June it's the fifth anniversary of the opening of the gallery. My proposals to mark the occasion are being considered by the directors and I'm waiting for their decision. I am nervous about it. It's a huge deal and I could be way off the mark. I wanted to impress them and I know I can pull it off, but I wonder if they'll think my plans are too ambitious.'

Judi stares straight into my eyes, giving me her no-nonsense look. 'I'm sure you've got it right. As much as I hate the fact that you're so far away, you're not stifled any more, and I'm honestly thrilled for you. And has being around all that arty stuff inspired you?'

'Maria's seventeen-year-old grandson, Luis, helped me to set up a little workshop in the garden.' I can't help breaking out into a huge smile.

'I knew that artistic streak of yours was still alive and kicking! Well, done, Seren. Freedom can be exhilarating when there is nothing, and no one, to hold you back.'

My father didn't want me wasting time on things that didn't further my career, but that need to create is a part of me. A part I've given too little attention for far too long.

'Well, freedom also comes at a price and if I mess up at work the rent won't get paid and my savings will begin to dwindle. Renting out my house in the UK keeps the mortgage ticking over and covers the cost of the management company, but that's only a temporary solution.'

'There really is no turning back for you, now?'

'No. Anyway, keep everything crossed for me that my ideas are well received and that I can prove my worth.'

'They're crossed,' she says, holding up a hand in front of the screen. 'But you won't need it as this job was made for you.'

'And in return I'll be sending calming thoughts your way. If this Alex guy unsettles you, just conjure up a mental image of him doing something ordinary. Like washing his hair in the shower. I'd say sitting on the toilet, but that's an invasion of a person's privacy. Even if it is just a mental image.'

She bursts out laughing. 'Oh, my focus wouldn't be on the bubbles in his hair, or the fact that he's just like everyone else. He is simply gorgeous, intelligent, super-organised and... fascinating. Alex has this wonderfully intimate little smile. It gives me goosebumps.'

Goosebumps? What has gotten into her?

'And you're getting this from faraway glimpses of each other?'

'Oh no, is that the time already? I'd better go or I'll be late for work.'

Her words come tumbling out and I wonder whether she's purposely cutting me off. 'Thanks for listening and for the advice. Good luck and a virtual hug, Seren! Speak soon.'

Ping, she's gone. I'm left shaking my head sadly. I can tell she still hasn't made up her mind what to do about the promotion and I can only hope I said enough to tip her in the right direction.

That's one of the disadvantages of being so far away. It's too easy to avoid talking about the real issues and I don't want to worry Judi, either. I am lonely at times and feeling a little isolated. A small fish in a huge pond and I'm anxious to make my mark. The big fear is that my father is right, and I think I'm more capable than I am. Was it his influence and money that backed up whatever skills and talent I have?

I groan. *Why do you keep doing this to yourself, Seren?* I ask myself. *You are your own person, treading your own path. Own it, girl, and show the world what you're made of.*

I think it's time to fire up the welding torch and work the metal. I can fit in an hour before I jump in the shower. The only monster in my world is the one I'm creating for myself. He's shaping up to be a gloriously majestic marsh sandpiper of epic proportions, because I don't do twee. I snapped him when I was walking along the banks of the Tagus estuary, and he's going to be the first sculpture in my new collection.

2

GO BIG, OR GO HOME

Walking into *A Galeria das Almas* – The Gallery of Souls – a thrill courses through my body, as it does every single time I step through the enormous glass doors. Everything is all about profit these days, but here the board of directors have a wider remit. Representing more than a dozen, wealthy investors, their aim is all-encompassing. From developing local talent, to liaising with artists from other countries – the focus is on thinking outside the box to surprise and delight locals and tourists. Yes, their individual businesses mean they have a vested interest in celebrating the cosmopolitan and cultural heritage of the capital of Portugal, but there is also a sense of pride in continuing to raise the bar on what has been achieved since the gallery opened.

Collaborations with other countries are viewed as a vehicle to grow the reputation of the gallery as a centre for inspiration for future generations. A recent exhibition featuring the art of jewellery making, included Portugal's much-celebrated and intricate, gold filigree designs. Artisans from several different countries came together to produce a unique and inspiring collection, in a series of live demonstrations. It was so successful that it has been turned into a roadshow and is now touring Europe. It also inspired an idea that I felt sure would make the board really sit up and take notice. Something fun, bold and daring to capture the audience's attention in a unique way before the exhibition opens.

I wanted to come up with an idea that would reflect the passion and dynamic vibrancy of Lisbon. The setting for the spectacular event playing out in my head was key and the monument of the Cristo Rei is a powerful icon. What I love about Lisbon I have decided, is that everywhere you look there are signs of the wonderfully rich past. It has survived everything from a devastating earthquake, a dictatorship, a disastrous fire, to a peaceful revolution in 1974 – nothing has dampened that air of optimism. So, a setting that looked out across the river Tagus and Lisbon was simply perfect.

The gallery doesn't live in the past, though, it embraces the future as it pays homage to creativity in all of its forms. It's housed in a sweeping, glass building, built on the tree-lined, waterfront promenade known as Avenida da Ribeira das Naus. Formerly an area that had fallen into decline, after a huge injection of cash it's now a hub, an area people gravitate towards. It's popular with joggers, cyclists, families, and tourists, situated an easy stroll away from the ferry terminal, Cais do Sodré. For me, it's a ten-minute crossing from Cacilhas on the opposite side of the river, so it's an easy commute each day.

When people think about an art gallery, first and foremost they expect paintings, but a true reflection of the arts encompasses all forms of expression. Here, we celebrate the skill and imagination of any visual form of creativity. Whether that's because of its beauty, the emotion it invokes, or the senses it touches. It's not simply about quiet rooms and walls lined with expensive canvases, but instead we try to acknowledge the vision and determination of those who seek to create. Previously unknown names are exhibited alongside those whose reputations draw crowds.

The exhibits are diverse. Everything from a beautifully turned piece of wood, a series of sketches capturing the abundant local wildlife, or a study of the colourful azulejo tin-glazed, ceramic tiles seen all over Portugal. Then there are the sculptures in stone, metal and ceramics – for me it's heaven. What if, one day, one of my sculptures finds its own space in the gallery... I can only dream about that for now, of course.

And this is the environment I stepped into, determined to build on what my predecessor had begun. Organising large events is second nature to me now, but every day I worked for my father was a battle due to his overbearing, manipulative style. Today, I'm standing tall and my stomach is filled with nervous excitement. For the first time in my career, I'm about to be judged solely on the proposal I've put together and it's a *huge* deal for me. But there's no personal battle of wills going on behind the scenes here. If my proposal is too ambitious, then I simply need to come up with another idea – and I have plenty of those.

Taking my seat around the table, I give an acknowledging greeting. 'Senhor Ferreira, Senhora Veloso, Senhor Portela. Thank you for calling this meeting at such short notice. While June seems a long time away, there is a lot of work to be done if you decide to move forward with this proposal.'

Within the first week of my arrival, I soon gave up trying to impress them with my limited understanding of their language. My pitiful attempts were met with appreciation but also amusement. It was a relief, as they assured me it was not going to be a drawback. I was being employed for my skills as an events manager and I was assigned an inter-preter by the name of Antero Medeiros. Whenever he's around, he pops in for a little chat, but, so far, we haven't formally worked together as I haven't needed to call upon his services.

Exhibitors at the gallery come from all around the world so virtually all the people I've dealt with have spoken a reasonable amount of English. Enough for me to conduct our meetings with ease, although it has left me wishing I were a seasoned linguist. Learning the language is a top priority for me this autumn.

'Have we all had a chance to consider Senhorita Maddison's proposals for our auspicious celebrations?' Senhor Ferreira takes the lead. His voice is heavily accented, but easy to follow.

The others nod their heads.

'And?' He raises an eyebrow. I find myself holding my breath.

'Impressive!' Senhor Portelo states, staring down at the document in front of him. 'Textiles are an area we have not yet explored. *Maravilhoso!*'

I'm delighted with *wonderful*. One down, two to go.

Senhora Veloso is next. 'It is ambitious with the spectacle of a fashion show but an inspired idea! Well done. It has my vote, too.'

'I am in total agreement,' Senhor Ferreira confirms.

I'm shocked when they give a little round of applause to seal their endorsement and I feel my cheeks begin to glow.

'You are setting yourself a tough timetable,' he continues, 'but we have no doubt about your ability to deliver. We have willing partners and our investors are looking forward to a most wondrous anniversary celebration. It is pleasing to see Portuguese photographer Rafael Osorio's name here. Bringing together fashion, art and textiles is a stroke of genius, Seren. And your initial approaches have been received with interest?'

'They have, Senhor Ferreira, all the potential contributors I've spoken to hold the gallery in the highest esteem.'

'Excellent.' His face breaks out into a warm smile. 'We will leave this in your capable hands then and will look forward to our weekly updates.'

I walk away from the meeting fighting the urge to punch the air. Selecting the three key figures around which to build this project wasn't easy, but the vision works on paper, and I can only hope and pray that when it comes to getting everyone to work together, there are no stumbling blocks. I have succeeded in gaining the confidence of my bosses, and now all I need to do is make it happen.

Heading back to my office, Antero approaches and the moment he spots me, his eyes instantly light up. Tall, dark and with a wicked smile, he offers his hand and we shake.

'Good to see you, Seren. When are you going to enlist my help?' he enquires in an admonishing tone.

He's always on call if needed, but as a self-employed contractor he's only around whenever his services are required. Usually, when a new display is being erected and Antero is instrumental in designing the multilingual signage.

'Soon. The chaos is about to begin.'

'Ah, chaos I understand. I look forward to it.'

I'm not sure he does understand. I have a feeling Antero is going to more than earn his fee once we get started.

'If you can spare me ten minutes right now...' I grind to a halt, waving to Carolina to attract her attention. 'Are you free?' I call out, as she strides towards us.

'Yes. It was approved?' she enquires, eagerly.

Both sets of eyes are now firmly on my face as I break out into a modest smile.

'It was and it's unanimous. Let's head to my office and I will give you both a copy of the proposal and a quick overview.'

There's the buzz of excitement between us and a little thrill courses through me as we come together as a team for the first time. On entering the office, I hand each of them a bound copy of the report, and while they settle themselves down, I walk around to the head of the desk.

'I can't believe what I am seeing,' Antero declares as he stares down at the document in his hands.

'Is this a fashion show at the Santuário Nacional do Cristo Rei?'

'Yes, but that's only one element of the celebrations. Good communication and a massive publishing campaign are going to be key in pulling this off.'

Carolina is leafing through the pages and I can see that her reaction mirrors that of the directors when they first received their copies. Surprise, no doubt, swiftly followed by the thought that if we do this well it could be spectacular.

'It's ambitious, I will admit. But I've been in touch with English artist Reid Henderson's personal assistant and he is keen to be involved in the project. You may not be aware that he is based in Lisbon, as well as having a home in London. His collection of paintings celebrating the birds, flora and fauna of the banks of the river Tagus was exhibited in an art gallery in London last summer. It created a lot of interest and resulted in the publication of a limited-edition hardback book, which raised a lot of money for Portugal's marine conservation efforts.'

I pause for a couple of moments, as they are now eagerly leafing through the graphics. A talented ex-colleague in the UK did an amazing job of taking the briefing and photos I sent him and turning them into a visual representation of my vision.

'Bernadette Brodeur, a French textiles designer, has confirmed she would be delighted to take part and is available to fly over for the day of the shoot. And fashion photographer Rafael Osorio is prepared to adjust his schedule to accommodate our time frame as soon as I confirm the board's decision.'

Carolina glances up at me, frowning. 'You do know of his reputation?'

I nod. 'Yes, I've read a few newspaper articles about him. But to make this work it had to be someone of his calibre so that limited my options. The photographer must be on a par with the artist, to establish a level playing field between the two different disciplines. One is translating the work of the other, but in a different – although equally as high-profile – medium. Liaison regarding the textiles will be much easier, as the intention is for Reid Henderson to have final approval, once Bernadette Brodeur has submitted the samples. For an up-and-coming designer, she's delighted to be offered the opportunity to work with us on this project and she has the full backing of her company. But from here on in it's important we make full use of you, Antero. While both Bernadette and Rafael have assistants who reply to my emails in English, we need to be holding regular conference calls to ensure our key players can voice their opinions to avoid any misunderstandings at a later stage.'

Carolina nods her head in firm agreement. 'I applaud the fact that you are being diplomatic, I see the need for that. Rumours are that Rafael can be difficult, but this will be a big project for him as well as for the gallery.'

'It is without a doubt the biggest spectacle the gallery will ever have hosted. With the filming of the fashion show kicking off the two-day celebrations in the shadow of the Cristo Rei, we will need that event to draw a huge crowd to cover the costs. But it will also raise the profile of the exhibition itself and, as word spreads, we hope to break all records for visitor numbers throughout the summer. So, the pressure is on, Carolina, to get the advertising up and running without delay.'

Her grin is ear-to-ear. 'I'm on it, as they say. Or I will be the moment I'm back at my desk!'

'There will be an invitation-only cocktail party at the museum on day two, formally celebrating the fifth anniversary. Our special guests will get a preview of the exhibition of Reid's paintings and

Bernadette's range of fabrics and soft furnishings based on some of his artwork. Once the video of the photo shoot has been finessed, the film will be projected on a specially made screen some nine metres high and twelve metres wide and will feature alongside the exhibition which will run through until the autumn. Bernadette speaks a little English, but no Portuguese. Reid is, apparently, fluent in Portuguese as his wife was born in Porto,' I confirm, turning to look at Antero.

'And Rafael, well, he's a law unto himself,' he informs me.

We grin across the desk at each other. 'Sorry. But this won't work without him. I'm hoping any temperamental issues will get lost in translation.'

Carolina bursts out laughing and Antero and I join in.

'You are both looking at me as if I'm a mad Englishwoman.'

They glance at each other for a moment, before redirecting their gaze back to me.

'It's crazy, but we can do this,' Carolina replies.

I give her an acknowledging smile and then look at Antero.

'As an interpreter I am both discreet and...' He stops short, casting around for the right word.

'Someone able to calm the flames?' I throw out there quite casually.

'I like that,' he replies. 'Most certainly.'

We have a mountain to climb, it's true, but as they head off, I can see that both Carolina and Antero are equally as excited as I am to roll up their sleeves and get started.

When my phone kicks into life, it makes me jump and, snatching it up, I see it's a text from Judi.

I start the new job in two weeks' time. You're right. I'm being ridiculous. It's all about the work and no one is going to rob me of the glory!

That succeeds in raising a smile as my fingers tap away.

Well done, lady!

I attach a GIF of a woman flexing her muscles before I press send. Seconds later she replies.

I was being a bit of a wimp, wasn't I? Any news at your end?

It's a go... eek!

Celebrations all round – nothing can stop us now!

* * *

'Good morning. You are through to Seren Maddison. How can I help?'

I glance across at Carolina, who is sitting the other side of my desk. Her fingers are tapping away wildly on her laptop as she massages the Gantt chart we've spent the best part of the last week poring over. We are on the verge of finalising the overall timeline, tweaking each operational strand as if it's a musical score.

'It's Reid Henderson, Seren. I thought it was time I made direct contact to express my sincere apologies for being so elusive. I've been travelling and bogged down with meetings in between, but I wanted to assure you that my assistant, Leonor, has been keeping me fully updated.'

The relief I feel at finally hearing his voice stops me in my tracks for a brief second or two. Three conference calls have already been held without him and the pressure is beginning to mount. Despite constant reassurances from his team, I was beginning to have my doubts over whether he was as invested in this project as I need him to be. To the extent that the last two nights I've woken up around three in the morning in a cold sweat, wondering if it's too late to find another artist to step in.

'Oh, no apology needed and thank you so much for the call, Mr Henderson. We're in the process of finalising the timetable for the various stages of the project as we speak and I'm hoping to get a copy emailed to you later today.'

'Great, and please call me Reid, if you have no objection to me calling you Seren. I've made a start on selecting which pieces I think will work best when it comes to the artwork for Bernadette Brodeur. I don't know her, of course, but my assistant has shown me examples of her work. This is going to be a most interesting collaboration indeed.'

His voice is smooth, like a voice-over artist. In fact, that velvety tone is something we should take advantage of if I can talk him into it. What if we could record him introducing the fashion show? Thoughts are whirling around inside my head and I realise he's waiting for a response.

'We are gearing up to begin moving things forward very quickly now. If your assistant can let me know when you are available, perhaps we could arrange a video call so we can run through any questions you might have?'

A mellow 'hmm' echoes down the line. 'I will most certainly make a list and if you can bear with me another day, two at most, it will allow me to tie up the last few loose ends. Then I'll make myself freely available to you. How does that sound?'

More than reasonable.

'Perfect. And if there's anything either I, or my staff, can do to assist you, then please don't hesitate to let me know.'

'Thank you, Seren, I will bear that in mind. It's been a pleasure talking to you and we'll speak again very soon, I promise.'

The blood is pounding in my ears as the line disconnects and I see that Carolina has stopped typing.

'That sounded positive.'

I let out a huge sigh, bowing my head and closing my eyes while I offer up a silent prayer of thanks to the universe. 'He hasn't been avoiding us, he's been travelling. You can go ahead with the press release.'

'At last! I will admit, no disrespect to you, Seren, but I was beginning to have my doubts about him.'

'Well, it sounds like he's equally as keen to get this rolling now, which is a big weight off my shoulders. Our timetable is dependent upon Reid being able to make some quick decisions and supply the prints we need to pass on to Bernadette. That must be the number one priority, given the lead time for organising the fabric samples. Naturally, Reid will be required to sign those off, in agreement with Bernadette. She'll then work closely with the manufacturers producing the garments and the soft furnishings. Leonor has already confirmed that Reid's business manager will arrange for the paintings for the general exhibition to be shipped over from London. Obviously, Carolina, if we can get hold of some photos of a few of the pieces for advertising purposes, that would be great, and I'll press for that when Reid gets in touch.'

'What impression did you get of him?'

'Well, considering his fame, he came across as very friendly, motivated, and about to get focused. Which is a huge relief. This is a big deal and the exposure he's going to get will translate into a nice little boost in sales of his paintings. Looking at the guest list for the official party, I doubt whether any of them would lose any sleep over the cost of acquiring an original by Reid Henderson. Goodness, if I could afford it, I'd love to have one of his pieces hanging on a wall, appreciating in value. It's a sound investment. But it's necessary to get those people in front of the actual artwork to tempt them.'

Carolina smiles at me. 'He is a very handsome man and a true gentleman, I hear. Lots of business meetings over lunch to look forward to?'

I shoot her a glance. 'I doubt that. He's much too busy to be wined and dined by an event coordinator. I'm sure the directors will want to arrange a special dinner in his honour, as an expression of their gratitude. Maybe even hosted at Senhor Ferreira's home as, naturally, the invite would also be extended to Rafael and Bernadette.'

It's strikes me as strange how people perceive these things as being much more fun than they are when you are taking part in person. I've had my fair share of sitting in expensive restaurants watching my father suck up to monied people and it's a chore.

'Of course,' she replies, nodding in agreement. 'Oh, how the rich and famous live; it must be a wonderful life. I might treat myself to a print as a souvenir of this momentous occasion, but my budget will be in the hundreds, not the thousands.'

My father might not be famous, but he has money and I can vouch for the fact that it doesn't make life wonderful at all. Well, not in the way Carolina means. I believe that happiness is a state of mind.

'I'm sure that we can wrap up most of the detail in a couple of online meetings. But I will be curious to meet him in the flesh, as I'm sure we all will.'

'Well, if, and I say *if*, you could get me a programme signed by him for my mother, I would be forever in your debt. My father bought her one of Reid's prints for their thirtieth wedding anniversary and she adores his work.'

'Ah, Carolina, that's a lovely idea. I'd like to think you'd get the opportunity to ask him yourself on the day, but we'll definitely make it happen.'

'I'd better start working on the design for the programme then. The pressure is on to make it extra special now,' she laughs. 'I bet I know where you're heading next.'

'Yes. Senhor Ferreira is going to be delighted to hear Reid has already begun to put the collection of pieces together. Things will quickly gather momentum and that's all the reassurance he requires for now.'

3

NOT QUITE THE SATURDAY I HAD PLANNED

It's chilly today and the sky is a bleak shade of grey. Here inside my little workshop in the garden I'm more than content to while away my day. My not-so-little marsh sandpiper has taken shape and the task of mounting him onto a substantial platform is making me break out into a sweat. In real life, this little guy would comfortably sit within my hands and weigh no more than eighty grams. The piece I've dubbed *Pássaro nobre* – Noble bird – is seventy-five centimetres long, and sixty-centimetres wide; he's so heavy that I need to bend my knees to lift him.

'This isn't quite right, is it, *meu amigo*?' I ask my new little friend.

Talking to him as I work, he stares back at me unblinkingly but with a distinct air of firm resolve. Voicing out aloud the questions that keep on whirling around inside my head is helping me to get my thoughts straight. Chief amongst them is whether I can fill the hours I'm not working enough to stop myself becoming nostalgic over the things I miss about the UK. Like being able to make a call and then head off to the cinema with an old friend when I'm in need of company. Or meeting up with Judi to go shopping. The statue's gaze is unrelenting and telling me to get a grip.

'You're going to make sure I'm kept busy, aren't you? I can tell you don't approve of wallowing.' His beady eyes stare back at me and I look down at the metal box I've only just finished welding together. It's too geometric and I realise I've just wasted three solid hours of work.

Turning off the welding torch and discarding my gloves, I feel disappointed in myself because this fascinating little bird deserves better. Raising the mask for a moment, it's a relief to fill my lungs with some fresh air.

When my phone starts to buzz, I snatch it out of my pocket, thinking it's time for a break anyway.

'Hello?'

'Hi Seren, it's Reid. I hope I'm not disturbing you.'

On a Saturday?

'No, of course not, Reid. Is there a problem?'

The sound of his slightly embarrassed laugh echoes down the line. 'No, not at all. But there's been a change of plan and I'm away again this coming week. I know you were hoping we could finally meet up in person and I'm home alone today. I don't suppose you are free for dinner this evening? It would be doing me a huge favour if you're not adverse to talking business as we eat. My itinerary is pure madness again, I'm afraid, as I'm involved in a charity fundraiser.'

Drenched in sweat from the heat of welding, my hair is plastered to my head as if I've just stuck it under a running tap and he's talking about dinner?

'Well, of course I can make myself available. I didn't know you were already back in Lisbon. I'm not even sure what time it is to be honest with you as I've been working, but I can most certainly make a reservation somewhere and would be delighted to grab the chance to talk.'

'Oh, no need for that. I'll pick you up and we can eat at my place. It's quiet here on the edge of the forest and only about a twenty-minute drive from the centre of Lisbon. Text me your address and I'll see you around seven.'

I swallow hard. 'I could hire a car to save you the drive if you give me directions.'

'It's no trouble, honestly.'

'Seven it is then. Thank you, Reid.'

The panic immediately begins to set in. What on earth am I going to wear? The dress code at work is conservative, with the men wearing the usual business suit, smart shirt and a tie. I usually wear a knee-length skirt, a jacket and a long-sleeve blouse, taking a lead from my peers. Learning the unspoken protocols took me a while. Punctuality is a given and excuses are seen as just that, no matter how busy the traffic might be. And no one leaves the office at a set time every day. Instead, the culture is to work until the job in hand is completed and never leave before your superior. But as for a business meeting outside of work hours, how on earth do I dress for that? Reid might be British by birth, but I'm still representing the gallery and I doubt he'll be in jeans and a t-shirt.

Yet, along with the questions, there's also excitement. I'm about to meet up with a famous artist and he's taking the time and trouble to come and pick me up. Maybe he isn't going to be a man with a big ego and I might actually enjoy this dinner.

* * *

Reid drives his silver Mercedes E-Class coupé with a sensitive touch and the journey is pleasant. I feel very safe as we speed along the open roads. I've said little, as he seems happy to talk about other projects he's working on right now. His life is as busy and varied as I suspected. That's why he's hard to get hold of at times.

When we eventually turn off onto a quiet country road and follow a long, sweeping drive up to Reid's house, it's even bigger than I expected.

'This is stunning,' I remark, unable to mask my admiration.

'I had Casa da Floresta built some eight years ago. This is where I will eventually settle, but for now I spend a fair bit of time in London. I'll get your door.'

He climbs out and walks around the car while I unhook my seat belt. Thank goodness I settled on wearing a pale blue, scooped-neck, lace pencil dress with a scalloped hem. It's one of those little dresses that is suitable for most occasions, as it's light and summery. Reid is looking casual, in navy blue trousers and a pale blue shirt. He's not an ostentatious man and in the flesh he's even more handsome than on a video call. His smile is engaging and lights up his eyes.

'Welcome to my little piece of Sintra,' he says, as he swings open the door and offers me his hand. As I take it and ease myself up out of the seat, I do so with practised elegance. It's ingrained in me now; my mother is all about poise and good manners, which she says will get you a long way in life.

As Reid draws me closer to him, I look away to focus on the property instead, nestled against a wooded hill at the base of the mountains. This luxurious country house has crisp lines and a contemporary feel. It's made up of two three-storey buildings linked by a single-storey central corridor on the second level, with the lower levels partially set into the hillside. There is a wonderful covered terrace to the front, beyond which is a wall of glass. The stark white exterior is in sharp contrast to the rich reds of the Roman roof tiles. But the backdrop of the trees as they rise up as far as the eye can see softens the whole appearance, wrapping it in a living cloak of vibrant shades of green.

'What an interesting design,' I compliment him, and he flashes me a wonderfully warm smile.

'Like a painting, you get out of it what you put in. It was a labour of love for me as the idea is that one day the east wing will become an art gallery. I'd like to teach here too when the demands on my time aren't quite so pressing. Dreams like that are expensive, so I need to be patient.'

I smile, surprised by his candour as he indicates for me to walk on.

'Have you managed to escape Lisbon yet and discover the delights of Sintra? Life here in the foothills of the mountains is very pleasant. We're lucky enough to be sheltered from the winds because of the way the land rises up.'

Reid falls in step alongside me as we climb a run of wide steps leading up to the terrace on the middle level.

'No. I'm still settling in and I haven't really ventured far. My goodness, you must find it a wrench every time you leave this place. What a wonderful setting, so relaxing, I should imagine, and such an inspiration when you are working.'

'Yes. It hasn't always been that way... relaxing, I mean.'

He leans forward to swing open an obscured glass door and what I assumed was going to be a corridor is in fact a massive, single-storey room with high ceilings. The walls either side display several large pieces of artwork, but, despite the proportions of the space, there are only two sofas in the centre of the room, flanked by small side tables.

'This will, someday, become a gallery showcasing up-and-coming artists, but, in the meantime, it is where I store some of my pieces. A few of them are destined for the Galeria das Almas exhibition. We're heading through here,' Reid indicates as we traverse the pristine, glossy tiled floor. He slides back bifold glass doors leading out onto a large inner courtyard. With the backdrop of the trees and the stone walls either side enclosing the space, it's delightful.

A large, circular table is laid out as it would be if this were a smart restaurant. With a white linen tablecloth, silver cutlery, and hammered metal charger plates, it's more formal than I'd expected. In the centre is a vase of pale pink hydrangea heads which couldn't be simpler, or more pleasing to the eye.

Reid hurries to pull out one of the two chairs for me.

'Thank you. I wish all business meetings were conducted in surroundings like this,' I remark, as I lower myself onto the seat.

Raising my eyes to give Reid an acknowledging smile, the genuine warmth in his gaze is unexpected.

He clears his throat, as if he's embarrassed that I caught him looking at me so intently. It panics me a little as I assume Reid is married, but I notice he doesn't wear a ring. He's so easy to be around, friendly and understated. There's no desire to impress, only to please – which is refreshing. And unexpected. Although, he's probably used to being a good host and doing his best to put visitors at ease.

'It's the least I can do considering I'm disturbing your plans for a Saturday evening. I appreciate you accommodating my request at such short notice. Sometimes my life doesn't feel my own any more, but busy is good.'

As Reid takes his seat, a man walks towards us and they exchange a few words in Portuguese.

'What would you like to drink, Seren?' Reid enquires.

'I'll... um, go with whatever you're having.'

The man smiles at me as I look up at him. 'I am Vitor. I bring you a

Tinto da Ânfora. Vinho clássico,' he informs me with pride, before striding off.

'Vitor and his wife, Gisela, run this place. It's too big for me now, of course, and I mainly use just the one wing.'

Now? It's a fight to keep my curiosity at bay, but I'm conscious that this isn't a social visit. Perhaps I should try to steer the conversation in another direction.

'It's nice to have space and so much easier to talk than in a restaurant. Although our publicity machine is busy putting out as much information as we can, so very soon everything will be common knowledge.'

Vitor returns, carrying a bottle of wine, accompanied by a much younger woman, who proceeds to place two large-bowled wine glasses in front of us. I defer to my host when it comes to the tasting and Vitor seems content when Reid nods his approval, but he doesn't leave us until I've taken a sip.

'This is lovely, Vitor, thank you. Cherry and blackcurrant... a wonderful choice.' I have no idea whether he understands what I'm saying, but he gives me a slight nod of his head, then wipes the neck of the bottle before placing it on the table and leaving.

'I often feel like I'm staying in a hotel when I'm here,' Reid admits. 'It was only a family home for about five years. When I married my now ex-wife, Beatriz, we lived in London where our daughter, Ana, was born. Beatriz missed Portugal and we came to live here seven years ago. Shortly before the divorce they moved to Porto, to be with Beatriz's family, and I'm left here wondering why I built such an enormous place.' He pauses for a moment, frowning, and I can see that his thoughts are elsewhere. 'Anyway,' he resumes, his expression brightening, 'here's to a successful collaboration, Seren.'

Reid raises his glass and I tentatively clink mine as he looks at me with an expression of curiosity on his face. I'm guessing he's in his early forties, as his unruly shoulder-length hair is still jet black. From time to time, he scoops it back and there's something curiously mesmerising about the action, which he does unconsciously.

'So, what is your story, Seren?'

I realise that he's trying to establish a rapport by telling me a little about himself and it's his way of breaking the ice. I've worked with clients before who need to understand what makes you tick before they can do business with you. Given that this project is so unusual, I'm wondering whether Reid is beginning to have second thoughts. Is that the reason he invited me here tonight?

'For the last six years I worked for my father as an events coordinator and marketing manager. He owns a large exhibition centre in the UK specialising in trade fairs.'

Reid frowns. 'And yet you've ended up here, in Lisbon. I'm surprised.'

How honest do I need to be to gain his trust? I wonder.

'It's not always easy working with family and it was time to find a new challenge.'

Reid twizzles the stem of his glass between his fingers, staring at me as he does as if he's sizing me up. 'I get that. My father is an architect, but I take after my mother, who was the one who encouraged me to paint. I still think my father would have preferred for me to follow in his footsteps. To try to make up for that, I involved him in the design of this place.' He casts around, a frown suddenly creasing his brow.

'But you are thrilled with how it turned out?'

'Yes. It's not that. Sorry, I miss my daughter and this house feels empty without her. It's her fifteenth birthday today. Beatriz and I aren't on speaking terms right now and I wasn't invited to the party.'

My goodness. Did Reid invite me here tonight because he's lonely and sad? I'm a little taken-aback and not sure quite how to respond, but I should say something. 'I feel for you, that must be tough. But you do get to see your daughter?'

He nods. 'Yes, from time to time, but not as often as I'd like. Ana has a good circle of friends and five cousins around her, but it's a difficult age. A father who hasn't been involved in her daily life for the best part of two years now isn't exactly a priority. I took her to dinner a couple of weeks ago and then shopping for her present. She's not an ungrateful kid, and I hope as she gets older our relationship will improve. Beatriz has a large family, so I should at least be thankful for that.'

A movement catches my eye and we both turn to see Vitor and the young woman walking towards us each carrying a tray.

'I promise you are in for a real treat,' Reid says, winking at me. 'Gisela isn't just a cook, she has a passion for food worthy of some of the best chefs around. Simple, Portuguese fare served with love and with a creative twist.'

It strikes me as rather sad that Reid is here alone and the only people around him are employees. And yet he's relaxed enough to let down his guard and treat me as if we are friends, rather than simply business acquaintances. It's not quite what I was expecting from this evening, that's for sure.

* * *

We end the evening in Reid's personal sitting room, which looks out over the extensive views from the front elevation, down over the valley. While the deciduous trees are only just in bud, it's still a vista of evergreen conifers, pines and cypress trees. The corner room has two large, panoramic windows, and both are open. It's a pleasant evening, although I'm glad of the little linen jacket I brought with me as a breeze has sprung up. It's wonderful to hear the slight whisper from the movement of the tall trees surrounding the property.

When Reid begins to quiz me about where the original idea came from to link the Cristo Rei and his art to a fashion shoot, he's not just making conversation; I can see that he's genuinely interested. It's difficult keeping my enthusiasm in check as I explain the thought processes, but Reid is a good listener and he doesn't interrupt my flow.

'It's hard to describe exactly what I'm visualising in here,' I tap the side of my head with a finger.

A look of amusement flashes over his face and I begin to feel embarrassed.

'No, it's fine,' Reid replies, his tone reassuring and gentle. 'As an artist I construct each piece over and over in my head many times before I even pick up a pencil, or a brush. By the time I'm touching the canvas there's already a master plan for each stroke. I would have been disappointed if you'd rattled off a well-rehearsed, one-liner sales pitch. Seeing the Cristo

Rei through the eyes of someone new to Lisbon, it's beginning to make sense to me now.'

I give him a grateful smile.

'I will have the portfolio of designs for Bernadette Brodeur sent across to your office by the end of this week. I hope she will be pleased. The fashion shoot element was a big surprise.'

There's a touch of reserve in his voice which makes me frown.

'You have concerns?'

He lifts his coffee cup, taking a sip and then placing it back on the low-level table between us.

'It's the first time any of my artwork has been brought to life in another form. How it will translate is making me feel a little anxious. You are a lady with big ideas and I'm a man who can appreciate someone who thinks outside the box. However, this is not simply ambitious, but also unique. And with that comes an element of risk, for all of us.'

The fact that he's a little cautious approaching this is a good thing and now it's my job to convince him he has nothing to worry about.

'Seeing a concept on paper doesn't bring it fully to life, does it? Let me paint you a mental picture of the vision. Humour me here, for a few moments. Imagine the models standing in the shadow of the Cristo Rei statue. The full length of the promenade is in front of us and it becomes a fashion catwalk. The backdrop is the stunning river Tagus and the iconic Ponte 25 de Abril suspended above the water. Overhead, the vibrant blue sky begins to mellow as dusk descends and the whole scene is lit up.'

I pause, to check that he's with me and he raises an eyebrow; I can see he's engaging with me as I walk him through it.

'Now close your eyes.'

Reid does as I ask, and I continue staring at him for several seconds, studying his face, before I realise he's waiting for me to begin.

'Gracefully, the models glide along, slowly twirling every ten or fifteen metres, arms outstretched and their silhouettes mirroring that of the statue itself. The ankle-length gowns will form a perfect T-shape as they unfold their arms to display your designs. Capturing scenes from your artwork celebrating this amazing part of the world, it's going to be a spectacle that has never been seen before. It will be an homage not simply to your work, but to Lisbon and to nature's beauty.'

I'm staring at him now in earnest. Since the second his eyelids closed shut, they haven't even flickered, and he takes a few moments before opening them. His skin is tanned, the line of his jaw strong and determined. He's a man used to being in control and I can understand his need to reassure himself this project is in good hands.

'That's a strong visual you're describing there, Seren. You have a creative eye. This idea of yours is refreshing, so many marketing initiatives are gimmicky. Let me hazard a guess... do you paint?'

I shake my head, tipping my chin down to touch my chest, as my cheeks begin to colour under his intense gaze. I'm enjoying this way too much for my own good. 'No.'

He waggles a finger at me. 'I'm not giving up that easily. You're a little uncomfortable, so I'm guessing it's a hobby... could be pottery, or jewellery making, maybe?'

Reid isn't going to let it go.

'Metal sculptures,' I reply. 'I like to weld.'

Tipping his head back for a moment, he cups a hand around his chin. 'That wasn't the first thing that jumped into my head, admittedly, but why am I not surprised? It's very you.'

What on earth does that mean? He hardly knows me and yet I get the distinct feeling he isn't just listening to what I'm saying, he's trying to read between the lines. Or is my body language giving something away? I sincerely hope not, because I'm beginning to feel a little exposed. Reid is an interesting man, but, given the situation, I wasn't expecting our conversation to get quite so personal.

'Bernadette is the right person to ensure your artwork is turned into catwalk masterpieces. And once you've approved the samples, she'll begin work on the range of soft furnishings that will go on sale in the gallery. You will be involved at every stage, I can assure you, Reid. This is going to grab people's attention and, hopefully, pull in a whole new audience of visitors to the gallery to view your work.'

It might be wishful thinking on my part, but he seems content – for now.

'Well, it will be the first time anyone has ever worn one of my paint-ings, so you will forgive a little nervous apprehension creeping in. But it's inspired.'

Our eyes meet and, for one second, it's as if everything around me has faded into nothingness. My ears begin to buzz, and my mouth goes dry. We aren't just looking at each other, we're experiencing something.

Horrified, I squirm around in my seat, edging myself forward and glancing down at my watch.

Reid takes the prompt and I sincerely hope he doesn't think I'm being rude. 'Right, it's time I drove you back home, Seren. I'd like to thank you for your company and for taking the time to set my mind at ease. It's true that I was excited about this project from the start, but now you really do have my full attention. Whatever you need, just ask. You can contact me any time of the day,' he pauses, 'or night.'

PART II

MARCH

4

NEW LIFE, NEW FRIENDS

Spring has officially begun and despite the early-morning chill, the sky is an unbroken blue canvas and the sun is already beginning to warm things up. It's Saturday morning and Carolina is due to arrive at ten a.m. I'm sitting in the narrow, elongated forecourt in front of the little place I'm renting. It's pleasant sitting here, waiting for my visitor and listening to the sound of the birds. I wave at neighbours who stop for a moment to catch their breath, calling out 'Olá, Seren' before making their way up to the top of the hill. I usually reply with a simple 'Bom dia', which is good morning. I figure it's a start, until I have the time to take classes, as I begin to commit a handful of words and phrases to memory.

To the left-hand side as I look out, the boundary is the side wall of Maria's house. Set within the imposingly tall, whitewashed wall is a door to her kitchen and above it a small window. On the opposite side, an equally pristine wall creates a private little courtyard, as well as providing shelter when the wind whips up.

Earlier this morning, Maria and I sat together for a while enjoying a cup of coffee. We often do this at weekends while she waits for her daughter-in-law and grandson to appear. It's a pleasant way to pass a little time before she makes a start on breakfast.

My new life is in sharp contrast to my former routine, where I always had a lie-in on my days off. And I rarely sat outside unless I had friends over for dinner. There never was an opportunity for me to sit and think, to simply unwind. Whether it's the more temperate climate here, I don't know, but I'm learning to take time for myself and it's both restorative and energising.

The charmingly rustic and bijou dwelling I'm renting belongs to Maria's brother and abuts the house their family has lived in for three generations. It makes up in charm what it lacks in size and it's more than adequate for my needs. With a mass of pots full of glorious colour lined up against the textured stone walls, it's a little oasis. It's located on the narrow, winding street named Fernão Mendes Pinto which leads up to one of Lisbon's most famous tourist spots, but it's off the beaten track.

Set back off the charmingly sedate street, the front façade of this pretty, wedge-shaped one-storey property captivated me. The width of two generously proportioned, country-style doors sitting side by side at the end of the courtyard intrigued me. Both are painted white but are set within solid stone pillars with lintels above, which are a gloriously summery cornflower blue. Offset with the faded pink, terracotta pan-tile roof, the frontage gives no real clue to what lies beyond.

The first door leads into the kitchen, which opens up into a quirky yet functional space. The second door leads into what was once just an alcove but is now a useful storage cupboard, then on into an open-plan sitting room which is almost totally square. With white walls and heavy, dark-wood furniture, the intricate Portuguese-tiled floor adds a rich vibrancy. Azulejo tiles can be seen everywhere in Lisbon and Maria told me, with a great degree of pride, that the tiles were made by her father and laid by her brother.

Three doors lead out of this room. One heads back into the kitchen, the other two on the opposite side of the room take you into an average-sized bathroom and a large bedroom. Curiously, the access to the rear garden is via the bedroom. It's a rectangle running the entire width of the rear of the property, consisting of a small patio and a grassy area bounded by shrubs. Beyond that, in the far corner, is a large, brick-built outbuilding which is now a workshop. My little residence doesn't have a name, just a number: 28a, Fernão Mendes Pinto.

What I love is that the little community here is mixed. The larger homes on the other side of the road are owned by more affluent people but are interspersed with terraces of smaller homes and a myriad of little courtyards such as this one – offering glimpses of hidden treasures. People are respectful of each other's space but, as I've found to my relief and delight, welcoming to all.

Carolina suddenly appears around the corner, stepping into the courtyard and waving out as she walks towards me. '*Olá*, Seren,' she calls out. 'This is a beautiful little spot. What a find!'

I stand and we greet each other with *beijinhos*, a swift kiss on each cheek as is the custom with friends and family. It's all new to me still, as the other people I mix with are simply colleagues. Here, one's working life is kept totally separate to one's private life, whereas in the UK when you start a new job, often a part of settling in is building friendships together outside of work. Popping into the pub for a quick drink is acceptable, whereas here it isn't common practice.

Meeting up with Carolina today is the next step in our growing friendship and it occurs to me that she, too, must miss her family. Even if you are Portuguese, leaving one's home behind means starting afresh in a place where you don't know anyone at all.

With Maria, my relationship is different again; she simply grabs both of my hands and brings them together, muttering something under her breath in Portuguese. She's a deeply religious person and I think it's a blessing of some sort. She has taken me under her wing and her kindness is appreciated more than I can possibly convey.

'It was a stroke of luck finding this place,' I reply to Carolina. 'Come inside. Have a look around while I get my things together. There are some beautiful old wall tiles in the kitchen.'

'It's perfect for you, especially being so close to the Santuário Nacional do Cristo Rei.' She laughs and I nod my head in agreement.

The statue of Christ is central to the success of my project and I wonder if I hadn't been drawn to this cosy little property, whether it would have been an opportunity missed. I'm sure that I would have visited it at some point, as it's a huge draw for visitors, but probably not so soon after my arrival.

The day I came to view the property, Maria suggested I make my way up to the monument to familiarise myself with the area. It was early evening and the gates were already shut, so I walked along the boundary of the extensive site until I could get the best view of the statue in all its glory. He's hard to miss, although partially obscured by the tall trees bordering the grounds. Standing on an eighty-two-metre high pedestal, the statue itself is nearly thirty metres tall and it can be seen from miles around. His hands reach out to the heavens and I noticed a halo of light sitting around his head as the angle of the setting sun encompassed him. I knew then that I was meant to stay here, in Almada.

Being on the south bank of the river Tagus isn't quite as convenient for work, given that I have the daily crossing by ferry to Lisbon. But it feels right, and when I popped in to see Maria on my way back to the hotel that first day, she was thrilled when I broke the news. That chance visit left an impression with me that didn't go away. But I could never have imagined it would inspire an entire project, or that my future career would then hang upon the wild thought when inspiration struck.

* * *

'Oh, my goodness! This isn't quite what I was expecting, I'll be honest,' I comment as Carolina looks at me knowingly. We are standing beneath a midnight blue canopy extending along the traditional, limestone-cobbled pavement. It bears the logo of the café, *Pastéis de Belém 1837*, in large lettering. I love the ambience these sweeping swathes of stone give to the streets. The cobbles are beautiful, but I've learnt that flat shoes are a blessing.

'You think this place is small for the size of the queue? This is nothing! In summer it goes on forever,' she informs me. 'But you will be surprised when you get inside, I promise, Seren.'

'It's infamous, though, isn't it? I mean, anyone coming to Lisbon will no doubt jump on YouTube as I did, and there are entire videos about the search for the most authentic custard tartlets. It's a part of the pilgrimage for sweet lovers coming here,' I acknowledge.

'Ah, that's so true. Now, of course, they make them all around the world, but here it is the real thing. The convents and monasteries in Portugal were shut down in 1834, including the Mosteiro dos Jerónimos, where the original recipe was created. When the clergy and labourers were expelled, a little shop began selling the tarts previously made in the monastery's kitchen. Three years later, the café here was set up and began making the infamous pastries following the original, secret recipe. Egg custard tarts are by far the most popular, see those cardboard sleeves bearing the logo?'

The vast majority of the people exiting the little shop are carrying elongated white boxes in their hands, decorated with a single, circular crest in pale grey. But some also have white paper carrier bags full of a wide variety of baked goods, and there's a constant stream of people going in and out.

'Once tasted, never forgotten. I keep on coming back and I always will,' Carolina chuckles. 'The queue is moving quickly today. In summer, people are usually foot-weary because of the heat and tend to sit at their tables for longer to recover.'

Carolina is a tall woman, very statuesque at around five-foot-ten. At five-six, she makes me feel petite, and I envy her those long, graceful legs.

'Anyway, we deserve this little treat for reaching yet another milestone on the chart,' she says, as we continue to inch forward. The queue snakes behind us down as far as the street corner. The small doorway to the café is within sight now, located to the left of the shop front. The pavement is full and people coming towards us have no choice but to walk in the road to navigate around clusters of family members, toddlers in pushchairs, and groups of friends meeting up. After two very overcast days, everyone seems eager to soak up the warm spring sunshine today.

'You're right, we have cause to celebrate. The first press release has triggered a phenomenal amount of interest. How far away are we from announcing that tickets for the fashion shoot at the Santuário Nacional do Cristo Rei are going on sale?' What excited me about the idea is that it's a unique experience and the perfect way to get people talking about this summer's exhibition at the gallery.

Carolina looks at me intently.

'It's all set to go, but the developers are running a week behind. I'm confident they will be able to confirm the link is live within the next forty-eight hours. So you can expect that email to pop into your inbox early next week.'

I'm sure Carolina can see the look of relief flashing over my face. Those sales are vital to help offset the costs, and without turning the actual shooting of the video into an event, it wouldn't have been doable.

'That's wonderful news. Once people start snapping up those tickets, word of mouth will help to spread the news. I will feel much happier though after Antero and I meet with Rafael Osorio for the first time, on Monday. I'm not sure what to expect, as he hasn't had a lot to say in the video calls. I'm told he's enthusiastic, but he comes across as being quite reserved from what I've seen so far.'

'Until he has something to say, apparently. He can be very insistent I hear,' Carolina replies, wincing a little. 'Ah, that reminds me. I told Antero we were coming here, and he said he would be delighted to join us.' She glances at me, nervously.

Goodness, Carolina and Antero? I didn't see that coming. I give her a reassuring smile and a tell-tale pink hue begins to travel up her neck.

'Oh, I do hope he can make it,' I enthuse. 'The more the merrier as far as I'm concerned.' Having wandered around Lisbon with a guidebook in my hands on several weekends, it's nice to go somewhere in the company of other people. I certainly wouldn't have come here on my own. It's not easy feeling like the odd one out, sitting at a table all alone surrounded by groups of friends and families.

'You are feeling sad?' Carolina enquires, frowning.

'No. But I appreciate this little trip out this morning. Oh, here's Antero!'

I wave when I spot him crossing the road and he breaks out into a huge grin as he approaches. Glancing behind us to check with the people who are next in line that they are happy for him to join us, he offers the two women his most dazzling of smiles. What a charmer he is – it does the trick.

There is a slight awkwardness, though, as he leans in to give Carolina the customary greeting and then turns to me. Our eyes meet and we exchange a meaningful smile. We are about to cross that dividing line and he kisses first my right cheek, then my left.

'We are friends too, no?' he enquires, and I nod, gratefully. 'So, are you ready for our meeting on Monday? Hopefully, Rafael will be in a good mood and eager to impress.'

'He's a perfectionist, I hear, which is a good thing as there's a lot at stake.'

Carolina joins in. 'It's exciting, though. Everyone is talking about it and the buzz has only just begun.'

I can feel their enthusiasm as they both turn to look at me. The pressure is building, and the impression I'm getting about Rafael is that he's temperamental. A chilly sensation hits my stomach for the briefest of moments before I shake it off with a laugh.

'Well, let's hope that his ardent followers start snapping up those tickets the moment they go on sale.'

'It will be something a little different. I'm sure people will be curious to see all that goes on behind the scenes when it comes to a fashion shoot. It's an experience few will ever get to see up close so it will be a novelty.'

A sudden mass exodus of people from the doorway ahead sees the queue eagerly pressing forward. From the outside, it's a grand-looking building set over three floors. Some of the symmetrical windows on the first and second floors have been replaced with patio doors that open out onto small, ironwork balconies. At street level, all I can see is a narrow entrance that I presume leads through into the café, and beyond that is the shop, which is packed with people.

When, eventually, it's our turn to step inside, we follow the snaking line in front of us. The first thing that hits me is the background noise level and the way the high ceilings and tiled floors amplify a whole range of discordant sounds: voices, footsteps, the clanking of metal on metal. The second is the delicious smell. The air is rich with that heavenly aroma of buttery pastry fresh from the oven, so gorgeous it sets the taste buds tingling. My mother wasn't the sort of person who baked, but for me it's evocative of Sunday morning brunches reheating croissants and pains au chocolat. The sweetness instantly makes my mouth begin to water.

We traipse behind a Portuguese family of five, into what feels like a labyrinth of corridors going off in various directions. It's bewildering and both Carolina and I hurry to follow in Antero's footsteps as we pick up the pace. All the tables look full as we move from room to room. Waiters walk purposefully, carrying loaded trays and I strain my neck to catch glimpses of pastries, cakes and coffees of all descriptions. Dressed in black trousers and waistcoats, with crisp white shirts, the demeanour of the staff is extremely efficient but friendly.

One stops to talk briefly to Antero, but I can't follow their conversation. Pointing to a room on the right as he effortlessly raises the platter in his hand above my head, the waiter throws me a fleeting smile. This is turning out to be quite an experience. If only cafés at home were like this one. It exudes its own energy, like a club for sugarholics. This isn't just a bakery, but a factory employing goodness knows how many people, and the further in we go, the louder the noise of the general background chatter and from the sheer volume of people moving around. The rooms are large with tiled floors, and swathes of wall tiling which amplifies every little sound and adds a cavernous echo.

We stop, briefly, to glimpse through a window into just one of the many preparation areas where two long, stainless-steel counters are laid out with enormous trays of freshly cooked tarts and squares of what look like a gooey, yellow sponge cake. It's a production line with rollers guiding the trays along a conveyor belt, trolleys waiting ready for collection, and huge cabinets that could be ovens, or steamers – it's hard to tell.

There's another long queue ahead of us for a large, open-plan seating area, but Antero diverts off to the right and we head into yet another small room of tightly packed tables. Weaving in and out, we make our way back out into the sunshine and discover a little courtyard where the breeze is so welcome, I greedily gulp in the air. Antero sprints ahead to claim the first available table we've seen so far.

'Well done, you,' I exclaim, as Carolina and I catch up and take a seat either side of him. 'It's certainly quieter out here. But what an amazing place, it has the buzz of a smart wine bar back in the UK. And I love the intricate blue and white tiles everywhere.' Some are friezes, others portray entire scenes made up of ceramic tiles. It's enchanting.

'I told you to reserve your judgement until you were inside,' Carolina replies.

A waiter appears to hand out the menus and take our drinks order. He informs us that he will be back shortly. Serving here can't be easy, as even outside in the fresh air, the sounds reverberate and it's a cacophony of noise.

'You cannot say you have lived in Lisbon until you have eaten your first *pastéis de nata* here,' Antero informs me, slapping his hand down onto the table. 'So many bakers have come up with their own recipes and it's worth giving them a try. Then you can decide for yourself who produces the most delicious one.'

I break out into a smile. 'I have already tried one, or two.'

They both laugh.

'Or a dozen?' Carolina enquires knowingly, and I nod.

'So, what else is good on this menu?' I ask, skimming down the little pictures of a wide variety of confectionary. I ignore the savoury section, today is not a day to worry about being good, or for counting calories.

'Shall we order a little selection of things to try as it's your first visit?' Carolina suggests and I nod.

Our espresso coffees arrive in tiny white cups and saucers bearing the iconic logo of the famous café. As Antero places an order, I glance around. There isn't a frown in sight, as I watch people filling their mouths with delight and going back for more. There are buns, slices of gateaux and cheesecake, as well as doughnuts and savoury items resembling pasties.

'It must be strange, Seren, settling into a new country as well as into a new job. You must miss your family and friends.' Antero looks across at me, a small furrow creasing his brow.

'At times, I do. But in the four months I've been here so much has happened that I haven't really had time to sit and think about my old life. It seems so far away now. At first it did feel a bit like being on holiday but that passed surprisingly quickly.'

'Did you know that Seren is a sculptor, Antero?'

He casts a quick glance in Carolina's direction before looking back at me. 'I had no idea.'

I shake my head, laughing. 'I dabble. It's merely a hobby.'

'But an unusual hobby. What medium do you use?' he asks.

'Metal. When I was a young child, I fell in love with a sculpture in our local park. It was a globe set within a frame, as though someone had put the earth in a metal box to protect it. I would run my hands over the solid bars, and it felt cold in winter and hot in summer, as if it wasn't an inanimate object. As a teenager, I went to evening classes at a local college to learn how to weld. My parents thought I was learning how to make jewellery.'

'You have always had an independent mind, then?' Antero replies, just as the waiter appears carrying a large, and very full, tray.

I nod briefly as we make room on the table for an array of plates, and hints of orange, cinnamon and vanilla begin to waft up.

The waiter fusses around, chatting away in Portuguese and, no doubt, making sure we have enough napkins and spare plates before he bustles away.

Both Carolina and Antero indicate for me to tuck in and I reach out for my first, original recipe custard tart. The flaky pastry is so crisp that flakes start to drop down onto my lap as I pick it up. It's the size of three, or four, modest bites and the top of the filling is a gorgeous lemony-yellow, obscured in places with patches where the top has caramelised. This is not the time to be shy, so I take one huge bite – almost half the tart in one go.

Then the taste sensation hits. The flavour of the warm, yet crisp flakiness is quickly replaced by the creamy gooiness of the rich egg custard. Cinnamon adds a little zing, but then the hint of caramel wraps it up like an encompassing hug. I let out a little involuntary groan of delight and my friends both burst out laughing. Swiftly followed by two gulps of espresso, the robust, roasted flavour is the perfect partner to offset the sweetness.

'It's official, this must be on a par with the nectar of the gods. And it was invented by the monks,' I comment, thinking they certainly knew how to eat. But this moment has been made even more special being able to share it with Carolina and Antero. 'This little trip here today was a great idea, thanks guys. Now, you'd better grab some of these quickly, as I'm not ashamed to say that one is not going to be enough.'

'She passed the test,' Carolina says, giving Antero a little wink.

He looks back at her and lingers for the briefest of moments, but it's enough to tell me there is something simmering away between the two of them. Carolina looks away, a little awkwardly.

'Antero, what do you do in your spare time?' I ask, eager to get to know a little more about him.

'I play guitar in a band,' he replies.

'It would be great if we could come to see you play sometime.' I can see that Carolina is delighted by my suggestion and Antero, too.

'We'll arrange something, very soon,' he replies, before popping a whole custard tart into his mouth.

Silence ensues for a little while and sitting here in the company of two people I haven't known for long, but with whom I'm beginning to feel a real connection, I'm starting to finally feel at home.

Carolina and Antero have both gone out of their way at work to help and support me as I've struggled to get to grips with the many obvious barriers. Their acts of kindness have created a special bond and have not gone unnoticed, or unappreciated. I will never forget the hands of friendship they have offered to me.

5

A MOMENTOUS MONDAY

The morning flies by but leaves me with mixed feelings as I sit with Antero after our meeting with Rafael and his assistant. Carolina has headed back to her office to tidy up the notes she took down, which in this case will not be an enviable job.

'My head is spinning, Antero. Am I right in thinking that his main concern is the background noise from the suspension bridge? What on earth are we to make of that? After all, there is nothing we can do about the Ponte 25 de Abril and the traffic that flows across it. It's a main artery and the nature of an outdoor fashion show is that life goes on as normal around it. Surely he understands that?'

Antero shrugs his shoulders.

Rafael kept using the same words, as if we weren't getting it. But he didn't always give Antero time to translate for me so that I could respond to him before he started speaking again. He talks fast and is expressive with his hands, and body. Several times I thought he was going to launch himself out of his chair and stand, to labour the point he was trying to make. Poor Antero had his work cut out and the pauses while he tried to catch me up on what was being said seemed to frustrate Rafael.

'He relaxed a little when I explained that the video would have a professional backing track and a voice-over for the exhibition in the museum. But he kept coming back to the noise, over and over. His other concern is that the waiting staff circulating with the platters celebrating the culinary delights of Lisbon will be a distraction. He's insisting there is a set break in filming while the food is served.'

'Well, that's not a realistic option, I'm afraid. Rafael is acting as if he is the star of the show, but each element is equally as important. The income earnt from promoting the Portuguese food industry is also helping to subsidise the cost of the fashion shoot. I'll have to come up with a solution that will satisfy both parties.'

'He wasn't in a listening mood, today, I fear.' Antero sounds almost apologetic, but there wasn't anything he could have done differently.

'I noticed! Were there any other demands?' I'm trying my best to remain cool, but the meeting felt more like one man having a rant. Antero did his best to placate Rafael and the man did shake hands with me before he left, but he came across as demanding and inflexible. The parting look he gave me seemed to imply that if I didn't already get the gist of his concerns, it was Antero's job to explain it to me in great detail, so I could then get them sorted.

'Rafael is not a very diplomatic man, Seren, but it wasn't as bad as it sounded. He has no limiter... filter. Whatever is in his head, he has to say it immediately. He asked that you get back to him as soon as possible to let him know what can be done. In my opinion, I think the wisest thing is to reply by email rather than invite him here for another meeting. That way we can deal with his response in a much more structured, and calmer, way. You agree?'

'I do, thank you, Antero, and I'm sorry it was such a rough ride. It was hard to get him to listen at all at one point, and I appreciate the enormous amount of patience you demonstrated. I'll work on this over the next couple of days and send the document to you for translation; we'll take it from there once we have his response. Right, I think it's time for a lunch break. I'm certainly in need of some fresh air and a walk to stretch my legs after that little fiasco.'

As we get up and head for the door, Antero leans in to place his hand on my arm.

'Passion is good, but it sometimes... what's the word... *boils* over.'

'Hmm. Well, let's hope I haven't made a huge mistake, and he's the right man for the job.'

* * *

'Hey, Seren. What are you doing?' Judi's voice sounds bright and breezy today.

'Sitting on a bench overlooking the water. It's been a tough morning, so I treated myself to a chicken pitta with curried mango sauce and it was delicious. How are things at your end?'

'Good. Really good. I promised I'd get back to you with some dates. The earliest I can get away is the second week of June, after that it's the third week of July. I haven't checked flights yet, but July might be an issue, being peak period.'

'The fifth and sixth of June I'm working as it's the weekend when everything is happening. We can get around it, though, as I can ask someone to pick you up from the airport, then, in the evening, bring you up to the monument where we'll be filming. There will be plenty to see and do. Afterwards, we can walk back to my place, it's close by.'

'It's sound exciting, but I don't want to put you out. You'll be under pressure.'

The truth is that I have no idea how exhausted I'm going to be feeling at that point after the hectic run-up to the exhibition, but I can hardly leave Judi to fend for herself for the best part of two days.

'How about I bring a friend? That way, you won't have to bother about me, as I'll have someone I can wander around with until you're free.'

'Well, aside from the sofa bed, I could sort out a blow-up mattress,' I offer.

'Ah, I hadn't thought about that. It's not a problem, we'd probably get a better deal on a shared hotel room with flights included, anyway. Leave it to me and I'll let you know if it's doable.'

'I hope it is, as I can't wait to catch up properly. And once that weekend is over, I fully intend taking some time off, so it will be great. Bring someone who is up for an inordinate amount of uphill walking and pack a pair of comfortable, flat shoes. Anyway, you sound really happy.'

There's a short pause. 'I am, actually. Mind you, I haven't heard a thing from anyone in my family for over a month and that's always a blessing. I bumped into your mum the other day. It was a bit awkward as she asked me how you were doing, as if she hadn't heard from you in a while.'

I let out a sigh. 'She hasn't and I do feel guilty. I'll send her another email, but whatever I tell her, she'll share with my father. So, the less I say, the better. My life here is different. There's still pressure of course, and plenty of it, but I'm happy. If I start dwelling on the past it will bring me down.'

'Aww... my dear friend. Happiness is different things to different people, isn't it? And sometimes what we think we want isn't what we want at all. Other times it turns our lives around.'

'That's rather cryptic!' I burst out, in surprise.

'No, not really. I'm learning to stand back and see the bigger picture.'

If that's what having no contact with her family does for Judi, then it's a step in the right direction. Or maybe it's the relief of having settled into her new job and realising that a guy is just a guy.

'Any developments you care to share?' I enquire, intrigued by this new, philosophical Judi.

'I might have had a couple of dinner dates. And a trip to the cinema with someone rather special, but I'll leave it there, for now.'

'Well good for you, lady. I was worried that without me by your side to keep you on track, you'd fall into the old trap of getting dragged into other people's problems. I'm impressed.'

'And I'm off to book a week's holiday. Lisbon is calling and I'm all ears!'

* * *

When I arrive back at the office, I think about how I'm going to pacify Rafael, as any solution is going to involve a compromise of some sort. It's funny how different things look on a full stomach, though, and on balance I think he might have a valid point. During the rush hour, or if the wind is in the wrong direction, the traffic on the bridge might well be an overpowering distraction. If not for the audience, then for Rafael when he's working.

This calls for a little research. I need to walk up to the location on a Saturday around lunchtime to gauge the full extent of the problem. It doesn't usually open evenings, so I can't test it out, but I should imagine the traffic on a Friday night between seven and ten o'clock is going to be no worse than a normal Saturday when people are heading into Lisbon to shop, eat and see the sights.

For me, the monument is a special place and I find the sounds of Lisbon intriguing rather than distracting. But I try to compare it to listening to music with an annoyingly pounding beat, which I find strangely disconcerting when I'm welding. My creative zone requires concentration and focus, and a more gentle, non-intrusive background of white noise. While classical music might enhance the mood, other sounds wouldn't.

As for the timing of the serving of the food, he's just being too demanding over that. People can take a bite-size canapé from a tray as it passes in front of them with the merest deflection of their eyes. Is that likely to spoil their enjoyment of the spectacle, as he insists? I'm sure a live shoot is going to be a stop/start process anyway. Judging by what I've seen of Rafael, he's going to stress over the slightest gust of wind and that, I know, is going to be an issue. Surprisingly, that was one concern he hasn't raised yet, but Lisbon is known for the way the winds can change and the Cristo Rei is on top of a hill. A big one.

With ten hours of daily sunshine being the norm here in June, the odds are in our favour for a dry day. The only unknown is the wind factor, which often carries with it sand and dust, which I would have thought was more likely to cause Rafael a problem. Rechecking the longer-term weather forecast yet again, I'm as happy as I can be this far out that we won't need to erect the covered walkway among the avenue of olive trees, which is our backup plan.

When my mobile kicks into life, I'm surprised to see it's Reid calling. He's up to date with everything we've requested, but maybe he's chasing the fabric samples. I know he'll feel happier once he's seen them and they are due in this week.

'Hi, Reid. How are you?'

'I'm good, Seren, and you?'

I try to keep my voice upbeat, for fear I'll let out a groan, because that's how I'm feeling. 'Great, thank you. I'm just thrashing out the finer details of the photo shoot.'

'Problems?'

Awkward.

'Not really,' I reply a tad breezily. 'But I've only visited the monument either first thing on a Saturday morning when it's quiet, or in the evening when the gates are shut. I like to stand and watch the sun setting behind the statue. Rafael thinks we might have a noise issue during filming.'

'From the bridge?'

Oh. It's a little worrying Reid immediately picked up on it.

'Yes. I need to take a trip up there and consider what options we might have to help soften it.'

He laughs. 'Good luck with that. The bridge has a sound of its own, it's the beating heart of Lisbon. Anyway, I'm ringing to ask if you'd do me a huge, personal favour.'

Why does it make my stomach flutter a little to hear him say that? Our paths haven't crossed since I visited his house in Sintra and our emails and phone calls have all been purely business.

'Fire away. If it's something I can help you with, then it would be my pleasure.'

'I'm having a little get-together the Saturday after next. My assistant will be there to help as a co-host, but some of my guests will also be attending the party at the gallery in June. You've managed to attract an incredible amount of interest and everyone is talking about the exhibition. The problem I have is that they're all curious and I'm anticipating a deluge of questions, things I wouldn't answer half as well as you can. So, I thought, rather than risk underselling the project you've masterminded, why not see if the lady herself is available?'

I'm a little surprised by his request. 'Isn't that rather like talking shop when your friends will be there to simply relax and enjoy themselves?' I point out, wondering what I might be letting myself in for; is it a little drinks thing, a party, or a sales pitch?

That gravelly voice echoes down the line with a throaty laugh. 'You don't know my friends,' he replies, and I can hear the sardonic smile in his voice. 'You succeeded in painting me a virtual picture and, I'll be honest, I needed that because even I didn't really grasp the full breath of the project. People are naturally curious about what's involved and many of them run local businesses. An art exhibition they understand, but someone asked me the other day if I was expanding into textiles. I suppose I am, in a limited way.' He sounds amused by that thought.

'Okay. I understand where you are coming from. Perhaps our marketing needs to be a little more cohesive, so that's really helpful to know, Reid. I'll pass that on to Carolina. And yes, of course, I'll be there to circulate and answer any questions people might have – it would be my pleasure.'

Reid Henderson is, without a doubt, the star of this project and if anyone is going to make waves, I would have thought it was him. Instead he's been easy-going and cooperative, even given the fact that he's clearly rushed off his feet, so this is the least I can do.

'That's great, Seren, thank you. My business manager will be delighted, as it's something he's arranged and he's flying over from London to make sure it goes well. I will return the favour, I promise. I'll get someone to pick you up at three o'clock on the day. You might want to consider packing an overnight bag in case it's a late one. Several of my guests will be staying over. We'll speak soon, then.'

As we disconnect, I feel it's only right that I make Senhor Ferreira aware of the commitment I've made. In the eyes of Reid's guests, I'll be an official representative of the gallery and it would be wrong of me not to inform him. When I pop my head around his door, he looks up with a smile.

'Seren, come, take a seat. How can I help?'

'I've just spoken with Reid Henderson and he's asked me to attend what sounds like a formal cocktail party he's holding at Casa da Floresta. I'll be there to answer any questions that arise about the events we have planned. I wanted to check that you don't have a problem with this?'

'Not at all. It's good of you to make yourself available. No doubt there will be some very influential people there.'

His response is positive and it's a relief. It wasn't until after I said yes that it occurred to me there might be an unspoken rule to consider. Reid is, after all, a famous and well-respected artist and it might be more appropriate for one of the directors to be present.

'It occurred to me that if Mr Henderson is fielding questions, then it means our marketing message isn't clear enough. Carolina and I will review everything and revise our strategy.'

Senhor Ferreira nods his head, cocking an eyebrow. 'It's a new concept, so the more information we get out there, the better. But it's timely you should appear, because I'm getting a flood of emails from people who would like to come on board and be a part of the celebration.'

I look back at him, straight-faced. 'While that is good news, Senhor Ferreira, my concern is that we are stretched to capacity with the programme as it stands.'

It's not always the most comfortable thing to question Senhor Ferreira, but sometimes it pays to tell the truth.

'I know and I appreciate your honesty, Seren. But when people see a good thing, they want to be a part of it. All I'm asking is that you give some consideration to possible ways of widening our partnerships for the duration of the summer. Success breeds success and we would wish to pursue whatever opportunities arise. What additional resources would you need?'

I smile back at him, politely, my mind in overdrive.

'If Carolina was promoted temporarily to become my assistant events manager, we could possibly enlist one of the general admin staff to support her on the publicity side without too much disruption. I would also need Antero to be permanently assigned to the team for the duration.'

Before I get to the count of three, he responds.

'Approved. Thank you, Seren. Your flexibility is duly noted and appreciated. Please congratulate your team for me.'

Walking back to my office, I'm still processing the news when Carolina catches up with me.

'I've been looking for you all afternoon. You're not finishing for the day, are you? I need a quick word.'

It's been a long one, and I've done all I can for today.

'If you're ready to head home, we could talk on the way if you like. I have a bit of a headache coming on and a little fresh air might help. I have some good news to share with you, I think you'll be pleased.'

In no time at all, we're on our way to the ferry terminal at Cais do Sodré. We've missed the first wave of the rush hour, but there's still a steady stream of people making their way in the same direction. As we walk, I break the news about the changes to Carolina. I don't know if she's more delighted at the thought of stepping up and having more responsibility, or the fact that Antero is going to be working more closely with us.

'You will find a way to work this out, Seren,' she adds encouragingly. 'And you know that both Antero and I will do whatever is necessary to ensure the project is a success. We knew Rafael was likely to be demanding. Nothing is ever easy, is it?'

As the mass body of people are funnelled into the concrete terminal building, we soon come to a standstill as we wait while the ferry in dock offloads its passengers. Then it's our turn to plough forward and cross one of the metal gangplanks. Carolina nimbly races ahead to make her way to the stairs leading up to the top deck. When I catch up with her, I sink down gratefully into the graffitied, faded orange and pale grey plastic seat, glad we don't have to stand.

'I haven't had time to tell Antero yet, but I'll phone him as soon as I get home.' I can hear the tiredness in my voice and Carolina casts me a sympathetic glance.

'This is wonderful, Seren. Senhor Ferreira will be pleased that the gallery is attracting such interest.'

She's right, of course. There's nothing I'm being presented with that I can't sort out. We settle back to enjoy the ten-minute journey across the river Tagus and take in the views. The scenery is stunning, and it never gets old, even though I do this crossing twice a day, Monday to Friday. It's the sort of commute to work I could never have dreamt about living back home, and one that many of my friends in the UK would envy.

Overhead, a silver bullet of a plane way up high glints, as the sun bounces off its wings. It looks like a bird flying over the Ponte 25 de Abril. At this level, the road noise is way above us and it's just a low droning sound.

Linking Lisbon to Almada, the suspension bridge is over two kilometres long and reminiscent of San Francisco's Golden Gate bridge. With six lanes and a train line suspended below road level, it's high enough to allow the massive container and cruise ships to pass underneath. Of course, the sounds emanating from it are going to travel. A fleeting smile passes over my face as I imagine myself handing Rafael and his assistant some earplugs to block out the offending hubbub.

Today, the water flowing beneath it is a rich turquoise blue. As I scan the sweeping coastline, my eyes instinctively home in on old-town Cacilhas and the cluster of dockside buildings, which include decaying warehouses long overdue for demolition. Beyond that, the white buildings of the city of Almada rise up, topped with the glorious hues of pinks and terracotta rooflines. My eyes automatically work along the coastline of the south bank. To the right, the tree-covered hill dips and as the land rises up again, there it is – standing alone, arms reaching out like a proud father ready to embrace his people, the statue of Cristo Rei.

With a wonderfully cool breeze coming off the water, I close my eyes for a couple of minutes and gradually the tension in my neck and the back of my head eases.

When we dock, Carolina and I take the short ride to São João Batista together, where we hug goodbye before heading off in opposite directions.

'I'm always here if you ever need company, or someone to talk to, Seren,' Carolina offers. 'Antero will be delighted and very grateful to you, as am I. His dream is to work solely for the gallery. This might be his chance to demonstrate that he isn't just an interpreter.'

I can see this means a lot to her and I have no doubt at all that they will both be eager to prove they are up to the challenge.

'That's good to know, Carolina. Thank you. We can work on raising Antero's profile, I'm sure. See you back here tomorrow, same time as usual,' I call out, as I begin the long uphill trek home.

I call Antero as I walk and he can't hide his enthusiasm, or delight.

Afterwards, I slow my pace, taking the time to consider what the easiest options are to appease Rafael. The complexities of managing his expectations have a wider impact and yet his standing dictates that I cannot gloss over anything he raises.

The company who are putting on the *Gostos de Lisboa* display represent a consortium of different restaurants and food-sellers, to present the tastes of Lisbon. The initial meeting simply outlined the companies involved, which the board of directors have now approved. Our next meeting will thrash out the details, such as where the catering vans will be parked and the mechanics of setting up food stations, from which the serving staff will replenish their platters. An idea pops into my head as if a switch has suddenly been flicked.

'Simple,' I say out loud, feeling pleased with myself. It's not too late to steer it in a slightly different direction. Keeping everything a safe distance away from where Rafael will be working is easy enough. It's a huge site, anyway, and the answer is to keep the waiting staff within a set area. If people are hungry, they can wander away from the promenade and return whenever they want.

As for the noise factor, well, hopefully I'll get to the bottom of that. I can't stop the traffic, so I suspect it's going to be a case of providing some distracting background noise of our own.

I'm foot-weary as I turn into the little courtyard, and when I pass Maria's kitchen door, she pops her head out.

'Ah, you are a little late today. I have just made a pot of *caldeirada de peixe*. Can you join us?'

A dish of Maria's Portuguese fish stew and a little company is exactly what I need this evening.

'*Maravilhoso*, Maria, *obrigada*.' It is a wonderful gesture, and I am grateful to end what has been an exhausting day in the company of my generous neighbours. We'll sit and chat, everyone sharing moments from their day, but I know it will be light-hearted, with a lot of laughter. Tomorrow is another day full of endless possibilities and when my head eventually touches the pillow, my mood is lighter and brighter.

6

FLYING HIGH

Inevitably the contours of life are not flat. Every dip, therefore, will eventually be followed by an upswing, and this week has been no exception. What felt, on Monday, like a setback has resulted in ending the week with a stronger team and a much clearer focus.

Delegating can throw up as many problems as it solves, as I've found to my detriment in the past. Some people rise to the occasion, and others sink. But when it goes well, it's so satisfying to see your colleagues step up with enthusiasm to take on a new challenge, eager to take it forward. Antero, I now realise, has been held back in the past by his own awareness of the boundaries of his remit. But with his expanded role, he is happy to throw out ideas in our meetings. It's obvious that he's going to be an asset in ways I couldn't have imagined at first. He's incredibly calm under pressure and he's also a master organiser.

As for Carolina, aside from her marketing skills, she is one of the most efficient administrators I've ever worked with. And the both of them are totally professional to the point that I doubt anyone, aside from myself, suspects there is a growing attraction between them.

My thoughts chunter on inside my head as I stand back to gaze with pride at my not-so-little bird sculpture. 'There, that's better.'

He gazes back at me proudly from his new perch. Gone is the geometrical metal box, which sits in the corner ready to be recycled. In its place is a stack of flat, metal tablets offset to resemble a pile of limestone slabs. My noble marsh sandpiper looks happy and a sense of elation hits me square in the gut. He's beautiful, but how on earth I'm going to get him out of the workshop and into the garden, I have no idea. He's way too heavy for one person to move.

Glancing at my watch, I see that it's almost eleven o'clock, and time I sorted myself out to head up to the monument. Walking back into the house, there's an insistent tapping sound and I head straight for the front door. Swinging it open, Reid is standing there, making me step back in surprise.

'Oh, Reid.' My T-shirt is patchy with sweat and my hair is lank against my head. 'Sorry, please come in. Excuse my appearance, welding is hot work.'

He can see I'm embarrassed, and he gives me an apologetic look as he steps inside.

'This is charming,' he comments, to fill the awkward moment of silence between us.

'It is, isn't it? It's plenty big enough for what I need, and I feel as if I'm in the heart of the little community here.'

We stand in the middle of the sitting room, looking at each other and he clears his throat. I watch as he runs a hand through his hair, an indication that he's nervous, maybe.

'I should have called first, Seren. It's rude of me to simply turn up like this, I'm sorry. You mentioned you were going to check out the background noise up at the site today and I've been thinking about it. I have an idea that might solve the problem at the same time as gaining the event some extra publicity.'

It's hard to wonder what on earth I must look like as he stares back at me.

'No, it's fine. And I'm intrigued.'

'It also occurred to me that you are still very new to Lisbon and I wondered if you'd appreciate some company. A second opinion is always helpful, I find.'

'It's a kind thought, thank you. I, um... I was about to jump in the shower and change. Why don't I get you a cold drink and show you through to the rear garden? I'll only be ten minutes and you can sit on the bench and listen to the birds. And the sound of my neighbours,' I grin at him. You can't hear another soul at Reid's luxurious country home, no matter where you sit.

I grab a soft drink from the fridge and Reid follows me out through the bedroom and into the garden. It feels a little awkward, but he seems content so I leave him to it, hurrying back inside. This is going to be the quickest shower and change of my entire life. I'm conscious of each second ticking by and a little annoyed that Reid didn't ring me before turning up. What if my plans had changed? Would he have driven up to the Santuário and wandered around looking for me? I am curious to hear what he has to say, though. I had been toying with the idea of a loop of classical music playing in the background. Nothing too distracting and easy enough to sort out, as long as it meets with Rafael's approval. But I could be way off the mark as I'm not really up to speed with popular music over here. Maybe Reid will be able to offer some advice.

When I reappear in the garden, hopefully looking refreshed and smelling a whole lot better, Reid points to the workshop.

'Aren't you going to show me your masterpiece?' he enquires, his eyes smiling.

'No. There isn't time,' I reply firmly. 'We need to head out now as Saturday lunchtime is when the traffic noise will be the greatest.' The mere thought of Reid's experienced eye appraising my work makes my stomach start to churn and that's why it's off limits.

I turn and, with a noticeable reluctance, he follows me.

'Artists are supposed to share the pieces they create,' he mumbles, but I ignore him.

As I lock the door behind us, and we make our way to his car, I turn the conversation back to work. 'So, you think Rafael has a valid point?'

'I do. I wonder if you are so taken with the views and the beauty, you haven't really stood there and listened to the throb of modern living. At night, I fear the growing darkness will tend to amplify it and so an alternative distraction is a great idea.'

His comments give me pause for thought, but it isn't until we're standing on the promenade in the shadow of the statue of Cristo Rei that I appreciate what he's talking about.

'Admittedly, today the wind is in the wrong direction and this is probably the noisiest it gets. But it's like a constant drumming, isn't it?' he prompts.

'How did I not register this?'

'The traffic flow never completely stops, but it's noisier when it's free-flowing, as it is now. Ironically, when it gets heavily congested, it slows to a crawl and the noise level is much quieter. The wind is carrying the sounds towards us as up here there is nothing to act as a buffer. The promenade is on a level with the bridge itself.'

We stop to lean against the waist-high wooden fence, the other side of which the scrubland falls away.

'Noise affects people in different ways. To some people, it's merely a nuisance, an irritation. To others, it's the sound of life happening all around us. It doesn't bother me, and it seems that it doesn't bother you, either, but it's there and it's a constant.'

'I suppose what matters is that it bothers Rafael. I'm thinking a little soft music in the background to take the edge off it. A soundtrack playing some of the Portuguese classical composers might do the trick.'

Reid nods his head, pursing his lips as if he's a little disappointed. 'Have you heard of the wave of new *fado* music?'

'No, it's not a term I've heard before. What does *fado* mean?'

Now it's Reid's turn to laugh. 'If I could convey the essence of it in a sentence, I would succeed where others have failed. It began in the early eighteen-hundreds and it's a type of Portuguese folk music. There's an air of sadness to it, a haunting, soulful quality, some might say has a hint of the blues. What I like about the way it's been reinvented and brought up to date in the last few years is that modern instruments soften it. It's a perfect solution.'

I stare at him, raising my eyebrows. Music is music, surely? 'Why?'

He indicates for us to begin walking and we trace the path the models will take along the promenade. Overhead, the sun beats down and I'm grateful for the cooling breeze.

'Off the record, Rafael is known for his temperamental outbursts.

This makes me sound old, but he's young and headstrong. He'll mellow as time goes on because, if nothing else, he'll realise it pays to make friends and not enemies, but that's a lesson to be learnt the hard way. I hope you don't think I'm speaking out of turn, but I thought it might be more helpful to you right now if I talk frankly. Rafael is extremely talented and has amassed a big following on social media, Leonor tells me. But he has a fiery personality and a short fuse. So your challenge is more about coming up with a solution he's unlikely to find fault with, given that it's not a problem you can take away.'

'Your honesty is appreciated as I would be mortified to come up with something that was equally as bothersome to him.'

As we reach the end of the promenade and are about to wander through the grove of olive trees, I stop for a moment to close my eyes, aware that Reid is watching me.

The gusty wind is playing havoc with my hair, and his, to my amusement. The whooshing sound rises and falls. I hear the chatter and laughter of the visitors around us, but it's overlaid by the constant clickety-clack of the vehicles travelling along the bridge. Overhead, circling birds call out to each other and somewhere, further down the coast, the sound of metal hitting metal travels on the breeze. I love all the sounds, because to me they are the beating heart of Lisbon and remind me that it is alive, but he has a point. By far the most dominant noise today is that repetitive rumble, and the more I focus on it, the more distracting it becomes.

'Well, thank you for pointing me in the right direction, Reid. I will most certainly look into your suggestion. It might be more to Rafael's liking and, naturally, I want to ensure he's happy.'

Reid waggles a finger at me. 'I can save you a lot of work and guarantee you'll get on the right side of Rafael at the same time. Come on, let's head over to the café and grab a drink. We can sit in the shade and I'll explain.'

We stroll across the grass and take a shortcut along an avenue of miniature palm trees. It's one of my favourite areas. With wide, squat, pineapple-looking trunks, and massive feathery fronds of green which hang like an arch no more than ten feet above our heads, this is my fall-back option – if it's too windy on the day of the show, then this sheltered area will become the runway.

I try to fathom out why Reid is taking the time and trouble to accompany me here, when a phone call would easily have sufficed. He must have better things to do in his spare time, surely? Or does he simply enjoy chatting with someone from his home country? His guard is down, and his general demeanour is relaxed today. He's different from the man who takes part in the video calls, who is polite but to the point.

Once we hit the gravelled area leading to the café, ever the gentleman, Reid seeks out a table tucked away in a shady area on the paved terrace. He leaves me to sit and wait as he goes off to join the queue.

With one of the two chapels a mere stone's throw to my right, the sound of monks singing emanates across the divide. The music is played on a continuous loop and helps to mask any background noise. It's relaxing, even though the chatter of tourists filling the tables around me partially drowns it out.

Today, the gusting breeze comes in waves but is partially deflected by the red and pale pink brick columns supporting the terrace roof. I'm content to sit and simply enjoy my surroundings, tucked away in a shady spot where my hair isn't being blown all over the place.

Reid appears carrying a full tray. I help lift off the coffee cups and place them on the table. He slides a plate of four egg custard tarts in front of me, then lifts off two glasses of water before placing the tray onto a spare chair. 'Who can resist, right? I'm hazarding a guess it won't be you,' he jests.

'I'm already a connoisseur.'

'Enjoy,' he says, his eyes sparkling as he lowers himself into the seat next to me. 'Anyway, where were we? Ah, yes. I'm reliably informed that a young woman who is well-known to Rafael – a fact that is not yet common knowledge – has recently recorded her second album. The first one did very well, but, as we all know, everyone with something to sell is constantly seeking new opportunities to gain exposure. I could put you in touch with Yolanda Abreu's agent, Senhor Sequeira, and you could take it from there. It's a simple solution all round.'

I pause for a moment to sink my teeth into one of the tarts. It's good but would benefit from a little more cinnamon, I reflect, as I mull over Reid's suggestion. Pandering to Rafael like this could be the answer. If Reid is correct, then at least it's less likely for Rafael to find fault on the day, I suppose. He's hardly going to criticise the work of someone he knows, is he? Whereas a random playlist could throw up all sorts of problems. 'I really appreciate the digging you've done to come up with this solution, Reid. It's very generous of you, as I know how busy you are.'

Reid has just devoured a whole tart in two bites, and he smiles at me from above the paper napkin with which he's wiping his mouth. With his shirt sleeves rolled back, the hairs on his arm look pale against his tanned skin, bleached by the sun. I find myself wondering if people around us think we're a couple but realise the glances we're getting are more likely for another reason. No doubt some people will recognise his face.

'It's the least I can do given that you've so graciously agreed to come to my rescue next Saturday. Besides, it really was no bother at all. I was at a friend's birthday party and happened to find myself standing next to a music buff.'

One look at his face and I can see that he's making light of it, and I suspect it's taken a lot more effort than he's letting on.

'It's all beginning to feel very real now, isn't it?' I murmur, more to myself than as a part of the conversation.

'Do you want to know the truth?' he asks, leaning forward and lowering his voice.

I shift around a little in my seat, wondering what he's going to say next.

'This came along at just the right time for me. I was becoming detached from my work, maybe even a little disinterested. That sounds petulant and ungrateful, I know. But my life has become one constant round of the same thing and the only time I'm happy, other than when I'm with my daughter, is when I'm in my studio, either here or in London. Which is less and less, because after an intense period of hiding myself away and being productive comes the slog of selling and being seen. My business manager, Tomas, is Beatriz's eldest brother and right now he's ramping things up and celebrating my renewed vitality, as he so eloquently termed it.'

We exchange a brief smile. 'That's kind of you to share that with me. It's a truly wonderful thing to have been blessed with such an amazing talent. It must be tough, though, to walk away from the easel and jump through the marketing hoops. The two worlds don't really sit well together, do they?'

'Exactly. I was born to paint, but the rest of it is an unfortunate necessity. However, I never lose sight of the end goal. Every hoop I jump through now gets me closer to setting up the gallery and the art studio. But, as they say, patience is a virtue and it's one I struggle with, constantly.'

I can see from his body language that there are things on his mind, and, for a brief moment, he seems full of conflict.

'My team and I are totally committed to ensuring that the exhibition is a huge success. And it will be,' I reassure him.

'Well, word is travelling fast, so whatever you're doing is working. I'd become a little too complacent and it's good to take a step outside one's comfort zone occasionally. How my work will hold up when it's being paraded along the promenade here, who knows? But I needed that jolt to get me out of a rut. Tomas convinced me it was the right thing to do and he was right.'

The way he's looking at me as I process my thoughts makes my heart miss a beat.

'Anyway, I'm grateful to you, Seren. And that leads me on to the other reason I dropped by today. It's a personal matter and rather delicate, so I would appreciate it if you could keep it just between the two of us.'

I was about to finish off the dregs of my coffee, but I put the cup down, anxious over the change in his tone of voice. Have I done something wrong?

He looks away and I can see that he's embarrassed. 'Sharing my fractured life story with you wasn't my intention, but my personal life is inextricably linked to my business. Leonor is Tomas's daughter. I'm well aware that she's Beatriz's main source of information, often without meaning to be, as my niece has always been incredibly loyal to me. But just lately, well, there's family stuff going on behind the scenes, so if you get any problems in your communications with Leonor, please email me direct, or text me.'

Reid gives me a pointed look, which I'm not sure I understand.

'I've always found Leonor to be extremely efficient,' I reply. She can come across as a little curt at times, but I assumed it was because she's under pressure managing Reid's timetable.

'It's rather complicated, I'm afraid. Beatriz still feels her views should be taken into consideration when it comes to my work, and Tomas didn't consult her before the decision was made to get involved with this project. That is a totally unreasonable demand obviously, but to her my art is a family business, despite the fact that we are divorced. We still have some financial links and she sees it as looking after Ana's inheritance. The truth is that she's only able to dabble because she has direct access to Tomas. He can sidestep her manoeuvres to a degree, but Leonor is a little more susceptible. Beatriz makes it her business to gather information and then waylay Tomas to find out what's going on. It isn't easy for him, as she is still very much a fervent, and active, supporter of my work.'

It's too late for Reid to pull out of the project to please his ex-wife and I get no sense that he wants to, but clearly he's worried she's going to cause problems. Thinking back over the last week or so, Leonor hasn't responded as quickly as usual and I've had to chase her a couple of times.

'I know it's a ridiculous situation to find myself in, Seren, but if you have any problems, I would be grateful if you could let me know immediately.'

'Of course, I will. And anything you say to me is in confidence, I can assure you. If there is anything I can do to ease the situation, please do not hesitate to let me know.'

He can see I mean well, but his frown shows the full extent of his concern.

'I can't risk inflaming Beatriz in any way. My daughter has a mind of her own, but her mother exerts total control over her for the time being. Beatriz has recently severed all links between Ana and my family in the UK and that has come as a total shock.'

It's obvious he's concerned about what's happening and when we were at the house I did think it was odd when he said his ex-wife wasn't speaking to him. It sounded petty, but I hadn't appreciated the full impact with regard to his daughter.

Despite my reservations, I reach out and place my hand on his arm, as it rests on the table. 'It's tough enough for two parents raising a teen, I should imagine, so it's not an easy situation to find yourself in. Is it possible to call on a third party to help get you and Beatriz talking again?'

'Tomas is a go-between at times, but he's growing tired of the constant battles. Other than to constantly give in to Beatriz's demands, there's little I can do,' he replies.

'You have a voice as a father, Reid, and you also have the right to live your life the way you choose.' The moment I finish speaking I regret my words, thinking it's none of my business and it sounds like I'm judging him.

'Wise words,' Reid utters, his voice low.

'And easy to say. I'm sorry, you are in an impossible situation.'

'Hmm. That sums it up, perfectly. A part of me can't believe that I've allowed it to come to this, but Beatriz will always have power over me and she's made that very clear. I fear I've ruined enough relationships for one lifetime to risk doing any further damage, even though that's tough to accept.' He trains his eyes on me and I feel a jolt, like a surge of electricity running through my veins. Am I that transparent, I wonder? 'When you stepped into my life, it was a pleasant surprise in the midst of a dark phase for me. You remind me what it's like to feel inspired and hopeful, when I'd become jaded and I was simply going through the motions.'

His words make my heart constrict. How terribly sad.

'But you must never give up on life. Moments of pure happiness need to be grabbed before they pass you by. Some things in life aren't meant to be forever, but that doesn't make them any less important, or special.'

To my surprise, my hand edges down his arm until our fingertips are touching and when we look at each other, they intertwine as if it's the most natural thing in the world.

Was Reid asking if I find him as attractive as he finds me? Well, now he has his answer. And so do I.

* * *

'This wasn't planned, Seren, please believe me. Quite the opposite. I had no intention of taking advantage of you by sharing my personal woes, other than to put you on alert. Being with you like this... well, it makes me think about the life I saw ahead of me, once – a long time ago now. But it didn't quite turn out as I'd hoped. Beatriz is well connected, and it doesn't pay to get on the wrong side of her. I pulled you into something you can't possibly understand by inviting you to dinner and now this happens, today. It was wrong of me to be so cavalier and I can't even begin to apologise.'

His remorse is purely down to his concerns for my well-being and any potential fallout. Doesn't Reid think he deserves a happy life if he can find the right person to be with? Lying in my bed, wrapped in his arms, the sincerity in his voice tells me it's not a rejection. The passion between us has been simmering since the moment we first met and yet we both fought it. Or tried to ignore it. But now it feels so right, even though I could list endless reasons why this shouldn't have happened.

For a few glorious hours, just knowing we were giving ourselves to each other freely and without any underlying motive felt honest; that need to be wanted, desired, and treasured, I suppose. And Reid has more than satisfied that emptiness within me, he has made me feel whole again when I didn't even know there was something missing. No promises and no expectations for a future – just a magnetic attraction that came from a place within me I didn't know existed. How can I explain that away?

'You didn't talk me into this, Reid, and I hope you know that.'

I'm well aware of the implications of this afternoon for us both, but I can't hide how happy I feel. And I can see Reid is happy too, even though his thoughts are now in turmoil.

'This is the last thing I wanted... well, *expected* – of course I wanted it since the moment I first set eyes on you. It's rare to meet anyone as refreshingly honest and straightforward; these days everyone has an agenda. I could tell you don't, Seren, and there's something so damned attractive and mesmerising about you. Just hearing your voice or being in your company lifts my spirits and pulls me away from the negativity that is stifling at times. But it's unfair of me to drag you into my complicated life.'

'I did have an agenda,' I remind him.

'I mean a personal agenda and not a business one. You know what I'm trying to say,' his voice softens as he leans his head against mine.

'Well, for my part you captured my attention in a way no man has ever done before. That's a good thing, isn't it?' Having voiced my thoughts, it sounds defeatist, as if I already know what Reid's response will be.

He groans, nuzzling his chin into my hair. 'No. It's a bad thing. Ten years is a big age difference, Seren, believe me. It's not something to take lightly. When I was twenty-five years old, I thought nothing would stop me achieving what I wanted. As each year passed, things began to weigh me down. Marriage, a demanding wife, even the birth of my beautiful daughter added a pressure I couldn't even have imagined previously. Fifteen years later and I've never felt less sure of anything. I've regressed. It's all become too much, too demanding, too impossible to sort out and I'm at breaking point. You, well, you are on the brink of discovering where your potential lies and nothing, and no one, should hold you back from that. Including me.'

A part of me feels more alive than I have ever done before, but if I tell him that, then I become another pressure to add to his burden. In a perfect world, our future would start here, but I know that's unlikely to be the case. Our paths are crossing for the briefest of moments and I have no choice but to accept that this can't go anywhere long-term. It's a little ripple in time, a glorious moment caught in the folds of life. A secret to remember forever, that can never be shared.

'It's not as if we're hurting anyone though, is it?' I ask, trying not to sound desperate. I'm grasping for a tenuous thread to tie us together because I can't help myself.

Reid pulls back to look at me in earnest. 'My conscience won't allow me to rob you of the future you deserve, Seren. The last thing you need is some jaded artist dancing to the tune of a bitter ex-wife and the daughter he failed. Those are my burdens to carry, alone. But this, today, is a memory I will treasure forever. Some people live their entire lives without having a moment like this and it will live on in my heart.'

I want to cling onto him, but I know there's no point. His mind is made up and there are too many obstacles in our way. A bitter sensation of numbness hits my stomach where moments ago a warmth was flooding through me.

The hours pass as we lie in each other's arms, savouring every second we have together. I talk about my childhood and then Reid shares a little about his early years as an artist. I begin to understand just how instrumental Beatriz was in the beginning and, given her connections, still is in many ways.

When, eventually, Reid takes his leave, it's dusk and as we reluctantly part, he turns to kiss my temple.

'I'll see you next Saturday?' I ask, fervently, hoping he hasn't changed his mind.

'Of course, my lovely Seren. But if you have second thoughts, I understand. I'm leaving you here with a heavy heart, but, believe me, it's for your own good. I'm past saving and I can't be a part of your future. Everything is about to happen for you and the bitterest pill in life is to look back with regrets. Trust me.'

Knowing that Reid is walking away depressed and dispirited after our afternoon of heart-stopping passion tears at my heart. I see it clearly now. He has it all wrong. It was meant to be, for whatever reason. Maybe an angel looked down and felt pity for two people struggling to put their lives back on track. How I wish I was on the same track and I can only hope there are no repercussions for two lonely people giving each other the comfort they so badly needed.

7

POPPING THE CHAMPAGNE CORK, BUT WHERE'S THE FIZZ?

'Seren, the samples have arrived! Senhor Ferreira's secretary just phoned through to say the boxes are in the boardroom. Our presence has been requested.' Carolina makes no attempt at all to hide her excitement.

'I was hoping reception would send them up here first, so we could take a quick look before the unveiling,' I groan. I'm still on my first cup of coffee and I always have at least two on a Monday morning before I'm ready to face the day.

'Take a deep breath, boss. I'm just going to find Antero and then we'll meet you up there.'

I stand, nervously smoothing down my skirt and running my hands over the crumpled areas. Grabbing a lipstick and a compact out of my bag, I carefully apply a thin film over my lips and then run my fingers through my hair. Everything hangs on Bernadette's ability to bring Reid's artistry to life in a way even he never imagined. Am I nervous? No, I'm terrified, and as my feet make their way to the boardroom my head is somewhere else. I have no idea when I'm going to see Reid again and our next contact is going to be awkward, to say the least. What if one of the directors suggest we find out if Reid is available online to witness the unboxing?

'Ah, Seren, come in. Are the rest of your team on the way? I'm sure everyone is excited this moment is finally here. You will do the honours?'

I cast around, wondering how I'm going to open the sturdy boxes, when there's a sharp tapping sound before the door swings open and both Antero and Carolina enter. To my relief, Antero immediately steps up to the side table and produces a knife to begin slicing open the boxes. Carolina very carefully starts lifting out the individual parcels, each encased in bubble wrap.

Carrying the first two across to the large conference table, the directors draw close as my fingers nervously lift the tape. Inside the first parcel is a folded length of fabric and the moment I gaze down at the print, a huge weight lifts from my shoulders. It's exquisite and, holding one corner tightly, I launch my arm into the air, letting the fabric unfurl and fall in folds on the table in front of us. Antero and Carolina immediately begin helping me to spread it out, as we all stare down in awe.

With an offset, half-metre pattern repeat, a flock of birds fly gracefully above the delicately drawn shoreline. In a dark grey against the white slightly silky fabric, the sky is tinted the lightest of blues and little streaks of green hint at the grasses along the banks of the river. The merest suggestion of colour here and there brings the scene to life and having seen the painting that inspired this, I know Reid will be thrilled. It's reminiscent of a pencil drawing and yet the depth, detail and trace of colour draw the eye.

Senhora Veloso reaches out to touch the fabric and runs her fingertips over it, approvingly. 'That slight sheen is wonderful, Seren. Is this the fabric for the fashion show or for the soft furnishings?'

I'm already opening the second, bulkier package and that answers the question, as it's a small, rectangular cushion in the same design.

'This is curtain fabric and the cushions are a slightly heavier weight. The gowns will be much bulkier as we want the fabric to hang without draping in folds. It won't have a practical use for anything else as it will be heavily starched on the day. The models will also wear specially constructed hoops, similar to those worn under wedding dresses.'

One by one, Antero, Carolina and I reveal the series of designs and I couldn't be happier. They would look as good in a contemporary setting as they would in a rural, country cottage. The lightness of touch to the printing is perfect and the scene is a true representation of Reid's artwork. Reminiscent of the vintage French toile designs, Bernadette has succeeded in pulling off the perfect transition from canvas to cloth. I spot some marsh sandpipers in amongst a sand dune on the shores of the river Tagus, which is represented as a hint of pale blue, like a ribbon blowing in the breeze, and the pointed beaks of the birds peck at the ground beneath their feet. Nothing distracts them from the search for a tasty morsel.

Carolina becomes a mannequin, allowing me to unroll the heavier fabrics to give an idea of what the model's gowns will look like.

'Ah, I see what you mean, Seren,' Senhor Ferreira joins in, walking around the table to get a better view. 'The patterns will distort if the fabric settles into folds. And the shape will be that of the Cristo Rei statue itself?'

'Exactly, Senhor Ferreira,' I confirm. 'When the models twirl, they will outstretch their arms and the fabric becomes the canvas.'

'Outstanding, simply outstanding. Congratulations and please pass on our thanks to Bernadette Brodeur.'

'Of course, and she will be delighted to hear such glowing feedback. The next video meeting is arranged for the day after tomorrow and I know everyone involved will be delighted with the results.'

'This calls for a toast. This is truly a milestone for the project. You have all worked so hard and it's fabulous to see it paying off.' Senhor Ferreira's delight is evident, and it fleetingly crosses my mind whether there is a hint of relief in his voice.

Antero is charged with opening the champagne and when we chink glasses, the atmosphere in the room is electric. All I can think of is that I can't wait for Reid to see the samples in person, because I know he was a little apprehensive. Leonor still hasn't responded to his invitation to the video meeting on Wednesday, but I want him to see these beforehand. I manage to convince myself that my motive is purely a matter of professional courtesy – well, almost.

Truthfully, though, there's a little place in my heart that feels empty now. I need to see him, and this is about as legitimate an excuse as I can come up with.

* * *

'Hey, girl, it's late. What's up?'

The sound of Judi's voice cheers me no end. I need her advice, but I'm nervous about what she might say, so I choose the coward's way out.

'I'm chilling with a glass of wine as I'm feeling a little homesick. How's life with you?'

'Everything is fine, actually.'

There's no hint of a sigh or any hesitation, which is a good sign. While I'm gathering my thoughts, Judi jumps in.

'Did you get my email confirming the flight times?'

'Yes, I did. That's partly why I'm calling. I'm sad you won't be staying with me, but at least you'll be here. Who's coming with you?'

'It's been a nightmare. I made the mistake of mentioning it when we were all in the pub and the hands flew up. I mean, who wouldn't fancy a trip to Lisbon? We ended up putting names in a hat and Claire was thrilled when her name was drawn.'

'Ah, one of our old posse at school. I haven't seen her for a couple of years. That's nice. A real girls' trip.'

'So, what's your latest news?'

'The fabrics arrived on Monday and today I had a video meeting with the designer and the photographer.'

What I leave out is that there's no sign of Reid and he hasn't responded to my texts, or emails, even though he suggested I contact him directly if I have a problem. Leonor doesn't seem to know his exact whereabouts – a claim which I find hard to believe.

'It's all beginning to come together, even though it feels like a never-ending project.' I manage a breezy little laugh. 'I'm ringing to ask your advice.'

I can't help squirming around in my seat and I take a big gulp of wine in the intervening seconds.

'Ask away. I can't imagine there's much I can say that you don't already know.'

'How did you get around your little problem with Alex? You don't mention him at all any more. Have the feelings simply gone away?'

She sighs. 'It was a taboo subject for a while and I'm sorry for not sharing. We went for a drink the day before I started my new job. Alex and his wife have lived separately for almost nine months and he was upfront about that, but she persuaded him to have one last attempt at fixing their relationship. He broke the news that he'd agreed to see a marriage guidance counsellor. That was the reason he was avoiding me, so I had no choice but to put a lid on my feelings.'

'And yet he felt the same way you did, at least for a while?'

'Yes. But, given the number of people with whom we come into contact in our daily lives, it's unlikely that there is going to be only one person we feel that instant sense of attraction with, is there? It was me believing all this crazy soulmate stuff. Lust isn't love, is it, and I don't know if I'd want to be with someone who gives up too easily when the going gets tough. It's too reminiscent of my family, so I'm always going to be cautious. Why?'

'There's a guy I've met, but it makes no sense to get involved. I just need to hear someone say that to me.'

I hear a low 'hmm' travelling down the line. 'That's rather vague, Seren. A little more information would be helpful if you really want my opinion. Every situation is different, isn't it?'

'Just ignore me. He's a client and it would be career suicide.' This time a heavy sigh slips out, which I instantly regret.

'But you're tempted?'

Does one afternoon of passion even count, when you part on the, albeit unspoken, understanding that it can never happen again?

'No. Not any more. When something is impossible from the start, it's unlikely to get any easier, is it?'

'Aww... you're sad. We were both insistent when we hit thirty last year that age was just a number. But psychologically it has an effect – I mean, we drew up our action plans and focused on the next stage of careers, didn't we? The point is that there are physiological changes, too, and the whole *body clock ticking thing* is triggered because it's a part of our programming, whether we want to acknowledge that, or not. We can't ignore the fact that if the plan involves settling down and having kids at some point, then the next decade is important.'

I scoff, trying hard to suppress a full-blown laugh. 'So, we're likely to grab the first passing man who glances our way? I'm sure it's a well-known fact that women tend to feel happier and more content in their forties. I read an article about it recently.'

'Maybe, maybe not. Anyway, I'm talking about women in general, to explain why you might be feeling a little desperate. It's a caution, that's all. You did ask for my advice.'

'I'm not desperate,' I throw back at her, trying not to sound offended.

'Sorry, poor choice of wording. I meant, more likely to jump into a situation without giving it your customary, detailed consideration. It applies to me, too.'

'Okay. There are going to be times when we're lonely and I guess that makes us vulnerable.'

'Don't let your guard down, Seren. You've told me that you really like this new version of you, that you're feeling more upbeat, more settled. If this is your future, I mean your forever future, then don't let a silly mistake risk messing it up for you as it nearly did for me until you talked me out of it.'

'Point taken. Thanks, Judi. And I am sorry about Alex. At least he was honest about his situation.'

'That actually made it worse. If he'd lied to me then I would have had a reason to be angry and hate him. Instead, I just felt sorry for him. He was as thrown as I was and we both agreed to put it behind us. We don't avoid each other, but we don't really talk about anything aside from work. It's for the best.'

I ask her about her family and shamelessly tune out as she recounts the latest drama. All I can think about is the fact that Reid was anxiously awaiting those fabric samples and I was hoping to take a run out to show them to him in person. At first, I assumed he was avoiding me, but to not even take part in today's meeting is unprofessional. I rang Leonor yesterday to casually remind her and she said the meeting was in his diary but didn't seem to know where he was, or when he would return. I can only assume it's a family matter that has dragged him away, so I try to remind myself that his personal life has nothing to do with me.

I shake off my thoughts when Judi mentions my name.

'Seren, why don't you give your mum a call? That day I bumped into her she was sad and desperate for news about you. There are things the two of you left unsaid, things that you're unlikely to put in an email. She knows you better than anyone and I always envied you that connection. The row between you and your father is just that, and it wasn't her fault. Imagine how hard it's been for her watching the two of you constantly sparring and it must have appeared that you were both pushing her away. She's always been a good listener. At least reach out to her in case you need a little extra support and you can't get hold of me.'

Judi means well and I say goodnight, placing the phone down on the sofa next to me with a heaviness in my heart. Mum said she understood why I had to get away, but the truth is that I felt as if I was abandoning her. At first, I avoided talking directly to her out of guilt, but now I know that Mum will instantly pick up on the fact that something isn't quite right with me.

I have to keep reminding myself that I have a plan and I need to stick to it. And hopefully it will be easy to fool myself that I'm being strong when all I'm really doing is taking one step after another to keep moving forward. But, deep down inside, my heart is breaking because Reid is constantly in my thoughts. And all of a sudden he's avoiding me, which risks people working out for themselves that something has happened between us. And neither of us want that.

Maybe Judi was right and I do need to hear a caring voice. Picking up the phone, seconds later Mum's cheery tones are on the other end of the line.

'Oh, Seren, how are you, my darling?'

'I'm good. Lisbon is wonderful, but it's been hectic. How is life treating you?'

'Well, a *little* better since I received your recent email. Honestly, children forget that parents worry, even when you're all grown up. A one-liner, *I'm here and I'm fine* isn't enough. And the next couple weren't much better. I'm sure the food is wonderful, but I want to know how *you* are doing. Are you making friends? Is there anything you need?'

Mum, too, has had a rough ride with my father. He takes everything that she does for granted and yet he wouldn't be where he is today without her constant support. In my book, she deserves a medal for putting up with him.

'I didn't mean to be so distant, but it's been a challenge.' And with that admission, a single tear begins to track its way down my cheek.

A sniff coming from the other end of the line tells me that Mum is tearing up, too. 'I was so scared you were turning your back on me for good. I keep going over what happened and berating myself for not doing something, anything, to stop it before it went too far. You were both so angry all the time and whenever I—'

'—Tried to intervene, one of us walked away. You did your best and I know that. I'm sorry if I didn't make that clear before I left. There was so much to do and it was overwhelming at times. My armour went on and I couldn't allow myself to dwell, because if I hesitated for one second, I wouldn't have gone through with moving. And then I was here, all alone, and I didn't know a single soul.'

Now the tears are coming thick and fast, and we're both snivelling.

'It's like a part of me is missing, not seeing you and with those silly emails that talked mainly about the weather,' Mum says, her voice breaking a little as she tries to laugh. 'It's hard to read between the lines when there aren't many of them.'

'I'm so sorry. I didn't mean to hurt you, Mum. But when you are starting from scratch, there isn't a lot to say, just a lot to prove. Fortunately, two of my work colleagues have become firm friends and my neighbour, Maria, treats me like one of her family. It's only now I can finally pause to catch my breath and let you know how much I miss you.'

'I understand that you need your space, Seren. My fear was that you'd feel isolated and there are times in life when we all need to hear a familiar voice. I don't want you burying your feelings like your father does. Eventually, that becomes the norm and look at the mess that landed us all in. I can't forgive him for tearing our family apart.'

I'm shocked at her anger, and I can tell she's seriously evaluating their life together. Now I understand why Judi told me to call. She had clearly seen for herself that Mum is struggling, and I haven't been there for her.

'I had my part to play in the argument, Mum. If only I'd left sooner, just got a job somewhere else, but I couldn't let it go. The way I disappointed him at every turn seemed to spur me on. It was destroying me and yet I couldn't stop.'

My heart constricts as I hear a troubled sigh echoing down the line.

'With hindsight, I can see now that he thinks that bullying is a way of motivating people to do better, but it's sickening, Seren, and I've had enough of it. I didn't intend breaking the news to you over the phone, but I moved out seven weeks ago and I'm renting a little flat of my own. Your father's not happy obviously, but I am. Where I go from here, I'm not sure yet. I've been helping Fiona three days a week. It's a real tonic as I meet lots of smiling, happy people.'

Mum's best friend, Fiona, runs a fabulous bridal boutique. I'm in total shock. I can't imagine my father being happy about Mum working in a shop and as for walking out on him, well, that's unimaginable. But before I can begin processing my thoughts, Mum continues.

'You rang tonight for a reason. You're not quite yourself, I can sense it.'

The pause is loaded.

'I... um... made a mistake and I'm struggling to put it right. It's my own fault, wanting the impossible. I'll get over it. We are both proof that life goes on, Mum, aren't we? Changes happen for all sorts of reasons, but we're survivors, you and me?' It's a question and not a statement.

'Yes, my darling. I'm only sorry I couldn't see why everything was going so badly wrong until I escaped. As soon as it was just the two of us, it was obvious that there was no love left between your father and me. We had nothing to say to each other any more.'

How sad that it also took this hurt I'm experiencing over a man I hardly know to make me finally reach out to Mum. To discover that I'm not the only person my father succeeded in alienating is shocking.

'Sorry that I've been so wrapped up in my own woes, that I left you all alone with him without even considering the impact it would have. That was selfish of me.'

'No, Seren, it was the right thing to do. We will get through this somehow, my wonderful, darling daughter, and end up happier for it. And thank you, from the bottom of my heart, for reaching out. Just know that you've been in my thoughts every waking hour of every day. And often in my dreams, too. Right, I'm off to bed as I'm up at six tomorrow. Us working ladies need our beauty sleep. Love you, darling. And if you need me, I'm only ever a phone call away, the miles don't matter.'

'Night, Mum, love you.'

8

WHAT HAVE I DONE?

This morning, my office door remains shut. I'm hiding myself away and making it clear that I don't want to be interrupted. I pretend to be oblivious to the fact that both Carolina and Antero walk past at regular intervals in the hope that I'll look up and spot them through the half-glass walls. Whenever I catch a shadow out of the corner of my eye, my head bows down even lower, as if I'm scrutinising the report in front of me.

I've messed everything up and I don't know what to do to sort it out if Reid won't talk to me. It's two days until the party and if he's too embarrassed to contact me to cancel, then the only solution is for me to phone Leonor and come up with a reason why I can't attend. That way we both save face. Having now made the decision, I can at least get down to some real work. I hope that by the end of the day a plausible excuse will pop into my head and I can make the call.

Ready now to join the team, I straighten my back, take six slow, deep breaths to calm myself and head out to catch up with Carolina.

'Sorry about texting so early, but there were a few things I needed to sort out and it was easier to work through them without any distractions. I wouldn't rob anyone of an extra hour in bed just because the birds woke me up early with their constant squabbling,' I muse, as her eyes search my face.

'Poor you. I had your calls diverted to my phone as I could see you were busy. There isn't a problem, is there?'

'No. Just catching up with the latest report from Bernadette. Are there any messages?'

'Only one. Senhor Ferreira said to let you know that he has confirmed his attendance at Reid's party on Saturday evening.'

I stare at her, unblinking. Well, I didn't see that coming. 'Thanks, um... did he say anything else?'

She narrows her eyes as she looks back at me. 'No. I assumed you'd know what he was talking about.'

'It was just a message and he isn't expecting me to ring him back?'

'I'm sure he would have said if he needed to speak to you,' she confirms. 'There's some good news, too. Antero and I didn't like to disturb you, but we've been dying to give you an update on the ticket sales.' She's beaming at me and I feel remiss that it wasn't the first question I asked as they have worked so hard on this.

'Good news already?' After a series of annoying technical glitches, the tickets have been on sale for a mere thirty-six hours, which is way behind schedule.

'There are only twenty-three left, if we stick to the original one-hundred and fifty allocation. The website actually went down yesterday afternoon for three hours, so it's been chaotic, but everything is fine now.'

'That's wonderful news and just the boost I need this morning. I'll pop in to tell Senhor Ferreira now and see if he'll approve raising the limit to two hundred. He'll be delighted that our cautious approach has paid off.'

She beams back at me. 'I know. There's nothing more likely to get people clamouring to buy, than to limit availability. But later today we'll be in a position to put up a banner saying sold out. Releasing those other tickets is yet another promotional opportunity and we must capitalise on that.'

Thinking as I walk, it's obvious Reid wants Senhor Ferreira to take my place at the party and while I feel hurt that he didn't have the guts to tell me first, it's also a relief. It's crucial he approves Bernadette's samples before the middle of next week, at the latest and if he's avoiding me, then at least this solves a rather pressing problem.

Senhor Ferreira is on the phone and I hang around in the corridor, trying not to stare through the glass as if I'm anxiously waiting for him to finish.

Moments later, the sound of his door opening has me turning around and he invites me in with a broad smile.

'I did walk past your office earlier on but could see you were busy. You signed in at seven this morning, Seren. I hope we are not overworking you?'

'No, not at all, Senhor Ferreira. I'm an early riser by nature and I was eager to make a start. I've just had an update on ticket sales and Carolina tells me that we expect to sell out by the end of the day.'

Senhor Ferreira raises his eyebrows, as if he can't believe what he's hearing. 'So soon?'

I nod.

'Well, that's incredible.'

'I've come to check you are happy for us to release another batch of fifty tickets to take us to the pre-agreed maximum number.'

'Ah.' The look he gives me isn't the one I was expecting. 'That's what I was coming to see you about, Seren. Here is a list of friends and associates of the gallery who have made direct contact with me over the last twenty-four hours, people who will be attending the anniversary party. However, they are also expressing an interest in attending the fashion show, too. It wasn't something we anticipated, of course, but it does put us in a difficult position as it would be impolite, and against our interests, not to accommodate them.'

Taking the list from him, my face falls. There must be nearly thirty names here.

'There may well be a few more, after the little gathering at Reid's house on Saturday.' He shrugs his shoulders, apologetically. 'I think, therefore, you need to take this into consideration before releasing any more tickets, I'm afraid.'

The plan for the event on Friday evening was for it to be aimed at the general public. The exclusive anniversary party at the gallery on the

Saturday is a pre-showing of the exhibition by invite only for the VIPs, so this news is frustrating.

'Can we not simply arrange a special showing of the final cut of the video before it goes on general display, here at the gallery? It could be held a week or so after the anniversary party and I'm sure your guests would enjoy an exclusive preview on the big screen.'

He appears to be considering my idea with some seriousness. 'Let me talk to the other directors, first. Rafael is a big draw, Seren, and this is a unique fashion show. We had no idea it would be so popular, though.'

As he's mulling it over, I scan down the list of names and third from the bottom, there it is... Beatriz Esteves and, alongside, someone has written *two tickets*. The blood rushing through my veins turns cold, as I realise Reid's fears aren't necessarily paranoia.

'Is something wrong?' Senhor Ferreira enquires.

'No. It's simply that the success of the exhibition throughout the summer will, I believe, be fuelled by the event at the Cristo Rei. When it comes to attracting visitors who haven't been to the gallery before, the best advertising to draw them in is by word of mouth.' I can't say what I really think, that it would be a waste of tickets. 'Your special guests would be more comfortable watching the video here, where we will be better placed to cater for them.'

'You may have a point there, Seren. I appreciate you being frank with me. I will call a meeting to discuss this matter with my fellow directors, then get back to you. I'm sorry this is something I overlooked and it's a mistake on my part.'

He's apologising because it's polite, but he used the word *frank* when it came to my comments, which might mean I've overstepped the mark.

'Oh, no, not at all. This is new territory, Senhor Ferreira, for everyone involved. I can't profess to have all the answers here. It's a fine line between being optimistic and unrealistic. I think, on balance, we've hit the middle ground but feel that this guest list is important enough to warrant a special arrangement. It would be my pleasure to arrange that, so we can release the other tickets if the board consider that is for the best.'

It's important that Senhor Ferreira sees me as a problem-solver, not a problem-maker, and I hope that my reply has set him at ease.

'Wonderful. I do have one small concern. Beatriz has asked me to attend the party on Saturday at the Casa da Floresta. She feels my presence is necessary, given that many of the people invited will also be attending the gallery's anniversary party. Tomas Esteves usually brings people together for mutual benefit and Beatriz sees the gathering as a perfect opportunity to preview some of the paintings that will be on display in the summer. But she also mentioned that she has a few concerns and we need to be prepared to answer her questions in full. I have assured her that we will be delighted to be of assistance, especially in the light of Reid's unexpected absence.'

It seems the whole of the Esteves family have a vested interest in this project, but they aren't all necessarily on the same side.

'I will be most happy to collect you and drop you back home afterwards, Seren. There is no point in our travelling separately.'

So now I have no choice in the matter. If my boss wants me at the party, then of course I'll have to be there. 'Thank you, that would be much appreciated.'

'You must call me Filipe, Seren. Few people have joined our team and made the sort of impact that you have. I appreciate how much work has gone into making it all look so effortless, when in fact it is quite a challenge. If you ever need my support, please do come to me. You've been thrown into an environment where you have no connections, and few could have coped with what we've demanded of you.'

'Thank you, Filipe. I appreciate that and also the way you have supported the team.'

I leave his office, resisting the temptation to screw the piece of paper in my hand into a ball out of sheer anger. Is Beatriz raising her profile to warn me off? From what Reid has already told me, everything she does is for a reason.

Yanking the phone from my pocket, I text him once again.

Two minutes of your time, that's all I ask. But I need to speak to you. Please.

Pressing send without a moment's hesitation, I stride into Carolina's office. She's chatting with her assistant, Inês, but immediately looks up.

'How did it go?'

'He was delighted by the news, but the availability of extra tickets has to be approved by the entire board.'

A look of disappointment flashes over her face.

My phone pings and I pause momentarily, before continuing. 'In the meantime, the minute we sell out, can you put out another press release announcing how delighted the gallery is by the uptake? If we get the go-ahead to release that last batch, perhaps we'll advertise it in advance of the tickets going on sale with a countdown on the website to create a buzz. I must go, but I'll catch up with you later.'

Hurrying away, my heart is pounding as I stare down at Reid's reply.

Make that five and I'll call you, I promise.

Antero approaches as I'm about to close the door to my office and I give him an apologetic look.

'I'm just about to take an important call. Can we get together after lunch, as I might need your help in pulling together a presentation rather quickly. Carolina has her hands full and if you and I put our heads together, I'm sure we can crack it. I'll know more after I've made a few phone calls.'

'Of course. I'll catch up with you later.'

As my phone kicks into life, I give him a parting smile before shutting the door.

The voice on the other end of the line sounds faraway, and there's a lot of background noise. 'Seren, please don't think that I'm ignoring you, but I'm dealing with a family emergency. It's difficult to talk right now. I've had to hand everything back to Tomas, but he's been rushed off his feet, too. This damn party came at the wrong time. Can you liaise with him until I get back?' He breaks off for a moment, as someone calls his name. 'I'm coming,' he replies. 'Seren, I have to go, it's a trying time, that's all.'

On hearing the tone of his voice, guilt instantly begins to gnaw away at me for thinking the worst of him: that he was ignoring me. Now all I feel is compassion. He sounds like he's at the end of his tether.

'I'm so sorry to hear that, Reid. Senhor Ferreira and I will be there on Saturday to field any questions. Forget about everything here, it's all in hand. I was just worried about you.'

'It's hard to think right now...' He pauses, sounding totally disheartened.

The silence continues to grow, and I realise that whatever has happened is serious.

'If you need anything, anything at all, I'm here. Now, go do what you have to do, but please take care of yourself.'

I click end call, my fingers trembling. There was a wretchedness to his tone that sent a shiver through me. Slumping down into my chair, it's hard not knowing exactly what's going on. I decide to phone Leonor and try to make contact with Tomas, in case there is anything I can do to assist him.

'Leonor, it's Seren. I know you're busy, but Reid said I should liaise with Tomas? I have a quick question about the party on Saturday evening,' I explain, in my friendliest voice.

'Has Tomas not been in touch with you?' She sounds put out and I can only imagine the nightmare she's having to sort out if both Reid and Tomas aren't easily contactable. 'I will ask Tomas to give you a call if you tell me your query.'

'Reid mentioned that there are likely to be some questions about the exhibition and the events surrounding it. I wondered if I should put together a short presentation?'

'I see. I will ask Tomas to call you on his return, Seren. Leave it with me.'

'Thank you for your help, Leonor. I will also bring along the fabric samples that Reid was waiting for, ready for his return.'

'I have no idea at all when he will be back, but I am sure he will appreciate that.'

Click. Well, whatever is going on, it's clearly affecting Leonor, too, as that's the most neutral she's been with me. It was as if she was simply going through the motions and her mind was elsewhere.

Then a horrible thought jumps into my head. Is Reid ill? He didn't sound himself at all and what if this isn't about another family member but the pressure is getting to him instead?

It's frustrating to feel so helpless, but I've done all I can. That doesn't make the pain I feel for what he's going through any less real, as I sit here conjuring up the image of Reid's face. Remembering the warmth of his body against mine that afternoon we spent together, I sensed he was at peace for the first time in a long while. I wasn't the only one who didn't want the afternoon to end; Reid, too, was reluctant to walk away. Did he know he was teetering on the edge and fearful of what might happen? I could feel the strength and depths of his emotions, which appeared to be in freefall. One moment he was genuinely happy, the next full of guilt. And now yet another problem has arisen in his life and he sounded like a man who was feeling swamped and struggling to cope.

* * *

'Seren, it's Tomas Esteves. My sincere apologies for the delay, but I've only just picked up your message. Trying to sort out what has, and hasn't, been done is proving difficult.'

'Well, thank you for getting back to me, Tomas. The signal might dip a little, I'm afraid, as I'm just about to board the ferry.'

'I appreciate you reaching out to help. If you can come prepared to do a short talk, I'm sure our guests would be very appreciative. I can arrange for a flat-screen TV if you have visuals. We are delighted to have both yourself and Filipe, now, joining us for the evening. I hear you will be arriving together, so I no longer need to arrange transport for you, as Reid requested. Are you staying overnight?'

My mind goes into overdrive as I step aside to linger at the opening to the terminal, fearing the signal will drop out. 'No. Filipe will be driving me home.' Did Reid mention that to him? Or is he simply trying to figure out which guests will be staying? It's hard to tell as he sounds so agitated.

'Ah, I haven't spoken to Filipe, myself, but he is an old family friend and my sister realised the oversight and extended an invitation to him. The arrangements have become a little muddled, I'm afraid, due to Reid's unexpected absence. He's in Porto and not expected back until shortly before the party.'

He is with Beatriz, as I suspected, and she's managed to involve herself in the arrangements for the party, too.

'We will pull together a special video for your guests to give them a sneak preview no one else has seen yet,' I explain.

'That's wonderful and most kind of you, Seren. If there is anything else you might need, please do not hesitate to call me on this number. I look forward to meeting you in person on Saturday. *Adeus*.'

Tomas sounds utterly charming and there wasn't a hint of negativity in his voice, which is reassuring.

'Seren, Seren!' I look up and see Carolina hurrying towards me. 'I thought I'd missed you.'

'Your plans changed?'

She gives me a half-hearted smile. 'Yes, unfortunately. But at least we get to travel back together. I'm exhausted, you must be, too, and I will be glad to get home and put my feet up.'

Oh dear, I hope the person she was meeting up with after work wasn't Antero, because she's clearly disappointed her plans have fallen through.

'Yes, the heat has got to me a little today,' I reply, genially. 'That's a shame about your plans, though.'

As we step onto the ferry, our conversation is brought to a halt as we slip into single file to find two seats together. Settling ourselves down, I can see that there's something she wants to say, but she's hesitant.

'Would it help to talk about it?' I ask, thinking she can always say no.

Carolina fusses with the bag on her lap, checking the zip is done up before glancing at me. 'Antero asked if I'd like to go for a drink. But he's had second thoughts about it. He feels it is not appropriate, given our recent advancement.'

By advancement, I assume Carolina means their temporary promotion, but I'm curious. 'It's only a drink,' I respond, breezily.

But I can see by her frown, she agrees with him.

'We would not wish anyone to feel we were not putting our work responsibilities first, Seren.'

'What you do in your own time is entirely up to you, Carolina. You are both single and your families are not close by. I can't see why Antero is concerned. You two get on so well and I suspect you have quite a bit in common.'

I can see she's uncomfortable talking about this and she shifts uneasily in her seat, staring out over the wide expanse of the river. I turn my head to catch the breeze face on and it's pleasantly cooling.

'It's the way it is here,' she explains. 'One's work life is separate to one's private life. The directors would not be happy. A close personal relationship might affect someone's ability to do their job.'

My stomach feels as if a stone has just sunk to the bottom of it as I can see she's serious. Senhor Ferreira and Senhor Portela are the sort of men whose families still value the old traditions. Senhora Veloso is more progressive, being significantly younger, but I'm only now beginning to realise the potential impact of my moment of madness with Reid.

'But you are both professionals, Carolina. I think you are more than capable of keeping it strictly business in working hours.'

'I'm sure you are right, Seren. But as for Senhor Ferreira, it would not be acceptable. He would insist one of us was moved to another position within the gallery. Antero feels that would be disruptive to the team, and I agree.' The softest of sighs escapes from between her lips. 'Once the project is complete, we will consider our options.'

Are they putting their potential relationship on hold out of loyalty to me?

'Carolina, who would know if you and Antero were seeing each other? I don't have a problem with it, at all, and I'd be happy to make that clear to anyone who asked.'

She shakes her head. 'That would not be wise, Seren, and we would not expect you to do that. Is it so different in England?'

I immediately think about Judi and the situation with Peter. But that was a very public meltdown at work, which was totally unprofessional.

'We tend to see socialising outside of work as a way of getting to know each other better. Like a team-building exercise. There is a little work talk, but mostly the conversation would be about hobbies, families, interests, that sort of thing. It's not uncommon for two people from the same office to date each other, and that's not usually seen as a problem. There might be the odd occasion when it wouldn't be wise, I suppose. If one member of a section is dating the boss, for example. But, certainly, whenever you start a new job, it's in your favour if you join in with the socialising.'

Carolina stares at me in surprise. 'Does the director go along, too?'

I laugh, thinking of my father joining his staff for a pint and a fish supper in the local pub. 'Anyone can join in. But some only attend special get-togethers, like at Christmas.'

'Oh, I see. It's different back home, of course, as everyone knows everyone, anyway.'

'Where are you from, originally?'

'A small coastal village to the south. My parents believe I will eventually go back to Aljezur when I am ready to settle down. They were not happy for me to move away but accepted my decision. But it's difficult because they don't understand how I feel. I wanted something different, to experience things beyond our small community.'

'It's not easy leaving behind the life you know, Carolina, and not having a support network around you. I know that. And I'm grateful for the kindness you have shown me. I don't mean to be disrespectful to your culture in any way at all and it's simply a lack of understanding if I get it wrong. But I'm always happy to talk in confidence and anything you tell me will go no further.'

'Thank you, Seren. It's a pleasure being a part of the team and I come to work every day excited about what's ahead. You are pushing the boundaries and all eyes are on us, so I think it's for the best that I focus on work, for now. It's why I came to Lisbon in the first place – to prove myself, and I can't let anything stand in the way of that.'

Our conversation has given me cause to reflect. I didn't realise how firmly the lines of what is and what isn't acceptable at the gallery were drawn. Not only have I risked my reputation but that of someone with a much higher profile than my own. And that, it seems, might be considered inexcusable.

9

TREADING CAREFULLY

I've been dreading this party, especially after my little chat with Carolina. Even on the journey here, the conversation with Filipe has been awkward. When Vitor answers the door, thankfully Filipe doesn't appear to notice the brief acknowledging nod he gives in my direction before he offers to take the briefcase from my hand. Vitor escorts us through to the large room that leads out onto the rear courtyard. It's already full of people and the doors beyond are open as guests wander around.

'Ah, Filipe, and this must be Seren, welcome. I am Tomas.' Giving Filipe a curt nod, Tomas holds out his hand to me and we shake, cordially.

'It's a pleasure to finally meet you, Tomas.'

I'm relieved he doesn't strike up a conversation with Filipe in Portuguese but instead leads us across to a very flamboyant woman in the middle of a small group standing in front of one of Reid's paintings. She has long dark hair and is wearing an elegant silver-grey cocktail dress. When Tomas calls her name, she turns around and immediately steps towards Filipe, throwing her arms around him, affectionately. She accepts a kiss on both cheeks and there is a little animated conversation between them. Pulling back, she turns her attention to me.

'Beatriz, I am delighted to introduce you to Seren Maddison,' Filipe waves his hand in my direction. I can feel Tomas watching, as if he's expecting something to happen.

'Ah, Seren Maddison,' Beatriz replies, sounding mildly amused.

I offer her my hand, giving hers a firm shake. To my horror, I see her wince a little, and her hand is surprisingly limp, something I wasn't expecting.

Her perfectly made-up eyes sweep over me, taking in every little detail as if she's committing it to memory. After showing Carolina the contents of my wardrobe and trying on half a dozen dresses, we had decided that it was best to play it safe. I opted for a plain navy blue, cap-sleeve shift dress by Karen Millen. It's my equivalent of a little black dress, but navy is more flattering to my skin tone. It fits like a glove and doesn't crease, so it's perfect for a business function. My only adornment this evening is a large silver bracelet and a pair of plain, silver stud, feather earrings.

Beatriz glances down at my gorgeous, pale blue Louis Vuitton sling-backs. They were a present from my parents for my thirtieth birthday. As her eyes sweep back up to my face, not a single muscle has moved. Nervously, I look away for a moment, scanning around the room in search of Reid, but I can't see him.

'We meet at last,' Beatriz continues. 'I've heard so much about you.' Her voice is soft, her accent charming.

To our left, a man calls out 'Filipe' and I turn my head as Tomas places his hand on Filipe's shoulder and they excuse themselves. I have no choice but to stand here and make polite conversation with Beatriz, but she's simply staring at me.

'I'm thrilled to be involved in the gallery's latest project and the exhibition will be the highlight of the summer.' I keep my tone light, but formal.

She raises a smile, but it's the type of smile you plaster on your face at a party and it doesn't come from her eyes. 'It was good of you to come tonight. Especially as Reid isn't able to make it and we are rather short-staffed.'

That put me very firmly in my place.

'My husband, well, technically my ex-husband – but you know how these things are... two passionate people with strong opinions.' Her tone changes, her voice containing a light-hearted laugh as if she's confiding in me. Which she isn't, she's laying down the rules. 'Reid was in need of a complete rest. There are too many people around him demanding his time.' She flashes her eyes at me, arching an eyebrow.

I look at her blankly. What is she implying?

'He is a famous artist,' she continues. 'His time is precious. He is not a solver of annoying little problems other people could so easily resolve without his input. Reid is a gracious man, sometimes too gracious for his own good. And that should not be misinterpreted. It would be unfortunate if anyone should feel he had time to waste on a little... whim.'

She is no longer looking at me, as if I've already been dismissed. I noticed as she delivered her little speech, her eyes were everywhere as she was constantly scanning the room. She's talking at me about me, and we both know it, but I'm the last person of any real interest to her tonight. I feel confident at least that she doesn't know what happened and it's just a general warning she's giving out. So I decide the best plan of action is to smooth over her concerns, not just because I'm here in a professional capacity, but because this is my chance to win her around. And, in doing so, make Reid's life a little easier.

'It must be very trying at times, Beatriz. Especially when Reid is so heavily involved in the preparation for the exhibition at the gallery. I can assure you that we have a whole team working tirelessly to make sure no detail is left unattended. But we will, of course, ensure that when it comes to the areas where we are collaborating across various disciplines, we obtain his full agreement. As the focus of our summer of celebration, it's my job to make sure Reid is completely happy with the way his work is portrayed, given the unique opportunity this presents.'

Her smile begins to wane and for one second the mask drops. Beatriz is the sort of woman who dominates a room and she's already bored with our conversation. I take that as a good sign, that she doesn't consider me a threat in any way.

'Then you will appreciate how important it is for him to have time to recharge his batteries in an appropriate environment. Somewhere he won't be troubled by annoying little details. While he relaxes, naturally it falls to me to help Tomas in any way I can. Did you bring the fabric samples for our approval?'

Beatriz is leaving me in no doubt whatsoever about the role she believes she still has to play, and who am I to challenge that?

'I did. They're in the car and I'd be delighted to set up a display for you and your guests.'

'Vitor,' Beatriz calls out, beckoning to him and I realise he's been hovering, awaiting her instruction. 'Please help Seren to set up her little presentation. I'm assuming Filipe will talk us through it, so I will discuss that with him now. We'll schedule it for half past eight, I think. I'm sure that's adequate time for you to prepare everything for him,' she instructs me, and I nod, playing my part.

Does Vitor's loyalty lie with Beatriz or Reid? It occurs to me that she may be aware this isn't my first trip to Casa da Floresta, which would put me on the back foot, whatever I do or say.

'Of course. Thank you.'

With that, she turns and hurries off in search of someone worthy of her time.

As Vitor and I head out to the car, I wonder if Reid is visiting some sort of spa facility. Did he ask Beatriz to stand in for him, or was that her own idea? Either way, it's none of my business, I know that. Whatever is going on, it's given her the perfect opportunity to step back into his life. She is a woman who commands attention and when she turns on the charm, she is mesmerising. But my gut instincts are screaming at me to be careful. How did someone as sensitive and kind as Reid end up with such a cold, calculating woman? I find myself shaking my head and Vitor turns to look at me, puzzled as we draw level with the car.

'I forgot to ask Senhor Ferreira for the keys!' I exclaim, cross that I let Beatriz unsettle me.

Vitor nods his head, putting up a hand to indicate for me to stay here, while he hurries back to the house.

As the heat of the day begins to cool a little, I step off the drive and onto the grass. Slipping off my shoes for a moment, it's wonderful to feel the soft, springy turf beneath my feet. Here, on the edge of the forest and with the mountains as a backdrop, it's heavenly. But the location is so isolated, and tonight demonstrates that this house needs people, it was made for entertaining. It's not a good environment for a lonely man who is doubting everything in his life right now.

I stand here, trying to imagine what Reid feels when he returns home. Alone, save for Vitor, Gisela and the no doubt constant stream of people needed to maintain it, does he feel like a prisoner of his success? It's sad to be surrounded by beauty in this stunning environment and yet this contemporary country house is little more than a smart venue for publicity events. I wonder if it's not Reid that Beatriz wants, it's the lifestyle, and tonight has reminded her of what it's like to step back into the limelight. From what I've seen already, it's a role she performs with ease and a sense of authority.

* * *

Beavering away in the corner, trying to shut out the noisy chatter of the party in the background as I set up the video, I'm glad to have something to occupy me. Tonight, it's all about networking and it's clear that Tomas and Beatriz work well as a team.

I begin to unpack the parcels of fabric and Vitor very kindly arranges for two of the waiters to bring in a long, narrow consul table over which I can drape them.

Filipe hurries over to me, glancing at his watch. 'I am sorry about the change of plan, but Beatriz is insistent. Is there anything I can do to help?' he checks, which is thoughtful of him.

'It's not a problem. Antero produced a short video and it's quite comprehensive. Beatriz would like to see the samples, so I'm going to set up a little display. I'm afraid with my limited Portuguese and Vitor's few words of English, he's gone in search of two things for me, but I'm not sure he understood what I need.'

'What do you require?'

'Something to lean this scatter cushion against, so that it will stand up and an item that is heavy enough to anchor these swathes of fabric, then we're good to go.'

Filipe gives me an encouraging smile and then hurries away, as I begin unfurling the bolts of fabric. Heads are already turning my way out of general curiosity and I need to be quick.

A few minutes' later, Vitor and another man appear, each carrying a small stone plinth. Filipe is close on their heels, and I can see that he's eager to make a start. I indicate where I want the heavy ornaments placed and I quickly anchor the corners of the fabrics. A smart smoothing out of the folds and the display is done.

'Wonderful job, Seren,' Filipe comments as he stands back to admire my handiwork. I begin fiddling with the TV remote, leaving it on pause at the start of the loop. I am pleased with the result, considering it's all been thrown together very last-minute.

Tomas walks up to the display, turning to look at me. 'Reid is going to be delighted when he sees this, the fabric has really brought his work to life. *Excelente!*' He beckons to Beatriz and she comes to join us.

It's time for me to stand back and melt into the background as the three of them gather around the display. There's a lot of gesturing with hands, as Beatriz inspects the designs and Filipe engages them both in a flurry of animated conversation.

The other guests are now beginning to assemble in an arc around us and the show begins. Tomas introduces Filipe, who raises his hand, indicating for me to start the presentation. Beatriz might not have thought this project was a good idea at the start, but judging by her expression now, I'd say she's on board with it.

There is a general air of excitement as Filipe draws his polished and well-received talk to a close. He turns to point in my direction, his flow of words unintelligible to me. To my surprise, there is a round of applause and an uncomfortable heat begins to rise up from my chest.

'Well done, Seren,' Beatriz suddenly appears at my side, leaning into me as she speaks. 'I misjudged the situation. I had no idea this project was your baby. This collaboration is a marvellous idea. I am happy to confirm that the designs meet with our approval.' There she goes again. Handing out a little praise before asserting her authority.

Instead of that half-glazed, fake smile she had earlier, she's now looking at me with interest. As far as I'm concerned, though, Reid is the only person who can sign off on the fabrics and I wonder if she's testing me. My instincts are telling me that she wouldn't hold back at putting anyone in their place if they dared to challenge anything she said, so I return her smile graciously.

Tomas and Filipe are already circulating, and they must be delighted by the response tonight. And yet the man himself, whose hard work and talent has inspired this, isn't here to receive the kudos. It seems wrong, but I know he wouldn't have enjoyed what is no more than a sales pitch and I'm sure by the end of the evening several of the paintings on display will have new owners. Mainly down to Beatriz's desire to prove she's back and she means business.

* * *

On the journey home, Filipe very kindly gives me feedback about tonight's event and the sort of questions people were asking. Interestingly, he confirms that Tomas has asked for a meeting with all three directors to discuss the possibility of forging even closer links.

'You mean a permanent display?'

'That would not be possible as the artwork is on loan only until the end of September. Anything that remains unsold will be shipped off to Reid's next big exhibition in the autumn. It is in France, I believe. No, Tomas is interested in developing a closer working relationship with Bernadette Brodeur's company. Beatriz is of the opinion that this is an opportunity that should not be missed. She was impressed, Seren, and she is now very keen to get involved and take some of the pressure off Reid. We will consider the possibility of the gallery expanding our gift shop to permanently carry a range of soft furnishings and developing some new designs over the coming year.' He sounds pleased.

'That's a great idea and I'm sure Bernadette will be delighted that there is potential to take this forward so positively,' I reply.

While that's true, I can't help wondering whether Reid is even aware of this development. It will look odd, though, if I ask the question as this is well outside of my remit.

It's dark now and Filipe's focus is firmly on the road, but as he tilts his head to glance in the mirror, he looks at me for a brief second. 'Great work, Seren, and please thank your team for their diligence. The video presentation was excellent, and I think we should consider putting it up on the website, what do you think?'

'Antero worked hard to get it finished in time and I'm sure he'll be delighted to sort that out on Monday.'

'He has IT skills?' Filipe queries, sounding surprised.

'Yes. He's been a real asset in so many ways.'

As the car draws to a halt in front of Maria's house, Filipe jumps out to retrieve my briefcase from the boot. He sees me to the door, thanking me for ensuring everything ran so smoothly before bidding me a very warm goodnight.

The moment I step over the threshold and close the door behind me, I kick off my shoes. My calf muscles are aching and I'm glad I only wore low heels, because anything higher would have been purgatory. The adrenaline is still racing around my body and I know it's going to take me a while to unwind. A light tap on the door surprises me and I wonder what I left behind in the car as I pad towards the door.

'Sorry to disturb you.' It's not Filipe, it's Reid, and my heart instantly begins to hammer inside my chest.

I quickly stand back, allowing him to enter and then look out to check no one is around.

'Are you okay? I've only just arrived back.'

'I know, I was parked further down the road, watching. I saw Filipe drive off.'

We stand looking at each other, awkwardly.

'I was about to make a cup of coffee. Will you join me?'

He nods, following me into the kitchen. 'I'm on my way back to the house, but I wanted to check that you were okay first. How did it go tonight?'

I can see how exhausted he is and yet his first thought is concern for me, which is touching. Does he feel that his absence might have been misinterpreted tonight? Or that he let me down in some way, which would be utterly ridiculous.

'I'm fine and everything went very well indeed. Tomas had it all under control, so you can relax.'

'Was Beatriz there?'

I pause, turning around to look at him. 'Yes.'

'Damn it! I guessed as much.'

So, he wasn't a part of that decision, then.

'You'd better take a seat. You look exhausted.'

As I finish making the drinks, I hear him drag out a chair and softly sigh as he sinks down onto it.

'It's been a tough couple of days, and I wanted to explain myself as I can't imagine what you must think. After what happened, the timing was the worst. I meant what I said, Seren, I had no intention of hurting you, but my life is in a total mess.'

I place the mugs on the table and take the seat opposite him.

'You must be tired, too,' he continues, studying my face. There's a sadness to him that wasn't there the last time we were together.

'Tired, but not sleepy, if you know what I mean. Do you want to tell me about it?'

His fingers lightly dance against the heat of the mug in front of him. He's on edge and I sit here, watching his every move and the subtle changes in his expression. Those dark grey eyes have shadows beneath them, but he's wired, too. When the tiredness hits him, like me, he'll sink into a deep sleep, but that could be hours away.

'My daughter, Ana, ran away. Beatriz rang me in hysterics, saying she thought she'd run off with a boy she knows at school. I simply jumped in the car and headed to Porto, of course, and shortly after I arrived, I discovered that Beatriz and Ana had a big row, about an hour before she disappeared.'

I sit quietly, watching his expression and I can see he's been through hell.

'I was ready to call the police, but Beatriz wanted it hushed up and left it up to me to find her. While Ana has led a sheltered life in many ways, we've never kept the dangers the real world can present from her. She's a typical teen, starting to push back against Beatriz's rather strict rules, but she's not usually rebellious. From what I gathered, she was angry after what ended up being a shouting match with her mother.

When Beatriz went to speak to her after she'd calmed herself down, Ana was gone.'

'But you found her? She's okay?'

'Yes. Early this morning. It was one of the last places I tried, and I feared if she wasn't there, then I don't know what I would have done next. A school friend of hers lives a short train ride away and it was a bit of a long shot. When I knocked on their door, the parents said they hadn't seen Ana, but fortunately they invited me inside as I was in a bit of a state. It was obvious when they called Sofia down to talk to me that she was hiding something. They were shocked and very apologetic, assuring me that if they'd known Ana was under their roof, they would have called Beatriz immediately.'

'Ana went to some lengths to ensure she wasn't discovered right away then. You must have been frantic.'

'I was and it was hard not to think that maybe something bad had happened. Ana simply wanted to make a point, which is what she succeeded in doing. It scared Beatriz, and it terrified me. She's not happy and something has to change. What exactly, I don't know yet, but she realises she can't pull a stunt like this ever again. I rang Beatriz straight away, but when Ana and I arrived back at their house, she wasn't there. I had no idea she'd driven to Lisbon. I took Ana to stay with her aunt and I didn't want to just leave her like that, so I stayed for lunch. And then the two of us went for a long walk and we talked for a while. I asked her about this boy Beatriz mentioned and she laughed, sounding scandalised. "He's just a friend, Dad. I mention his name when Mum is being impossible," she told me. I laughed and it seemed to ease things between us, the fact that I didn't tell her off. I told her that this has been a wake-up call. In future, if she's upset about anything at all, I made it very clear that I need to be involved.'

'That's a great outcome, Reid. What a horrible time, though. A parent's worst nightmare.'

'One I don't want to relive, ever. As soon as I arrived back in Lisbon, my first thought was about you. I was surprised that it was Filipe who dropped you home, tonight. I expressly asked Tomas to arrange for a car to collect you and drop you back home.'

'When Beatriz invited Filipe along, he suggested we travel together. The party went well and it triggered lots of interest, so you can relax on that score.'

'She's been busy, then,' he comments, sounding cross. 'I bet Beatriz worked the room as if she still belongs there. I hope she wasn't rude to you in any way. She can come across as quite condescending at times.'

'She was... polite and said that the collaboration was a marvellous idea.'

'Well, that's something, I suppose. Tomas wouldn't have invited Beatriz to attend without checking it was okay with me, first. I can't even begin to imagine his initial reaction when she turned up. Making amends with Ana after their falling out should have been her first priority and I bet he was shocked, to say the least.'

Reid is so tired he's just voicing his thoughts out loud and I sit quietly, sipping my coffee as he rambles on.

'Tomas was sold on your project from the start, but when Beatriz heard about it, she wasn't happy. Of course, she wasn't speaking to me, until she needed help. Ironically, this little episode with Ana seems to have worked in her favour.'

He sighs, lapsing into silence, and I say nothing. It's calming, and a little time passes while he sits staring down into the mug in front of him.

'Reid, there really is no need for you to feel you have to explain your actions. I'm just glad that Ana is safe.'

'Please, Seren, I need you to understand what's going on because you matter to me. Beatriz is using our daughter as a pawn between us and it sickens me. Our divorce was acrimonious, but the family ties will remain forever, so it's something that needs handling. But it's as if Beatriz is trying to punish me by turning Ana against me, insinuating I don't care that she's unhappy. Now it's backfired on her because she's gone too far, and her family agree. They've been extremely supportive these last few days.' I can see he's relieved about that at least.

'If you continue a dialogue with Ana, hopefully you'll be able to find a solution that works for everyone.'

'Well, at least Ana is now aware that I never stopped caring. Tonight's party was important, and everyone will wonder why I wasn't there, but putting her first made her realise I will always drop everything if she needs me. It's taken her two years to settle down after Beatriz insisted that they move to Porto. It was the third big move in Ana's life and although she still misses the friends she made here, it would interrupt her studies too much to change schools again now if they returned to Lisbon. At least that's something on which both Beatriz and I are agreed. But I will encourage Ana to come here for weekends and during the holidays.'

Just Ana, I wonder, or Ana and Beatriz? Whatever Beatriz has to say about him, she can't dispute his love for his daughter. But if she's looking for a way to ease herself back into Reid's life on a daily basis, would she consider putting her daughter's best interests second to her own?

'It sounds like you are moving forward positively, Reid. It isn't all your fault, though,' I reply, trying to comfort him.

'I know. Beatriz has her own agenda, too, and she is good at extracting information from the people around me. I don't think she regrets the divorce, but she feels it's her right to keep an eye, not only on her share of Casa da Floresta, but on our daughter's inheritance. That's the excuse she uses to keep meddling in my affairs, despite the divorce settlement. She no longer has any financial interest in the London property, or any of my other assets, but it is still all about money. The problem is that there's no way I can raise half the value of the place and I can't sell it. It cost way too much to build and it's too big a hit to take. When I finally get to realise my dream, as an art school and a gallery, it would fulfil its potential and bring it to life. Until that happens it's simply another drain on my finances.'

'That's a tough situation to find yourself in. But you still have a life to lead in the meantime, Reid, and everyone is entitled to their privacy.'

'Beatriz is trying to back me into a corner before it's too late and that's what triggered this incident.'

'Too late for what?' I ask. Now I'm confused.

'You're an intelligent and beautiful young woman, Seren. You might not be aware of it, but your presence has caused a stir. Beatriz perceives you as a threat.'

Now I understand the icy cold look behind those eyes of hers.

'Oh, Reid. If she knew...' I feel sick to my stomach.

'And if she knew how I felt about you, she could make both of our lives unbearable if she had a mind to. Beatriz isn't above portraying someone in a bad light if it suits her. That's why I'm here now to apologise for my stupidity. I had no right to drag you into this because I couldn't help myself and that's pathetic. She won't target me, because financially that would affect her and Ana's future, but she has Filipe's ear as the two families have had a close relationship for many years. It's something she nurtures whenever it suits her interests.'

Is Reid trying to imply that my career – and my life in Lisbon – could be over if Beatriz sets her mind to it? And if things turned nasty, it could set back any progress he's making with Ana. Tonight, Beatriz made it crystal clear to everyone that she still sees herself as a big part of Reid's career, if not his life. How that fits in with his own plans, I have no idea.

It's heart-breaking. Reid and I aren't doing anything wrong. We can't ignore this connection we feel and why shouldn't we be allowed to explore it? My eyes fill with tears that I'm unable to hide. It's not fair and it's not right.

'Now I've upset you and that wasn't my intention at all. I'm just steeling myself for what comes next. I know that when I get back home, I'll probably say something I'll live to regret.' He lets out the deepest of sighs, as he reaches out to touch my hand for a few moments.

'Then stay here, with me, tonight. Things will look brighter in the morning after a few hours' rest.'

Reid stands, reaching out his hand to draw me up out of my chair, holding me close to him. After several minutes, we head into the bedroom and lie in each other's arms, until exhaustion allows an uneasy sleep to claim us both. It's enough to reassure me that what we feel is honest and it's real. Despite what's going on around us, we have this innate trust in each other and that's something I'm experiencing with someone for the first time. It means I'm letting down my guard and I don't quite know how I feel about that.

10

A NEW DAY DAWNS

I wake early, disturbed by the birds, but reluctant to move as Reid is sleeping peacefully after a fitful night. Are all divorces this messy? I wonder. Money doesn't solve problems, I reflect, it creates them.

At just after six a.m. I turn over to look at Reid, knowing he'll begin to stir when he feels the movement next to him.

Slowly, he opens his eyes and blinks rapidly for a second as he stares at me uncomprehendingly. Then he smiles in the tenderest of moments. We look at each other mesmerised, before everything comes flooding back.

'Good morning,' he mutters, softly, reaching out to touch my cheek. 'I should go before your neighbours stir.'

'I know. We can't make any mistakes now, Reid. I've been mulling it over and, at some point, Ana will leave home and begin a life of her own. Everything will change then, and adulthood will give her a different perspective on life. That would allow you a sort of freedom, wouldn't it, and lessen the hold that Beatriz has on you?'

He shifts position to lie on his back, so that he can slide his arm beneath my head and pull me closer to him. 'I guess it would. But Ana is only fifteen, she might not leave home until she's twenty-something. I can't expect you to put your life on hold. I come with too many problems, Seren. What's that saying... you get what you deserve, or something like that. I made some bad decisions and yet if I'd done things differently, I wouldn't have Ana in my life. So, I guess there's always a price to be paid. But you don't deserve to pay that price, too.' He tilts my chin with his thumb, forcing me to look directly at him. 'Your best years are yet to come. This is just the start, Seren. My advice to you is let go before you get pulled even further into this madness. Can you imagine how difficult it would be going forward, constantly having to be careful whenever we are around each other? It wouldn't be easy and that's no way to begin a relationship.'

We lapse into silence.

'I agree, but you are entitled to have a life of your own, Reid. Nothing changes that fact. You aren't married any longer.'

'To Beatriz that's a small, insignificant detail. In Portugal, it is family first and foremost. Her connections were what helped establish me and it was a true partnership in that respect. Without her influence, I wouldn't be where I am today and everyone around us is well aware of that fact. Including me.' He begins to laugh at the irony of the situation. 'I'm not just trapped, my hands are also tied.'

Reid needs Tomas and Beatriz if he's going to plough forward. If not, the sacrifices that he's made will all have been for nothing.

He holds out his hand and we intertwine our fingers.

'Do you think we knew each other in a previous life?' he muses. 'The moment we met in person for the first time, you took my breath away. You walked towards me as I opened the car door, and the connection was there. That's crazy, isn't it?'

Closing my eyes, the image of Reid's face doesn't fade away, it remains strong like an imprint and I wonder if he's right. Was it a coincidence I ended up here, in Lisbon, or is there a thread that runs through time, joining people together?

'I'm not sure I've figured out what I believe when it comes to fate and what lies beyond this life. My mother always says that like-minded people gravitate towards each other. Maybe it's more about empathy. We're two individuals who are determined to make a better future for ourselves and perhaps we give off a vibe only fellow sufferers can feel,' I suggest.

Reid laughs. 'Of what – desperation?'

'No!' I retort firmly. 'Of optimism and of welcoming change into our lives. I came here believing it was time to live each day without regret and that meant turning my back on the negativity that was around me. It's still my aim,' I reply with sincerity.

'Well, I'm good and ready for change but I'm a little short on optimism at the moment. Realistically, for the foreseeable future, it's a case of creeping around and snatching moments together until I manage to undo all of the constraints,' Reid's tone is sombre. 'The risks are very real, Seren, and I can't labour that point enough.'

'If you can live with that, so can I. Let's not pre-empt what might, or might not, happen. Dreams often change over time and people do, too,' I reply, gently.

Could there be a middle ground between us? I wonder. A perfect compromise where our very different aspirations could live side by side?

'You're not going to give up on me, are you?' His smile is tinged with sadness. Reid seems to feel his situation is hopeless and that it's a battle he can't win. But the decision is his entirely and I can't understand why he doesn't see that.

'I believe in fighting for what matters. It's the way I've lived my life so far, and I'm not about to change.'

'Let's take it one day at a time, Seren, but if you tire of it, you only have to say. Now, I think I'm going to need a strong coffee before you push me out the door. Beatriz will be feeling triumphant, having wheedled her way back into the house. Goodness knows what trouble she's stirred up in the last twenty-four hours. Let's hope it's as easy to get her to leave as it was for her to slip back in without my permission.'

* * *

Left alone with my thoughts, I decide to head out to the workshop. It's time to start a new sculpture inspired by one of Reid's atmospheric paintings looking out over the Tagus Estuary Natural Reserve. He had captured a kestrel in flight and its wings were spread wide as it seemed to float on the breeze. There was something about that solitary little bird that resonated with me. It wasn't that he was alone, but that he was free to glide and wheel over a landscape that stretched out over a massive expanse beneath him. He looked so regal, as if that split second in which Reid managed to capture him was his one defining moment in time. There was a sense of total freedom, as if the wind, the sky and the landscape had been created solely for him.

I blew up the photo and printed it out, and today it's time to make a start. There's always a little bubble of nervous excitement which rises up within me whenever I begin a new piece. Every single detail matters. The size, the perspective, the right technique to bring the vision alive. Reid's brushstrokes are light and the beautiful markings on the bird's feathers seem to shimmer, like tiny individual mosaic pieces. It's going to take hours of work to recreate this and it will be a labour of love, a tribute to the quest for freedom. Each individual piece will be hand-cut from thin aluminium sheets and hammered over the bevelled edge of the old vice on the workbench.

As I begin using the tin cutters to form the largest feathers, the repetition is calming, the effort and concentration involved stilling my troubled thoughts. Even the sounds filtering in through the open door of the neighbourhood as it stirs around me aren't a distraction. I feel peaceful and I'm grateful that life has brought me here. For all the problems and the anxieties that I've been through, no one can take away the promise of tomorrow and what it might bring. I refuse to give up, to let other people place constraints upon me and I won't live in fear. Reid and I will grab our moments of happiness and if that's all we are destined to have, so be it. It harms no one and, if we are discreet, the days and weeks will pass and who knows what might happen in the future?

I look down at the phone lying next to me as it lights up and begins to skitter across the pitted wooden bench. Pulling off my gloves, I snatch it up and see that it's Carolina.

'*Olá*, Seren. How are you this morning?'

'I'm good, thank you, and you?'

I lean back against the wooden bench, gazing out over the garden.

'Antero just called to see if we were doing anything at lunchtime. The band he's in are doing a little performance at the Time Out Market. He says if we are interested to head over early, elevenish, and they will do their best to reserve some seats. You know how busy it gets. What do you think? It sounds like fun, yes?'

'I'd love to come along. Shall we meet at the ferry? What time?'

'Ten-thirty?'

'Perfect, see you later and I'll look forward to it.'

I continue working for a while, thinking about Carolina and Antero, and how excited she sounded. It's good to be able to accompany her, because something tells me she would have felt awkward turning up on her own. It's nice to do something for her for a change, to repay the kindness she's shown me. The world is full of good people and yet isn't it ironic how the bitter, vengeful and selfish minority grab our time and attention as we battle to undo their harm.

* * *

Everyone who comes to Lisbon ends up walking around the Time Out Market. The food hall is located in the Mercado da Ribeira, taking up over half of this old area of the city. A stone's throw from the Cais do Sodré ferry terminal, it opened in 2014 and tourists and locals flock here. Without a doubt, it is one of the top ten places to visit for anyone perusing the guidebooks and planning a trip.

Some people drop in to grab a quick bite, others are weary tourists grateful to rest and refuel, but the atmosphere is always lively and congenial. You hear languages from all around the world and if you can't understand what someone is saying you simply smile, point and show your delight at the wonderful food you are tasting.

Carolina and I hurry through the huge fruit and veg hall. Staff are still in the process of setting up and clearing a long line of trolleys piled high with the morning's deliveries. The hollow space, and the metal support structures overhead, seem to take each little noise and expand it. It's like watching a machine in action, where you can hear the constant workings of the interior. Metal upon metal as the trolleys make contact, the clatter as a newly emptied tray is thrown onto a growing pile. People call out to each other and it's a general hive of activity.

Hurrying past the fish stalls, where the scallops look like white pearls, the pungent smells of the sea assault our noses. Then we approach the meat section, where our ears are filled with the sound of heavy cleavers crashing down onto well-scrubbed butchers' blocks.

We walk into the next part of the market, along an aisle of booths. There's a florist's, every inch of the space burgeoning with blooms that spill out into the gangway. Then a little stall where two servers are busily slicing buns, the sign above their heads advertising *hot dog de polvo à lagareiro* – octopus. We take a right turn as we weave in and out of the staff, everyone in a hurry to prepare for the mass influx of people who will soon begin to stream in through the doors as lunchtime approaches.

Carrying on past Garrafeira Nacional, the walls lined with glass-fronted cabinets and an Aladdin's cave of wines, liqueurs and spirits, we even resist the temptation to stop and admire the next concession. An array of mouth-watering cakes and tarts are being rearranged and a woman calls out in Portuguese, offering us a sample plate. We smile apologetically, as we move on.

Crossing over into the main food hall, there are probably less than a hundred people in here, but it will fill up very quickly now, as it's almost eleven o'clock. Scanning around, it's easy to spot Antero and a group of guys towards the far end of the cavernous room. The interlinking metal structures supporting the roof, which is made up of opaque panels, make it light and airy. A long run of lights is suspended the full length of the beams which traverse the open space. All four sides of the hall are lined with eateries, counter after counter tightly packed together, and within each, a team of chefs turning out the most exquisite food.

Everything here has been chosen, tasted and passed by a panel of Time Out's own journalists and critics; make no mistake, this is a five-star dining experience. With representatives in all of the various food categories, it celebrates the true taste of Lisbon's gastronomic experience together under one roof. This place is the main reason I was keen to tie in a celebration of the local cuisine with the gallery's fashion shoot. If we can create even a little of this buzz, I will be delighted.

These micro-restaurants belong to some of the most well-known Portuguese chefs in the business and I could spend all day walking around the vast rectangular space, watching them beavering away and fussing over the smallest of details – incredible given the sheer volume of customers they serve each day.

Carolina glances at me, her eyes sparkling as we walk past the vast run of tables which extend along the entire length of the room. As we take a short cut, passing one of the handful of small bars and gaze briefly at two large tanks filled with lobsters and crabs scuttling around, Antero hurries forward to greet us.

'Just in time. Come, meet the guys.'

Antero is looking so different today and it the first time I've really seen him casually dressed.

He proudly introduces us to his friends, as if he's known us both forever, which I find touching. The singer, a man named Miguel, stops tuning his guitar to shake hands, while the other two standing behind him giving a brief nod and a smile.

Carolina and I are conscious that we've interrupted their preparations and are eager to leave them to it.

'Shall we settle ourselves on the end table?' I prompt as Carolina and Antero gaze back and forth at each other, trying to downplay the moment.

'Sure. We're performing four sets over the next two hours. It's a promo for a concert here that we're supporting next month.'

'Oh, that's interesting. I took a quick look online at the Time Out Academy where they run the cookery courses, but didn't realise they held musical events here, too.'

'Yes, the Time Out Studio hosts some big international names and this is an important gig for us. Is there anything I can get you both before I re-join the guys?'

I glance at Carolina, smiling. 'Don't worry about us. It won't be long before we take it in turns strolling around to find something to eat.'

Antero scoops up a guitar case to pull out two tall stools for us. He lays it across a couple of the seats opposite.

'Two more people will join us shortly, so if you can try to reserve eight seats in total, we're sorted. I'll see you in a bit. Enjoy.'

Carolina pulls a purse from her bag and indicates for me to take a seat. I ease myself up onto one of the two stools at the enormous table, which is like a huge breakfast bar. Other seating areas comprise long bench seating with lower tables. All the seating is communal; it needs to be, due to the popularity of this place and adds to the unique atmosphere and experience.

'What would you like to drink?' she asks.

'A coffee would be perfect, thank you,' I reply, and she tips her head in the direction of the nearest coffee booth.

'I'll be as quick as I can.'

The early-bird diners are streaming in now to make sure they can get a seat. In an hour's time, the place will be full, with disappointed late-comers endlessly trailing around hoping to grab someone's seat as soon as they are ready to leave. But people often linger, and what I adore about this place is that it's perfect for people-watchers like me.

When I first arrived in Lisbon, I'd happily spend a couple of hours on a Saturday, walking around the market. Then, grabbing a variety of small snacks and waiting patiently until a space at one of the tables became available, I'd sit and watch the world go by. At weekends, time dragged a little for the first couple of weeks until Maria's grandson helped me sort out the workshop. It was crammed full of old furniture and boxes that were literally falling apart. I had no idea if it would be possible to make enough space for it be usable. However, with a little direction from Maria, and a garden bonfire one evening, it was soon sorted. I spend most of my free time there now but being here today and making new friends is exactly what I need.

Two women approach, waving to Antero and the guys. One of them immediately comes across to do the introductions. None of them speak any English, but I get the drift that the taller of the two ladies is his wife and the other one is the girlfriend of the guy who plays the keyboard.

Carolina appears a while later, apologising for the delay but the queues are already growing. She has two small coffees and, in a babble of conversation with our new companions, is no doubt checking what they would like to drink. After some back and forth, and a little laughter, Carolina turns to me.

'They are saying it's cocktail time. If we all put in ten euros, Luana is happy to wait in the line.'

Looking across as the cocktail bar, the queue snakes back quite a way, so it could be a while, but she smiles pleasantly as we hand over our notes.

Carolina enters into a conversation and while I try to grasp whatever words I recognise – the number is growing by the day – I'm happy to tune out, until, behind us, the band strikes up.

All around, heads start to turn in our direction, but I suspect only the diners sitting in the first couple of sections will be able to hear the music clearly. Already the background noise is escalating, but gradually my ears become accustomed to it.

By the time Luana returns, the group are on their third song, which, to my surprise, is in English, although it's not something I recognise.

I lean in to Carolina, 'I assumed it would all be in Portuguese.'

'Antero told me once that both he and Miguel did several tours around Europe with their former band and they performed some titles in English and in French. They were hoping to make a name for themselves, but eventually there was a split. He doesn't play very often these days, he says there's no money in it and it's ceased to be a dream for him. He helps Miguel out from time to time if he's one short.'

Finishing off our coffees, Luana passes across two large glasses, half-filled with sangria. We toast and the drink is a wonderfully refreshing taste of raspberries with a hint of alcohol and a blast of fruitiness from the sliced apples and strawberries floating on the top.

This is just the fun kind of relaxation I needed today.

When the guys break for lunch, Carolina and I relinquish our seats as we offer to go in search of food. We're two stools short and Antero heads off in the opposite direction on a mission.

'What shall we get?' Carolina asks, as we saunter past the gourmet burger bar and another little place selling sandwiches that bear no resemblance at all to the sort I often grabbed for lunch in the UK. We have a fistful of euros ready to feed us all.

'Antero asked if we could get some pastéis de bacalhau. Shall we look for some sharing platters, too?'

'Oh, I love those salt cod fritters and that's a great idea. Let's head for Manteigaria Silva, then.'

'Ah, we share the same favourite delicatessen.'

As we anticipated, the queue is long but orderly and eventually it's our turn.

'What do you think we should choose, Seren?' Carolina turns to me, as the woman behind the counter hovers.

'Two large cheese platters and a selection of cooked meats, to begin with.' I leave her side while she begins placing our order, to walk along to look at the display. Craning my neck to peer over people's shoulders to catch brief glimpses of the tantalising food, I head back to her.

'Why don't we ask for a basket of ciabatta, some of the stuffed figs and a few of the *patanegra grande* cones. I've tried them before and the ham is delicious.'

'Great choice,' she confirms, 'although how we are going to carry it all back, I have no idea.'

We pay and stand to one side, and I suggest Carolina enlists Antero's help to carry back the trays.

Their affection for each other is clear when I spot them weaving in and out of the constant stream of people as they hurry towards me. Antero's body language is demonstrative – he even places his arm around Carolina's shoulder, seemingly to avoid someone bumping into her. But she's enjoying his attention and happy to let him fuss over her.

When we eventually arrive back at the table, we offload the slate platters, to everyone's delight. Antero takes it in turns with Carolina to interpret for me, when the conversation begins to flow thick and fast. At one point, Miguel, who is the only one who speaks English, and Carolina change seats to save passing food around the table.

'How long have you been in Lisbon?' he asks, making polite conversation.

'I arrived in the first week of November.'

We lean forward to refill our plates. I take two thin slivers of toasted ciabatta and a fig stuffed with *patanegra*, a thinly sliced, cured ham.

'Would you like some of the cheese? If you lift your plate, we can hope we don't lose any,' he smiles at me. The cheese he's referring to is in a ball, which is fast spreading out over the almost black slate.

'I'd love some, thank you.'

He reaches over to grab one of the spare forks in the centre of our section of the table and digs into the melting cheese, quickly scooping it up and depositing it on my plate, where it begins to softly ooze.

'Surviving the homesickness must be the worst. I lived and worked in the UK for two years and then ended up touring around Europe before returning here.'

I wait while he serves himself.

'It hasn't been too bad. I have a little hobby to fill my time at weekends and I've done some sightseeing.'

'If you are ever in need of some company, or someone to show you around, let me know. Antero will give you a contact number.'

It's a genuine enough offer and I thank him. If he was coming on to me, he'd have asked for my number, I'm sure.

We begin eating again and I laugh at his attempts to get the cheese onto a small piece of bread, which results it in falling off and dropping down onto his shirt.

'There's a knack,' I explain. 'I've had this before. You need to scoop it up like this.'

He watches as I demonstrate, sliding the crispy ciabatta up close and, with my knife, flipping a portion of the cheese onto the bread. It has a life of its own, but most of it ends up in my mouth.

'It's worth the effort, isn't it?' I remark as he follows suit.

I look over his shoulder and see Carolina and Antero, their heads close together as they chatter away. I'm glad I came, it was the right thing to do.

At the end of the performance, Carolina and Antero disappear for a while and eventually it's just me and Miguel. I grab us a coffee and we end up having a pleasant chat about all sorts of things. His career has had its ups and downs, but he's at a point now where he's thinking of focusing more on song writing.

'Life is disjointed when you are constantly travelling. It's time to ease myself back into my old life and put down some roots. I have been a bad son, I think.'

I can't imagine that's the case at all. 'I'm sure your family have missed you and are simply delighted that you're back to stay.'

'Um, yes,' he replies, sounding a tad hesitant.

I give him a quizzical look.

'Putting down roots means one thing only to my mother and two sisters. It's time I settled down.'

I glance at Miguel, sympathetically. 'Oh dear. Good luck with that.'

He grins back at me. 'Thanks, I'm going to need it.'

11

IT'S ALL ABOUT PERSPECTIVE

This morning, I awoke feeling anxious and unsettled, and I can't seem to shake it off, even though everything in the office is fine and the text that Reid sent an hour ago confirmed that all his guests have finally left. Our secret is safe for now, so where is the huge sense of relief? I can only assume it's paranoia. It can create monsters where there are none and I suppose reality is setting in. I fear that the risk of Reid and me continuing to see each other is too great, given his precarious situation, and everything could change in an instant.

There's a tap on my office door and Filipe enters as I beckon him inside. Standing, I indicate for him to take a seat before I sit back down.

'I thought I'd come along and let you know that the board have agreed to the issuing of the remaining fifty tickets. Senhora Veloso will call in a personal favour to extend our limit by another thirty people. If you can arrange for a marquee to be set aside for that purpose, the directors will act as hosts and effect introductions. However, it would be useful to make someone available to chaperone the VIPs around the site at some point during the evening.'

'Of course. I'll make the necessary arrangements and ensure our special guests are well looked after.'

'Appreciated. I also wanted to pass on the thanks of the entire board, after giving them feedback about the little presentation on Saturday night. Everyone is delighted with the progress being made, Seren. Your attention to detail has not gone unnoticed and the only outstanding problem is that of the issues raised by Rafael.'

Filipe doesn't miss a thing and I need to be mindful of that.

'It's all in hand, I can assure you. I'm going to reach out to the agent of an up-and-coming singer to see if we can get permission to play her first album as a soundtrack for the entire evening.'

A slight frown settles on his forehead. 'Is that not a risk? Would it not be better to go with a more established singer?'

I can't really pass on what Reid told me in confidence, so I need to tread warily here. 'Forgive me, as I'm not an expert in this field, but there is a resurgence in a new wave of *fado*?'

His face brightens. 'Ah, yes! I don't suppose the person you have in mind is Yolanda Abreu?'

'It is. I was under the impression she's only recently started recording.'

'She is new, but a rising star. I know her family, so I will make enquiries. Excellent, Seren. I will leave you to your work as you obviously have everything under control.'

As soon as he leaves, I call Carolina.

'Good news! You can release that second batch of tickets. The downside is that Senhor Ferreira has asked if someone could make themselves available to chaperone the special guests around the site throughout the evening. In your opinion is that something I should do myself?'

'I think you will be needed to troubleshoot any problems, Seren. I can do that for you and find someone to step in for me. How does that sound?'

'Great and much appreciated. I doubt I will be straying far from Rafael, as it's imperative he is happy, and things go smoothly. So, thank you.'

'Oh, Antero asked me if you needed Miguel's number? I'm not sure why.'

'Ah, yes, he was kind enough to offer to accompany me when I'm on the tourist trail. But, to be honest with you, that's the last thing on my mind for now. And I've just started a new project in my workshop, which I'm rather excited about. I fear it's a little ambitious, though.'

'Ooh... I'm curious. You must invite me around to see it. One day you will be exhibiting here, I have no doubt of that.'

I start laughing. 'I will definitely invite you round, but I'm not so sure I'll ever be exhibiting here! But this piece is rather special as it's a gift for someone.'

'An admirer, then.'

'No. Just a surprise and I hope a good one.'

Putting down the phone, I see I have a new email from Reid, sent to both myself and Filipe. It's quite formal, saying how delighted he is with the samples and could we pass on his grateful thanks to Bernadette and her people. I had no doubts at all he'd approve, but his business-like tone is a stark reminder for me to be alert, for fear of letting anything slip. I'm curious there is no mention of Beatriz at all, though. It could mean that she's had to step back in line with Reid's wishes, of course. But it serves to reiterate that it's a delicate situation and likely to become more complicated as each day passes.

* * *

When I return home, later than usual, as I'm turning my key in the lock, Maria suddenly appears at my side. She's carrying a casserole dish, which is clearly hot as she's wearing oven gloves.

'*Olá*, Seren. I keep missing you. I was going to invite you in, but we have already eaten. I kept this warm for you in case you returned hungry. I hope you like duck, we call it *arroz de pato*.'

'That's so kind of you, Maria. Lunchtime seems like a long time ago,' I reply gratefully. 'I'm too tired to cook, so it was going to be bread and cheese for me.'

She steps inside, following me through to the kitchen and placing the dish down on a trivet.

Maria turns back around, studying my face intently. 'How are you?'

'I'm fine,' I reply slightly hesitantly as Maria is never usually this direct.

'Everything is going well?'

'I'm busy, but it's good.'

'You know where to come if you have any problems, or if you need anything. No matter what time of the day, or night.' Maria looks directly at me for a second or two, as if to labour the point. 'I will leave you to eat, then.'

'Maria, I am happy here, you know that, don't you? And I'm so grateful to have the use of the workshop.'

'Then I am happy, too,' she says as she turns and walks away.

The smell emanating from the casserole is enough to make me immediately grab a towel and lift the lid. It appears to be a toasted rice dish with a crispy top layer. I can smell red wine and there is a scattering of sliced, smoked sausage that fills the kitchen with a peppery aroma. Grabbing a fork, I can't resist digging in and discover that the chunks of duck meat literally fall apart. I end up carrying the dish across to the table and sit, too tired to bother decanting it onto a plate, because it's so delicious. Half of it is gone before I know it and I set the rest aside to cool.

Yanking open the door below the sink unit, I pull out a brown wooden box. Inside are a few spare keys and Maria told me there's one in here for the solid oak door set into the wall at the rear of the garden. As I'm searching through, my phone lights up and I see that it's Reid. I grab it, smiling as I put it to me ear and head off into the bedroom.

'How was your day?' The sound of his voice is comforting as I lie back, resting on the bed.

'Good. Productive. A long one, actually. And you?'

'I'm back in my studio. I've been commissioned to produce a set of watercolour prints for a private collection and Tomas has asked me to focus on that. He says I've had too many distractions lately. It's partly his fault for arranging functions and parties, but it does generate a lot of interest in my work.'

'That's a good thing for you to have quiet time, though, isn't it?'

'Yes, as long as he isn't being manipulated. Beatriz might be behind this, making sure I'm within easy reach. Ana is back with her now and things appear to have quietened down.'

He sounds mellow and I wonder if Tomas can see the anxiety

building up in him and this is as much about giving Reid space as it is deadlines.

'Beatriz's name is on a list that Filipe sent me. I wondered if you recognised any of the other people on there?'

'Can you send it to me?'

I was hoping he'd say that. A couple of clicks and I hear the ping. A few moments elapse. I'm sure there's nothing to be concerned about, but as Beatriz's name seems to be cropping up regularly at the moment, I can't help being a little suspicious.

'Let me see... four of them I don't know at all. Three of them are joint friends of ours. Two are a celebrity couple; he's a producer and his wife runs a marketing company. I don't know them personally. I'm not sure Beatriz would have any close links with them, either. What is this list for, exactly?'

'They are to be the VIPs attending the fashion shoot and I've arranged for Carolina to escort them.'

'I'm pretty sure Filipe has known the producer for a while. Maybe the four names I don't recognise are linked to the other directors? Beatriz may well be repaying favours, of course, and they could simply be new acquaintances she wants to impress. She has known Filipe's family for many years and if she presented him with this list he won't refuse her request. It's probably for the best that Carolina is looking after them, though. This is just the sort of tactic Beatriz uses when she wants to get under my skin and I don't expect you to have to pander to her. Going via Filipe is Beatriz's way of reminding me that all doors are open to her.'

'I did wonder, as the other invitees aren't being chaperoned. By the way, I've been thinking... the next time you come to me I wonder if it would be a little more discreet if you use the back gate. You can park a few streets away and I'll give you a key. The key is almost as big as a phone, but at least it's a private entrance.'

'Problems?'

'Not really, but I don't want to upset my neighbour. It's her brother's house I'm renting, and she's been so good to me. I don't think she'd approve of night-time visitors.'

'Creeping around isn't easy, is it? Maybe you should come here.'

'Is that wise, Reid? That would be a big risk to take.'

'It's the same for you,' he replies, softly.

His voice is so gentle, and I close my eyes, imagining that he's next to me.

'You've gone quiet, Seren.'

'I want you to do me a favour. Do you know how wonderful your voice is, Reid?'

He laughs. 'Wonderful?'

'Warm, genuine and mesmerising. You need to be the voice for the video. It's the perfect solution. Who could possibly talk about your work as well, or as passionately, as you?'

'Only you would say something like that, Seren. You don't think you're a little biased?'

'I'm sure Filipe will agree with me, but I wanted to ask you first.'

'I'll go along with whatever you want. There are no guarantees I won't mess it up though, so maybe have a back-up plan,' he muses. 'And as for getting together, maybe you are right. I'll give it some thought, too, and see if I can come up with another solution.'

My spirits instantly lift a little. I have no idea if Tomas has told Reid about the meeting Filipe mentioned on the drive back from the party. It might not come to anything, but Beatriz is behind it, I have no doubt about that. Something is making me hesitate about mentioning it, though. Reid is on board with the fashion shoot but has shown little interest in the product range that will go on sale in the gallery. Tomas has been liaising directly with Filipe and Bernadette, so I'm not involved. But Reid doesn't seem to be, either. That puzzles me a little, I must admit, and I can only assume that he's happy to let Tomas run with it.

The other thing that worried me a little that night was that Vitor seldom let Beatriz out of his sight. Whenever she wanted anything, he was there. It would be wrong of me to cast suspicion on him when he has shown me only politeness and respect, but I wonder where his allegiance truly lies. With Reid, or with Beatriz? To me, it appeared that Vitor was treating her as if she was mistress of the house still.

'Some time alone together would be good. But I understand the pressures on you.'

'I don't want you to be lonely, though. You can't waste precious time waiting around for my problems to resolve. I'll work something out, I promise, but in the meantime, you must enjoy yourself and I understand that.'

The responsibility he's feeling towards me is touching.

'I've just started a new sculpture, a special one, so that's going to keep me occupied for a couple of weeks.'

'Ah, good. Not that I think you should confine yourself to that little workshop, but I'm glad you have something you enjoy and that's relaxing for you.'

As we say goodnight, it's with a heavy heart that we end the call. Neither of us wants to be alone, but that's the way it must be for now. Getting ready for bed, loneliness threatens to overwhelm me and the only way I'm going to lift my mood is to settle down and read.

Pulling the e-reader from the bedside drawer, I trawl through my library. I miss my paperbacks so much. They were my security blanket, because sometimes you need to smell the print on the paper as you turn a page on a well-thumbed book. I have boxes of them in storage.

What I need now is something uplifting, a story that will give me hope that love can triumph, when what I fear is that sometimes there are too many obstacles. One title seems to jumps out: *The Trouble with Being Me* and when I read the blurb, it makes me smile. It's about a woman who doesn't give up on her dream, but the road she travels isn't an easy one. And as I begin reading, I'm hooked from the very first paragraph.

My mother once told me that if something is meant to be, things will fall into place. If the path is tortuous, then fighting against one's destiny is for fools. I now realise that I'm a fool, a complete and utter lovesick fool...

* * *

The next day, Carolina and I spend the entire morning working on the limited-edition programme for the exhibition. It's coming together, but we're not quite there yet. Tomas has yet to provide Reid's official biography and a portrait photo of him. I ask Carolina to chase him. For the time being, I want to keep my contact with Tomas to the minimum.

By lunchtime we are beginning to flag as we were both at our desks by seven-thirty this morning. I'm hungry and I'm sure Carolina is too, but we're loath to break off.

My office door is open and Filipe unexpectedly appears in front of me.

'I will be unavailable now for the next couple of hours as I have a meeting with Tomas and Beatriz. Your diligence is admirable, Seren, but a break is healthy,' he points out. 'It's a lovely day, but I suspect neither of you have noticed. Why not grab a leisurely lunch? My favourite place to stroll is around the Padrão dos Descobrimentos. Take some time, enjoy!'

As he disappears out of view, Carolina and I exchange glances. 'I think he's worried we are overworked. That's a compliment,' she remarks.

However, my smile turned into a frown the moment I heard Beatriz's name mentioned. Filipe's tone was friendly but encouraging. Has Beatriz said something about me and he's simply making sure our paths don't cross?

'Have you already visited the Monument to the Discoveries?' Caroline asks.

'No. It's on my list. I've visited the Torre de Belém. The day I went, there was a big queue for the tower, but I waited in line and it was well worth it. The views are glorious, and I was hoping to head back along the riverbank to the monument, but I couldn't find a direct route, so I gave up.'

'There is no way to cross the exits where the yachts that are moored up at the marina access the river. You have to head inland and circle around. Why don't we jump on a tram, it's only a short ride, and find somewhere shady to sit and eat a sandwich at the monument?'

'Why not?' It's time I put all thoughts of Beatriz out of my head and this could be the perfect distraction.

We gather our things together and spot Antero as we leave the building.

'We're going for a stroll and to grab a snack. Can you join us?' I ask.

'No, afraid not. I'm just printing off a few things for Senhor Ferreira's meeting. He said not to bother you about it, as you were about to go to lunch. It's a pity though, as I'm meeting up with Miguel shortly. We could have gone together.'

He hurries off, a wad of papers in his hand. It's unusual for Filipe to call upon Antero to assist him and it is a little unsettling.

Outside, the first thing I do is put on my sunglasses and Carolina follows suit.

'This way. We need to take the number fifteen tram and we'll get off at the Mosteiro dos Jerónimos, then it's a short walk across the gardens.'

'Ah, the monastery is next to our favourite bakery and café. It's a pity we'll be walking in the opposite direction,' I reply sadly.

'You have a good sense of direction, Seren.'

'When this project is over, I can't wait to take some time off and continue working down the list of sights I'd love to see. Two of my friends are flying in from the UK on the day of the fashion shoot and will be staying in Lisbon for a week. I've asked Filipe if I can take five days holiday once the celebratory weekend is over.'

'I'm glad for you. It can't be all work and, what is it you say? No play. What did you think of Miguel? I only ask, because he has never come here to meet Antero for lunch before. It seems too much of a coincidence.'

As the tram pulls away, our shoulders knock together and we laugh, but she raises her eyebrows at me.

'He's a nice man and his English is good, so we were able to chat. But—'

'You aren't interested in him? He's attractive, sincere and he has a beautiful voice.'

Is she trying to encourage me?

'I know.'

Suddenly, she narrows her eyes, searching my face, questioningly. 'You have a special someone back in the UK?'

'No. Not at all.'

'You have someone here?' The question is tentative, but we're friends now and Carolina has shared confidences with me. She's expecting the same in return.

'There's a huge difference between liking someone and being in a position to begin a new relationship.'

Whether Carolina will interpret that as an interest in Miguel, I don't know, but the statement is an honest one. Protecting Reid is, however, my first priority.

'That's understandable. It won't always be this hectic, I hope.' The way she shrugs her shoulders indicates that she, too, understands the difficulties. Reid doesn't want me putting my life on hold, but you can't choose what your heart wants, can you? Even when it's the impossible.

I stare out the window as the colourful buildings flash by, a mixture of pastels interspersed with vibrant blues and yellows. They are interrupted only by buildings adorned with the wonderful, vintage azulejo tiles, reflecting that sunny, Mediterranean feel.

We lapse into silence for the remainder of the short journey and when we alight outside the monastery, the lunchtime heat seems to bounce up off the wide, limestone-cobbled pavement.

'Your intention really is to settle here, isn't it? I know you said you were going to start learning Portuguese, but I wondered if your ties to home would pull you back there.'

'I don't think so, but I know you will appreciate how there are moments when it's easy to long for the familiarity of the life you left behind.'

We are both deep in thought as we cross the road. Wandering through the swathe of gardens ahead, the path leads us to an underpass beneath the busy main road. Stopping at a small stand to buy a cold drink, it's too hot to eat anything substantial. I point to some little round cakes with a hole in the centre. The woman says they are called *pão de ló* and Carolina nods enthusiastically. I ask for two, which the vendor carefully wraps, putting them into a bag with some napkins.

There's a steady stream of people coming and going in both directions, but it's not packed. However, when we reach the monument, it feels as if everyone who works in the area has chosen to join the tourists today.

'It must get really busy in the height of summer,' I comment, as we hurry across to a bench set back in a nook in the wall. There's little shade, but it will be pleasant to sit and enjoy our cake.

'It's mostly tourists then, as the locals prefer to come when it's cooler. We'll take a wander around when you are ready. These are delicious, aren't they?'

The sponge is moist and there's a hint of sharp lemon, which makes my tongue tingle. I gaze across at the monument as I sit here savouring the flavours.

'Yes, and perfect when you are hungry and in need of a sugar fix. The monument is bigger than I expected.'

'Did you know you can go inside and climb up the statue? It's worth a visit to spend a couple of hours wandering around in general, too.'

'The monument is the prow of a ship, isn't it?'

'Yes, a caravel – a light sailing ship used by the Portuguese navigators. The shield of Portugal is on both sides. This is where the ships departed to explore India and the Orient. At the prow is the Infante Dom Henrique, known as Henry the Navigator. One of the inscriptions says he and his peers discovered the roads of the sea. I like that thought.'

Even from this distance, the monument towers high into the sky and it's remarkable.

We finish eating and the water slips down easily to quench our thirst. I'm eager to get closer, but I'm also conscious of the time.

'Come, we can take another twenty minutes before walking back. Senhor Ferreira will be pleased we followed his suggestion.'

I'm trying my best not to stress about the reason why Filipe was so insistent Carolina and I take a leisurely lunch today. If Beatriz suspects something is going on between Reid and me, did she convey the need for discretion? If that's the case, not only does it not bode well for my reputation, but could it also mean she's going behind Reid's back? It's hard to shake off my concerns, but I don't want Carolina picking up on my unease, so I try to relax.

Today, the breeze coming off the river Tagus is light as the sun beats down on us and here there is no shade. As we saunter closer, the water alongside is like liquid silver. Overhead, a solitary plane passes over the bridge, which hangs like a necklace behind the monument. Of the people around us, many are office workers taking lunch breaks, but there are families, too, pushing strollers and tourists with bulky backpacks.

The wide promenade beneath our feet changes as we step onto the more traditional design of the cobbled limestone floor from which the monument rises majestically. In sharp contrast to the buff stonework of the statuary, the small cobbles are arranged in a pattern. It has been laid in a chequerboard style, with ribbons of dark grey cobbles that twist and turn among the general buff-colour stones.

Before we leave, I want to go up close and touch the statue with my hand. Carolina follows me, no doubt having visited many times before and having done this herself.

The figures standing on the sloping ledges either side are each unique, and my eyes are drawn to the navigator who holds a ship aloft in his hands. From a monk, to a knight in battle dress proudly brandishing his sword, and even royalty, the monument tells a story of generations. It's a homage to bravery and the quest for knowledge, trade and adventure.

When I place my hand on the stone, it occurs to me why the ability to create something lasting is so important. The work is a legacy so that the past will not be forgotten, but also the creator is aware that they are leaving something behind that will continue to exist long after they are gone.

'You are touched by this place, Seren,' Carolina remarks, placing a hand on my arm.

'You're right. It has inspired me.'

'That's the artist in you,' she adds softly.

Is that what attracted me to Reid? And yet he's right, I *am* only just beginning my journey and I have no idea if it will lead anywhere, but I owe it to myself to give it a chance.

Suddenly my heart dips, as I reluctantly follow Carolina to head back. Traipsing a pace or two behind, I wonder what on earth I'm doing. Reid is a famous artist. He socialises with the people that Beatriz can mix with easily, because her family is well-known and respected. As far as Lisbon is concerned, I have no history and no connections. Reid's life represents everything I'm hoping to turn my back on as soon as I can afford to do so. How ironic is that? Almost too ironic, and if I believed in signs, I'd say this might well be one.

Is it foolish to blindly follow a dream in the belief that I will end up feeling empowered and free? The thought that pops into my head is that those intrepid, Portuguese explorers didn't dwell upon the dangers, the unknowns, and the risks of never returning to see their families again. They lived in the hope of discovering new frontiers and uncovering a wealth of new opportunities. With great risk comes great reward.

For Reid, it's about creating something much bigger than simply achieving success as an artist. For me, it's about having the freedom to discover who I am and what will make me truly happy. His dream will, I'm sure, bring great financial rewards and mine probably won't – and that doesn't matter to me. But does it matter to him?

12

FEELING THE KARMA

When we arrive back at the gallery, there is no sign of Filipe's visitors and a casual enquiry aimed at Antero turns up nothing. It would be wrong of me to press him and I console myself with the fact that if it was anything directly linked with the project, then Filipe would have had no choice but to involve me.

It's unusual for Filipe to leave early, but he does today and stops by first for a little chat. He asks if I enjoyed my visit to the monument and I tell him that I will go back again. He seems pleased. Filipe also confirms that he has spoken with Yolanda Abreu's father and I can expect an email very shortly from her publicist. And just like that the problem is sorted. I express my appreciation, as his intervention has saved me from what could have been a long dialogue going back and forth. However, I have to let go of my disappointment that he doesn't mention anything at all about his meeting.

Just before I finish for the day, Carolina appears and taps on my door.

'I'm just a messenger here. Antero was too late for lunch with Miguel, as he was tied up with Senhor Ferreira. So, they are going for a meal after work. We are both invited.'

She looks at me expectantly.

'I can't, I'm afraid, but you must go,' I reply, emphatically. I can see she isn't convinced.

'It wouldn't be appropriate for me to go alone, Seren.'

'Friends get together, and you know them both. A threesome can't be construed as a date, can it? Please say you'll go, or I'll feel bad about it.'

'Can't you come for just an hour?' she presses me and I can see she really wants to go.

'That might give Miguel the wrong impression. This way the message is clear, and everyone knows where they stand. But Antero will appreciate you making the effort to join them. Go on, you'll have fun!'

She pauses for a moment, before wishing me a good evening, and I prepare to head for the ferry terminal. I'm in no mood to socialise and I know that I wouldn't be good company.

Checking my phone, I have two missed calls from Judi, and as soon as I get home, I give her a ring.

'Sorry I missed you, I was still in work.'

'Ah, I forget you can't sneak off and take a private phone call.'

'It's not that,' I chide, 'it's just not the done thing here. What am I missing?'

'More of the same, but I was ringing because I was worried about you.'

'Why?'

'Well, you rarely text these days and we haven't spoken for over a week now. What's going on?'

'Work, work and more work. I could level the same thing at you.'

'Yes, but the last time we spoke, Seren, you mentioned a man and something about "career suicide". Isn't dating a client a little risky? I mean, foreign country, new job and, well... it sounds like a bit of a recipe for disaster to me.'

The last thing I need now is a lecture.

'It's going nowhere, so there's no need to worry.' Inwardly, I groan. I'd hoped that would come out sounding reassuring, but it just sounded lame.

'Now I'm really concerned, because that means you won't talk about it because it isn't over. This isn't a one-sided thing, is it?'

I sigh. 'No. He's genuine, but it's complicated.'

'Oh dear.'

'What does that mean?'

'You're on the defensive, Seren, and that means one thing. You think this might be for real. I can't even bring myself to say the word out loud: L – O – V – E. Every feeling you have, every decision you make is no longer trustworthy because you have lost the ability to be objective. Seriously, you need to sit down and think this through.'

She's right to sound disapproving as it is a mess I could so easily have side-stepped. It wasn't so long ago I was the one warning Judi about her own situation and look how that fizzled out. It turns out that any advice I gave her was naïve, because at that point I had no idea what it felt like to be in love. Theory is one thing, real life is another and it isn't as simple as maintaining self-control, being practical, or even sensible.

I look up at the ceiling. *Universe, I'm sorry – forgive me please, because I had no idea what I was doing. I'll be kinder, wiser, more understanding in future, I promise.*

'Okay. You aren't going to like this, but here goes. I know what you stand to lose, but what about him?'

Her words are devastatingly clear.

'An ex-wife and a daughter.'

'And are you really prepared to risk your reputation over someone you hardly know, when there's no one around to help put you back together if it goes wrong?'

'I know what I'm doing, and it won't come to that,' I assure her.

'Can you hear yourself? That's classic self-denial. You are so far outside of your comfort zone that you've lost any sense of reality, Seren. Don't you think there was a part of me that didn't want to let Alex go? I could have talked myself into thinking everything happens for a reason and being in therapy means his relationship is already on the rocks. But I couldn't do that to him, or to myself. I thought you and I were on the same wavelength, but now I just want to jump on a plane to rescue you from yourself.'

The reason I love Judi to bits is because she has my best interests at heart, but on this occasion she's wrong. I'm prepared to settle for what little I can grab before the inevitable happens. And I know Beatriz is never going to let Reid go completely. It's obvious that he's more likely to get where he wants to be if Beatriz is involved because of her vast network of connections. And that's a fact.

'I already know how this will end, Judi. I'm not under any illusions because the chances of it going anywhere are so slim. His ex-wife doesn't seem to realise he has the right to a life of his own and he's the sort of man who carries his responsibility like a burden. But we need each other right now, just to get us through the next phase in our lives. Is that really such a bad thing? Neither of us will hold the other back when the time comes; we're adults, fully capable of looking at the bigger picture. And I know how it sounds, but if you met him, you'd understand.'

'Well, I will when I fly over – won't I?' she replies, in a matter-of-fact way, and my stomach does an involuntary somersault.

'Oh, he'll probably be in London when the exhibition is on.'

'Well, I hope not. If you are still in the same frame of mind by then, I need to meet this man and see for myself why you're prepared to waste a few months of your life for so little in return.'

As long as I don't let any real details slip, like a name, I can get around this, I'm sure. 'We're just two lonely people, enjoying each other's company until our lives naturally move on. We both know what it's like when the life you knew has come to an abrupt halt and you are trying to fathom out where it goes next.'

There's a loud, 'hmm' echoing down the line. 'Why can't you choose someone without baggage? I'm sure Lisbon is full of sexy, attractive, single men looking for love.'

'Did it occur to you that might be why I'm going for the more difficult option?' It's difficult not to sound a little cranky as I reply. After her angst over the situation with Alex, Judi, of all people, should understand that sometimes these things just happen. And, often, when you least expect it.

'You mean the impossible option, there's a difference. I'm ticking off the days until I can jet off on my rescue mission. Someone needs to get you back on track and it looks like it's going to be me!'

The truth is that I don't want to be saved. Well, not yet, anyway.

* * *

Before I know it, it's Saturday morning and, sod's law, I'm awake with the birds. I lie still for a while, but it's hardly restful as my thoughts are churning. By chance, I found out yesterday that Antero was asked to give Tomas and Beatriz a tour of the gallery after their meeting and yet he didn't share that with me. I've heard nothing, so maybe I should simply relax about it. What I do know is that Filipe is aware that the pressure is on to get the programme finalised and I assume he's doing his utmost not to distract me. If he had any concerns, I'm sure he would express them to me sooner rather than later. I mustn't let Beatriz get into my head, because for all I know that might be precisely what's she's hoping to achieve.

Instead of weekly video meetings, Carolina is now sending out an update via email to Reid, Rafael and Bernadette. It keeps everyone up to speed on the progress and any new developments. The big news we were able to share yesterday is that Yolanda Abreu's first album will be the backing music to accompany the fashion shoot on the night. And that Reid will be doing the voice-over for the edited version that will be screened in the gallery to accompany the formal exhibition. Rafael has gone quiet, so we're all hopeful that he's satisfied with the arrangements we have in place.

We are in the lull period now, where it's all about behind-the-scenes organisational stuff. The next big milestone will be when we take delivery of the first costume sample and give it a test run.

After a quick shower, I head out to the workshop. It's too early to start banging around, but I can sit quietly on the old wooden stool and continue cutting the petal-shaped feathers by hand. I've decided my kestrel isn't going to be a big bird, so the framework for his wingspan is only sixty centimetres across. However, the hollow metal box I discarded and set down in the corner of the workshop will become his launchpad. He'll sit on top of a single rod of metal, tilted on an angle, as if he's in flight.

The photo I took of Reid's painting is pinned to the wall in front of me and whenever I look up at it, I smile. What I love about his work is the simplicity of his style. He doesn't draw every single line, so it's as much about what he leaves out as what he chooses to put in. The way he then applies the watercolours with a delicate touch makes something one-dimensional come alive with depth and feeling. It's also clear that he is inspired by his father, because there is an architectural quality to the way he structures his work. Reid's mind is orderly, precise.

Two hours later and it's time for a break. I know Maria's kitchen door will be open by now and she'll be wondering where I am. As I step out into the courtyard, she's sitting at the little tiled bistro table and greets me with a cheery '*Bom dia*, Seren' as I take the seat alongside her. She immediately heads inside and returns with a mug of coffee for me.

'It's another glorious start to the weekend, Maria. This coffee is very welcome this morning, I've been in the workshop since five a.m.'

'I did wonder. And you are doing well?'

'I'm good, thank you. How are the family?'

'Good. Rachel has a new boyfriend. She brought him home to meet me on Tuesday. He came to lunch.'

It's difficult to tell from her expression how she feels about that. I have no idea when her son died, or how long Rachel, her daughter-in-law, and her grandson have lived with her. Rachel is easy to talk to and was very helpful when I first arrived. But she works two part-time jobs and our chats are usually fleeting, as we pass each other coming and going. On the occasions Maria invites me inside and Rachel is there, we usually talk about her family back in the UK, or how I'm settling in; never about her husband. Luis is usually around, so it's difficult to tell whether Rachel is being diplomatic out of respect for Maria or her son. I suspect it's Maria. It does make me wonder how Maria will cope, all alone in that big house, if they move out. They are the centre of her world.

'Are they a good match?' I ask, knowing that Maria isn't the sort of woman to begrudge anyone their happiness.

Maria nods, a look of acceptance creeping over her face. 'Yes, so it seems. I am content, but hope he understands what a lucky man he is.'

Her concern is only natural, given the circumstances.

'Everyone needs somebody,' Maria explains. 'But opening up one's heart to someone is always a risk. The pain of loss can last a lifetime. One loss is too much, another loss would be disastrous.'

As a mother it must be heart-breaking to support one's family through a tragedy from which you may never recover. How do you go on when a part of you is missing forever? And now this marks a new stage that only serves to remind Maria of her loss.

'It is easier for you now? You have friends?' she asks. Maria is worried about me and I'm touched.

'Yes. I have grown close with two of the people I work with – you've met Carolina. One lunchtime this week, she took me to see the *Padrão dos Descobrimentos*.'

'It is a long time since I visited. It is good, though, to honour the past. But you have another friend, too, who visits? That makes you happy?'

It's obvious that Maria spotted Reid. Whether it was arriving late at night, or leaving early the next morning, it looks like what it is, and I can't hide that.

'It does. I am sorry if it disturbed you. My friend had a problem and needed someone to talk to.'

'Is no problem. But if anything goes wrong you can always knock on my door, Seren.'

I know that Maria is simply looking out for me, and I suppose I'd be concerned if the situation was reversed and I saw a stranger going into Maria's house late at night when I knew she was there alone. 'Thank you, Maria. He is a good man and someone I trust, who has been kind enough to help me. But life isn't easy for him right now.'

She looks at me, the corners of her mouth turning down as she nods. 'There is so much unhappiness in this world. People have forgotten how to live simply and to be kind to each other. *Aqui se faz, aqui se paga.*'

I look at her apologetically, as the phrase means nothing to me, and she shrugs her shoulders. Grabbing the phone from my pocket, I type it in. The literal translation is *here it is done, here it is paid.*

'I think I understand. We say *you reap what you sow.*'

It's Maria's turn to look vague.

'Karma?'

She smiles, nodding. '*Sim, carma!*'

Luis appears in the doorway just as my phone pings. I ignore it as he calls out, '*Bom dia*, Seren.'

I give him a friendly wave and there's a quick exchange between him and Maria. She smiles across at him fondly, before easing herself up off the chair.

'He is hungry, Luis is always hungry and that's good. I like to cook,' she laughs. 'You come for breakfast?'

'No. But thank you. I have work to do.'

She leans over to place her hand over mine, as it lays on the table. '*Até logo.*'

'Yes, see you later, Maria. *Obrigada!*'

Glancing at my phone, it's a text from Reid, but I wait until I'm back inside to read it.

I was going to suggest we meet up, but Beatriz has just phoned. Ana is coming to spend the weekend with me. I'm picking her up from the station at lunchtime. I'm sorry.

He shouldn't be apologising to me for grabbing some quality time with his daughter.

Don't be. Enjoy your time together. It's what you both need. I'm happy for you.

And I am. It's a good sign that she's reaching out to him so soon.

It's a big step forward. Are you working on your newest sculpture?

I am. I'll be cutting and shaping little metal discs all weekend. It's a labour of love.

It's going to be a gift for Reid when it's finished.

I'm hoping you are free next weekend. How do you fancy a two-night stay at the beach?

A weekend away together with no worries about who might be watching. Bliss.

Of course, I'm free! It sounds perfect.

It will be, I promise. Speak soon.

This isn't just good news, it's brilliant news, I reflect as I head into the kitchen to grab something to eat. Any doubts I had about Beatriz wanting to meddle are beginning to fade fast. To encourage Reid and Ana to spend quality time alone together, when she could so easily have driven Ana there and invited herself along, is thoughtful. I wonder whether her attitude is beginning to change, as she begins to see that Reid has the ability to calm Ana down.

Maria's words echo around inside my head. Was I being suspicious because I'm a little jealous of Beatriz? She will always be a part of Reid's life and she's a force of nature. Anyone can see that. But a weekend away with Reid is something I can grab onto, a memory I'll have forever. I know he isn't mine, but a little piece of him will be for a short while and that's all I can realistically expect.

The fact is, Reid's long-term ambitions and my own bear no resemblance at all. The very things that made me loathe my old life are the reasons why Reid needs a woman like Beatriz in his. His dream to start up an art gallery and run art classes requires capital, and a lot of it. And if it goes well, I'm sure it will be very profitable and allow him to step away from the constant demands to attend parties and exhibitions in order to sell his work. He'll be going back to basics and doing what makes him happy.

As for me? Well, I don't always want to live to work. Once I'm financially stable and, yes, proven to myself that I can do anything I set my mind to, then I intend to work to live, quite literally. And that's what sets our dreams apart. Reid is intent on building an empire and I'm doing what I must so I can ultimately set myself free. But if what I feel for him is truly love, then it's not wrong to grab a little happiness along the way, surely. The fear is that I might never feel like this with anyone ever again.

Will I then regret not having taken the time to enjoy every single moment we have together?

I have this mental picture of me in years to come, slopping around in leggings and T-shirts, my collection of sculptures turning the garden of my home into a gallery of its own. I may even be lucky enough to sell a few pieces, but if not, I'll get a little job working just enough hours to pay the bills. I'm quite content becoming the single woman that no one in the village really understands and who is regarded by her neighbours as eccentric. The woman who decided that a handful of golden memories can sometimes be more fulfilling than a life spent with the wrong someone.

As I pour my passion into what I create, I console myself with the thought that I will think back on this time in my life with fondness. But I hope I'll also feel proud of the fact that I had the courage to do what felt right for me. I've seen what happens to couples when one person gives and the other constantly takes. All it causes is constant heartache and that's no way to live your life.

Each month I'm here my savings grow and I can't wait for the day when I have enough to buy my own little place somewhere fairly close to the city. But today I have metalwork to form while I patiently await the opportunity to make another precious memory with Reid. It's taken me a long time to finally understand what it means to live in the moment.

13

THE EXCITEMENT BUILDS

It's Monday morning and we arrive at the office to hear the news that the fashion shoot is now sold out. Not only that, but I receive an email from one of Filipe's contacts I've met with several times now and he'll be ready to come in to do a short presentation to the board later in the week. The company are hoping to gain approval to produce a selection of organic hand soaps and toiletries as a part of the *Inspired by Reid Henderson* range. It will complement the bathroom furnishings, which includes roman blinds and hand towels embroidered with birds and flowers. They are going to mock up some of the packaging based on the prints we supplied to Bernadette. I know Filipe will be delighted, and so will Tomas if we manage to pull this off. As for Reid, he'll probably just shrug his shoulders, amused that his face could end up on the back of a soap dispenser.

Antero knocks on my door, gingerly swinging it open. 'I just had a call from Bernadette. She'll be at the factory later today to see the first of the dress samples and wondered if you wanted to be in on it. She's suggesting a video meeting at two o'clock?'

'Two days ahead of schedule, that's marvellous news. As long as that suits you, Antero, I'm fine with it. It's a pity Carolina will miss it.'

'Yes, it is.' He looks at me sheepishly and I can't help wondering whether it's because she did go along to spend time with him and Miguel. He should know by now that I don't have a problem with it.

Today Carolina is up at the Cristo Rei, meeting with the site manager to draw up the parking plans to accommodate the trailers. With catering vehicles, facilities for the models to change, and the lighting people all vying for space, it needs to be carefully coordinated.

My morning is going to be spent looking over the budgets now that all the tickets are sold for the Friday evening. Achieving break-even is still going to be tight, even levying charges from the companies giving out their food samples and the people who will be selling the drinks. To walk the catwalk, we enlisted students from a local modelling school, who jumped at the chance to take part. We are footing the bill for the costs of the hair and make-up team but managed to negotiate a good deal in return for featuring their artists and hairdressers in the programme.

At lunchtime, I settle myself down on a bench and polish off a scrummy, traditional Portuguese pork sandwich, called a *bifana* – it's no wonder that the waistbands on my skirts are getting a little tighter. Then I call my mother.

'Hi, Mum. Only me, just checking in to say the parcel you sent arrived safely. How was your weekend?'

'We had great fun. I spent it at a manor house helping Fi out, as she was showing dresses at a wedding fair. The weather wasn't the best, but we were indoors much of the time, anyway. How about you, darling?'

'I spent most of it bashing metal around, you know me.'

'That warms my heart to hear you say that, because I bet you were in your own little world and happy as a lark.'

She's right.

I suppose that out of politeness I should give her the chance to talk about my father, even though I don't really want to know as she sounds happy enough. 'Any developments?' I casually throw out.

She hesitates for a moment. 'Same old, same old. Your father isn't happy and he wants me to *come home*, as he put it. But having made the break, Seren, I'm not regretting it at all. My time is my own, and I know this sounds selfish, but if I don't fancy cooking, I just grab a takeaway or make a sandwich. No more having to worry about dinner being on the table at seven every evening and making sure I don't serve the same pudding twice in one week. Seriously, when you are down to just two people eating, it should be more relaxed and not such a big pressure. I happily eat from a tray in front of TV, most nights. But you know what your father is like. The table must be laid and if I dared to use a paper napkin instead of a linen one, he'd think I'd lost my mind.'

It's strange to hear Mum talking like this, when I had no idea how trapped she felt.

'You don't think he's capable of change?' I ask, not wanting to let my feelings influence her.

'No. Nothing he's said to me is about compromise, it's all about getting things back to normal. I'm afraid, Seren, my mind is made up.'

You think you know the people you love, but Mum hid her true feelings for a long time. My happiest memories were as a young child, when my father was struggling to set up his business. We lived in a small, semi-detached house and most of my school friends lived close by. I remember him coming home from work and in summer we'd go into the garden to practise my netball shots, while Mum cooked dinner. In winter, he taught me how to play chess and Mum would often have to call us several times to get us to the table. Life was simpler then, for us all, but I didn't realise his dream wasn't necessarily Mum's, too.

'Do you have a plan?' I ask.

'No,' she replies, sounding bright and breezy. 'I don't need one. Your father will get fed up and realise I'm not going back. Then he'll get angry and start divorce proceedings. Then he'll be too busy trying to make sure I walk away with as little as possible. That's how it goes, isn't it?'

'But you supported everything he did, Mum. You pandered to his every whim, accompanied him to all those boring functions and you were both Mum and Dad to me, as he was rarely around. Don't settle for less than you are due.'

'My darling Seren, don't you worry about me. I can earn enough to keep a roof over my head while he gets on with it. Fi has offered me her spare bedroom, but I like the little flat I'm renting. It's cosy, has everything I need and I don't have to spend hours cleaning it. It's heaven.'

I can't stop myself from laughing as I think back to what I said to Judi when I first arrived here. It took me three years to be able to afford to put a sizeable deposit on a home of my own, the fact that it was mine more than made up for the fact that it wasn't the big, dream country property I'd left behind. But if someone had said I'd swap that for a rustic, bijou dwelling where visitors walk through your bedroom to access the garden, I'd have laughed. 'Oh, Mum. We are so alike in many ways. Bigger doesn't mean better, does it?'

'It most certainly does not. And I'm always in charge of the remote control these days. Can you imagine that? I didn't realise how many channels there are. I've even found a programme about quilting; I'm thinking of taking it up again.'

I can't remember the last time I heard her sounding so carefree and enthused. She has a new lease of life and one that is long overdue.

* * *

Bernadette's face stares back at us from the screen and while I did French for two years at school, she babbles away so fast that I can't keep up with her. She stops to allow Antero to interpret. I so wish I had his linguistic skills as he seems to be able to switch languages effortlessly.

'Bernadette says the quality is excellent, but she's concerned that the specially constructed undergarments, um, nets or hoops she calls them, are too flexible.'

I move a little closer to the screen.

'Can you ask if we can see the model walking towards us? Maybe Bernadette can then point out the problem.'

Antero turns back to talk to her and she listens, nodding her head, her hands constantly waving about in the air. There is a smile on her face, so I suspect she already has a fix in mind. She spends a minute or so talking to the young woman who is wearing the first test sample. It's the beach one with the sandpipers. I know I'm not seeing a close-up, but it looks even better than I'd hoped. I was dreading this moment in case the design just looked like we'd turned a pair of curtains into a tent. So, I'm delighted with what I'm seeing, despite a potential problem.

As Antero and I peer intently at the screen, the model glides towards us. Bernadette jumps forward, pointing to the hem of the dress which hovers an inch or two above the floor. She then begins to explain, lifting the edge of the skirt and tugging at the hooped structure beneath it.

'She's saying that it's an undergarment, I think. I'm not sure what exactly, but it hangs from two straps, one on each shoulder. There are three graduated, horizontal hoops sewn into it. One at chest height, one at the waist and the third in the calf area.'

He pauses as Bernadette tells us to wait a second and bids the model to do the walk again.

'Ah, got it! It's a petticoat. Look how the fabric doesn't hang straight to the floor. As she's walking towards us, between the waist and the hem it indents. Hmm... that doesn't work, it spoils the whole effect.'

It sounds like Bernadette is saying the exact same thing. She talks for a few minutes and Antero indicates that he understands.

'Bernadette is saying there are two solutions. One is much cheaper than the other.'

'I like cheap,' I reply. 'What are they?'

He gives me a brief smile and turns back to the screen to reply on my behalf. Bernadette hurries off and returns with one of the petticoats, holding it up and indicating that a fourth loop needs to be added.

'She says that the only other alternative is to use an even heavier weight fabric, which might restrict the models and the range of movement they have when they are walking. And she's worried that it would be harder to steam out any creases. The idea is not to allow anything to detract from the way the design appears to flow.'

Poor Antero, this isn't the easiest of conversations for him to relay.

'Please thank Bernadette and tell her that I'm happy to go with the additional hoop. The fabrics have already been approved and if anything changes, we would be obliged to go through another round of sign-offs. Tell her I'm very appreciative and the result is even better than I'd anticipated.'

And with that it's job done.

* * *

'How did the weekend go with Ana?' I'm sprawled out on the sofa, my stomach full. Maria doesn't like to think of me eating alone, so supper with her family had been an invite I couldn't refuse. It's like having a restaurant on my doorstep.

I readjust the angle of my phone so that I'm in the centre of the screen.

'Great. She was very relaxed. We spent some time in the studio together and she enjoyed that. On Sunday, I let her invite five of her old school mates here for lunch. Poor Vitor and Gisela were kept busy, but they loved it. It was life-changing for all of us when Beatriz took Ana away.'

I can feel his sense of loss, but it hadn't dawned on me before that of course Vitor and Gisela would have missed the busyness, too. I'm sure Beatriz entertained more often than Reid seems to do and having a child around is a distraction for everyone.

'Oh, before I forget, I saw the first of the sample dresses today,' I throw in as a distraction.

'Okay. You can't leave it there. Tell me more.'

'Aside from one tiny, technical hitch which Bernadette is about to resolve, it was amazing. You have never seen anything like it, Reid, none of us have. Your artwork, the beauty of the shores of the river Tagus, floated like a mirage in front of our eyes.'

'You're happy, then?'

'I'm ecstatic. It's not fashion, it's art. The models will truly be living canvases.'

'Now you're making me a little worried, because there's an element of surprise in your voice. You're the one who conjured up the images and reassured me this would work. Don't tell me you had your doubts about being able to pull it off?'

He's teasing, his throaty laugh shaming me, but I can hear the delight in his voice. Not just for himself, but for me.

'No doubts at all if I was successful in communicating the vision I had inside my head. But even if I succeeded, it was still a big ask of both you and Bernadette.'

Reid gives me a knowing smile. 'Ah, now I understand. At the very beginning, you didn't have my full attention and it must have added to your stress levels. I'm sorry for neglecting you, Seren. It was thoughtless of me.'

I flash him a forgiving smile, loving his playful mood. 'You were busy, I understood that. It all hinged on Bernadette taking your stunning artwork and translating it into another medium. That's no mean feat, because the gowns have to work as garments, as well as art, or it could have been a total disaster. The way she has pulled together various elements from one of your paintings to create such a unique piece is inspired and I can't wait to see the full collection.'

'You are amazing, do you know that?' Reid's voice softens and a fuzzy warm feeling begins to radiate out from my stomach. 'You breeze into my life making all sorts of things happen that remind me how jaded I'd become. Life had lost its sparkle and now you're turning everything upside down.'

'Is that a good or a bad thing?' I ask tentatively.

'A good thing. I remembered what you said to me about talking to Ana to find a solution, a way around this mess we've gotten ourselves into. So, I did just that. She said that she missed her friends here and that's why I arranged the ad-hoc little get-together for her. But she also said she was tired of seeing her parents fighting and not knowing what to do about it.'

The sadness is tangible.

'What did you say to her?'

'I said that it wasn't her responsibility and that if we made her feel she was in the middle of this, then we were failing her.'

There's a pause and my heart is now thudding against my chest wall, as if it's trying to break out. Will he give in to Beatriz and try to rebuild their broken relationship for the sake of Ana? If that's the case, then I hope he truly believes that there is still a chance for him and Beatriz to make it work for them as a family.

The seconds pass and each one feels like an eternity.

'I've asked Tomas to arrange a meeting with Beatriz and make it clear that it's to discuss business.'

Now I'm confused. Is he negotiating with Beatriz in order to pacify her, so that she'll be more receptive about Ana's needs?

'But how that does help the situation?'

'It's not straightforward, because a divorce isn't just about signing a legal document but also managing the financial burdens that come with it. Beatriz is never going to let go until my obligations are fully discharged because, as it stands, potentially, every decision I make impacts upon my ability to support them. It's time to renegotiate and then go back to the solicitors. I should have seen this coming and you've made me realise problems don't just disappear, it's a case of managing expectations and searching for a solution to appease all parties. I'll continue my dialogue with Ana and have a frank talk with Beatriz.'

It all sounds very practical, but we both know it won't be easy. As far as I can tell, nothing about Reid's circumstances have changed, only his desire to end the animosity.

'Think twice before you do anything rash. I've chosen a simpler life going forward because that's what is going to make me happy, Reid. But please don't let anything I say or do influence your decisions, because that wasn't my intention. I am glad you are listening to what Ana has to say, though, because I know what it feels like to...' I struggle to find the right way to phrase what I'm feeling.

'... Be distanced from your father?'

'It's not that. I saw my parents' relationship change, and unravel, as the years went by. With hindsight, I did feel a level of responsibility. I thought that if I went to work for my father, as he expected, then it would strengthen us as a family. But it was already too late because the love had gone. Did Ana run away because she wanted to bring you and Beatriz together in the hope that there was something left between you?'

Reid never talked about what happened when he left me and returned to Sintra the morning after the party, only that Beatriz returned home to Porto. I can't even imagine what was said between them, but it was obvious to me at the party that she had a master plan.

'I fear it was more a case of Beatriz taking out her frustrations on Ana. They both have a fiery temperament,' he acknowledges.

'I don't want to add to your problems, Reid, please believe me.'

'Listen, none of this is down to you. You're just the person who made me realise I need to take back control of my life. That's my decision. And this weekend I'm going to show you how grateful I am. You've been working far too hard and I'm going to spirit you away to somewhere quiet and secluded.'

The anxious thoughts whirling around inside my head get swept away as his words calm me. A whole weekend together.

'What relaxes you? Are you a sunbather, a swimmer? Long walks?' He's trying to lighten my mood.

'Walking, reading and eating. I'm a simple woman to please,' I reply softly. I appreciate that even though he has so much to occupy his mind, this weekend is important to him.

'Well, I have a surprise for you, too, which I hope you are going to love. Will I be seeing you at all this week?' His tone lifts, but we both know it's unlikely.

'It's too hectic at work to find a reason to meet up that couldn't be handled online. We're all staying late. One of the other directors is assisting Filipe now, after his discussions with Tomas. I'm not involved in that, as I'm progressing the toiletries line.'

'Toiletries?' Reid sounds slightly amused and mystified.

'Yes. I assumed Tomas had told you about that.'

'He probably tried, but my mind was elsewhere. Remind me where the idea came from, it might jog my memory.'

'It's a contact of Filipe's. He emailed Filipe after the party. His company produce a wide range of organic products, but we're focusing on hand soap, shower gel and bubble bath. They're making a presentation to the board on Friday to show samples of the packaging. It's going to be available in three designs if you agree, to match in with Bernadette's range. If the board like what they see, hopefully I'll be able to arrange a meeting with Tomas and you to get your feedback sometime next week.'

'Tomas is insisting he take the pressure off me while he's back for a while, and I do need that, but I honestly can't remember anything about it.'

'He's on top of it and so is Filipe, so you can relax.'

Reid merely shrugs his shoulders, but he doesn't look bothered about it. 'When I'm working in my studio, it's easy to switch off. Do you mind if I do a little sketching at the weekend, while you're reading?' he asks.

'I'd love that; it's a chance to see you at work.'

'I warn you, my cooking skills are sadly lacking.'

'Mine aren't much better,' I laugh. 'I'm sure that between us we won't go hungry.'

Neither of us wants to end the call and I can tell when we say good-night, there is that urge to be reckless hovering on our lips. We are a twenty-minute drive apart, but it isn't about the distance, it's about the delicacy of our respective situations.

The call leaves me feeling sad on the one hand and elated on the other. Hearing the excitement in his voice and knowing how much effort he's putting into planning our weekend away is beyond touching. And it's thrilling. My head is sounding warning bells and yet I've never felt so happy. Now I finally understand the meaning of the words 'love hurts' because it does. Nothing about our relationship is normal.

Reid's life has shades of my past that are so uncomfortable, it grates on me. I can't ask him to give his family and career up, no more than he could ask me to let go of my dream of a simpler, more relaxed lifestyle. Is there a middle ground? Am I really prepared to settle, make no demands and end up alone and bitter if Beatriz reaches out one day to reclaim him again? Or worse, he begins to understand what I'm doing now is simply a means to an end and the life I see stretching into the future is of no interest to him. Honesty is the only way forward and it's time I made Reid aware of my plans.

PART III

APRIL

14

A GLIMPSE OF PARADISE

It's been agony counting down the days, and, today, the hours, until I could leave work. If ever I had that 'thank goodness it's Friday' moment, that was it, multiplied by a hundred, and Carolina could see I was excited about the weekend ahead.

The smile hasn't left Reid's face since he picked me up fifteen minutes ago, but his attention is firmly on the road ahead.

'Are you going to tell me where we're going?' I ask.

'No. It's a part of my surprise. Be patient, it's a thirty-five-minute drive if the traffic heading away from Lisbon at this time of the evening isn't too heavy. But first I'll lay out the rules.'

I turn my head to stare at his side profile. 'Rules?' I reply, sounding mortified. 'Surprises don't come with rules.'

'Mine do. Rule number one is that we don't discuss work.'

I'll give him that one. 'Agreed.'

'Rule number two is that our first stop on the way is a supermarket and we go food shopping together.'

That makes me laugh. 'Okay... we need to eat, that's only fair. Let's hope that between us we can rustle up a few meals that will at least be edible. How long is this list?'

What I don't tell him is that Maria has been giving me lessons and I now have two traditional, Portuguese dishes committed to memory. I wanted to let Reid know that I appreciate this weekend, a little respite for us both during a frenetic period of our lives.

'Two more. Rule number three is that at some point when you are reading, you let me sketch you.'

'Really? Okay, but I'm not sure how good I will be at sitting still. Last one, then, and that's it.'

'There's an envelope in the glove compartment. I want you to open it and when I explain, I want you to say *thank you, Reid* and accept it with good grace.'

I continue staring at him, noticing his thickening beard – it seems he doesn't shave when he's in his studio. And his hair could do with a trim. But I can see he has switched off from all his worries and he's happy to live in the moment, with me.

'Go on,' he bids me.

I reach forward and, sure enough, there's a padded envelope with my name written on the front. Holding it in my hands, I can't imagine what's inside. It's surprisingly bulky.

'Open it, then.'

I tip it out onto my lap and two sets of keys fall out. Left inside is a little bundle of paperwork which I slide out, but it's all in Portuguese.

'Keys? Is this some sort of treasure hunt?'

I watch as Reid's tongue moistens his lips, he's so happy he can't stop beaming and I can see that he's dying to turn his head to look at me.

'The set of keys with a fob is a birthday present.'

'But... you don't know when my birthday is, Reid,' I reply, haltingly, because it's clear that he does.

'Why do you think I arranged this weekend? I have contacts everywhere.' He begins to laugh as I look at him, amazed. 'It's on Monday, my informant tells me. Unfortunately, it would have meant contacting Filipe to arrange for you to have a couple of days off and I knew that wasn't the right thing to do. So, I hatched a plan. It's a car and it'll be delivered in about a week's time. Someone will be in touch to sort out the insurance for you. I'm assuming you have a driving licence as you were talking about hiring a car at one point.'

'Yes, of course I have a UK licence, but I can't accept a car as a present, Reid. A box of chocolates, a dinner out... but not a car.' This isn't right.

'You know how hard I work, Seren, you are no stranger to hard work yourself. If I can't give someone a present because I want to, then what's the point of earning money? I want to do this, and I will be offended if you refuse it.'

He's serious.

'Reid, I don't need something expensive to impress me.'

'Ah, now I've made you cross. That wasn't my intention at all. You make me happy, Seren. Whatever happens from here on in, I have no expectations or demands because that's not my right. But it makes me happy to do something for you and, believe me, it wasn't easy finding out when your birthday was, because I had to do it discreetly. Allow me a moment of joy, please. You know what they say about gifts, the pleasure is in the giving. The car is yours and I hope you like it. I'm confident you will. For me, planning all this has been more exciting than Christmas.'

His delight is genuine, but I'm not sure how I feel about it. I don't want to appear ungrateful. No one, even my father, has ever done anything like this for me before. However, I can't help but wish that Reid hadn't.

'Please indulge me and I'll explain why. When I was eight years old, I often stayed with my grandparents down in Devon, for the weekend. Their neighbour, George, was a great old guy who spent most of his time tending his garden. He'd hear me kicking a football against the side wall of the house and he'd shout over the hedge, "Ready to pick a few veggies, little 'un?" and I'd make my way down to the lane at the back. There was a communal path and I'd walk the few paces as he unlocked his rusty old gate.

'It was like wandering around a market garden. Row after row of neatly planted onions, lettuces, carrots, potatoes, and canes bearing runner beans and peas. He'd head off to find me a box and we'd wander around picking a bit of this and a bit of that, chatting as we went.

'You see, George didn't have any close family, no one knew why, but I was happy to spend time with him. He was very patient and a kind old guy. In fact, it was always one of the highlights of my trips. As an adult, I looked back fondly on those times, realising that it delighted George to share the results of his labour and teach me a thing or two about horticulture. He said nothing you bought in a supermarket could compare to something you grew in your garden. And he was right. But I also enjoyed listening to him explain what each plant needed to grow strong and healthy, and how to keep the slugs at bay by sinking yoghurt pots full of beer into the soil. Yes, beer. He once told me: "Always give without remembering and receive without forgetting, and you won't go wrong in life" which didn't really mean anything to me back then. But it does now. I wanted to make your birthday special, because you're special, and you're far away from the people who have known you all your life. That can't be easy.'

How can I be cross with him?

'What means more to me is the thought you put into this. My father would give very generous presents every birthday and Christmas, but it wasn't until I went to work for him that I found out his secretary bought them. Not just for me, but for Mum, too. It was diarised and each year she'd take a couple of hours to go shopping on his behalf. I always thought it was strange he bought such appropriate gifts, things I'd certainly have chosen myself. But she had a daughter of about the same age and it must have been easy for her. A nice little break from the office, too.'

'Oh, Seren, I'm sorry to hear that, it's sad.'

'The one thing he knew how to do was to write a cheque. No thought went into it for him, it was just like any entry in his diary, an obligation that required an action.'

'I didn't mean to hit a raw nerve. Forgive me.'

'It's fine, you have nothing to apologise for, Reid. You weren't to know and it's my hang-up. A car is way too generous, though.'

He steals another quick glance at me. 'Can you find it in your heart to forgive my exuberance and accept the gift in the spirit in which it's given? I had this picture in my head of you driving along the road, the top down, sunglasses on and your hair floating on the breeze. The thought made me smile. It's in pepper white, but that's the only thing I'm going to tell you about it.'

We burst out laughing.

'Oh Reid, you are impossible to resist. I feel ungrateful saying this and I don't mean to be, really, but it has to be a one-off.'

'I've never known a woman get upset over a present before. Next time I'll make sure I get it right. I'll take you shopping, that way I won't get myself into trouble.'

'Expensive presents aren't my thing, that's all.'

He can feel my discomfort. 'Maybe you are placing a value on money that it doesn't have, did you ever think of it in that way? Money can never buy love, can it? And I'm not the sort of man who throws money at people. If I give you something it's because I want to and, personally, I can't see anything wrong with that, but I will respect your views in future.'

He's probably right, but for me expensive gifts are a trigger. My father thought money was the solution to every situation and I ended up despising him for it, because what Mum and I wanted was his time.

'The other set of keys are to the place we're spending the weekend. I've rented it for the entire summer and it's yours to use whenever you want. Not just when you're with me, but if you decide to take a break from work or use it when your friends fly over from the UK. It will sleep six people in total.'

I'm speechless. 'That's really thoughtful, but, I mean, well—'

'Please don't overthink this, Seren. I want you to be able to get away. I appreciate everything you've done for me, personally. I know you aren't comfortable at the Casa da Floresta. And I really don't want to upset your neighbour, so that rules out late-night visits and early-morning departures.'

I can feel the heat rising up from deep within. A little place we can escape to, together.

'Now, are you ready for an entirely different kind of shopping experience?' Reid adds, putting on a silly voice as if he's doing a commercial and I groan at him as we turn off the main road and pull into a supermarket car park. Drawing to a halt, he unhooks his seat belt and does a half-turn to sit looking at me. 'Just because my life is the way it is right now, doesn't mean it will always be like this, Seren. I can change, but nothing happens overnight, it's a process. Just hang onto that thought.' And then he grins at me, before easing out of his seat to walk around and open the passenger door. 'Right,' he says as he offers his hand to help me out. 'My one impressive signature dish is fish stew. What's yours?'

'Duck, *arroz de pato* and Maria's version is amazing.' I search around in my bag and produce a little list of items, waving it at Reid. 'I came prepared and I also make a passable *pastéis de bacalhau*.'

He pulls me close, leaning in to place a swift kiss on my cheek and lingering for a second as if he can't believe we are here together.

'For the first time in years, I feel able to switch off and I couldn't be happier,' he whispers softly into my ear. 'It's all because of you, Seren.'

* * *

'I need you to close your eyes now and don't open them until I say you can.'

'Seriously?'

'It's an order. What do you not understand about the word *surprise*? It's about time someone spoiled you, and before you give me one of your fixed stares, I simply want to make this a fun experience for us both. I'm excited and I want you to feel the same way. Humour me and relax.'

I do as Reid asks and I wonder why I find this all so difficult to cope with; is it surrendering myself to someone else's control that I find hard, because I've spent my entire adult life fighting that? Every man who has tried to step into my life, however briefly, has failed to keep my interest. I don't want a man whose ego means he's constantly trying to prove how superior he is and showing off doesn't impress me. Reid is the first man I've met who is making an effort to understand what makes me tick, because it matters to him. What's not to trust? He's done nothing wrong, it's just too much, too soon, and I can forgive that because his motives are genuine – can't I?

'You're not peeking, are you?' he chastises me, as my fingers begin to drift apart and I quickly draw them together as they linger over my eyes.

'Of course not!' I exclaim, offended. 'I love surprises, who doesn't?'

'That wasn't at all convincing. Sit still, I'll come and get you out of the car. I want your first glimpse of the view to be unobstructed. You're in safe hands, I won't let you fall, I promise.'

Seconds later, he's lifting me to my feet and then he wraps an arm around my waist, gently leading me forward. At first, there is loose gravel, then the soft, springy feel of turf beneath my feet. I can already hear the sea and the soft lapping of waves. We are walking up a gentle incline and I take a deep breath, filling my lungs with the pungent smells wafting around me. The sea air is invigorating, as the light breeze catches my hair and whips it back and forth against my hands.

'You can open them now,' Reid says, tightening his grip around my waist and turning me slightly to my left. Then he draws me even closer to him.

I stand, slowly scanning around to take in the panoramic view. Directly in front of me, as the grassy mound on which we are standing drops away, is a swathe of empty beach and beyond that the blue sea ripples gently, the brilliant sunshine turning it into a mirror of light. The breeze forces the water up onto the beach like arms reaching out and, as it ebbs, the sun's rays turn the tips into a myriad of sparkling little jewels. It's a tiny little cove, the beach part sand and part cobble. We stand in total silence for several minutes enjoying the beauty and tranquillity of the moment.

Reid eases his arm from around my waist and uses his hands to swivel my body to our right. A mere fifty or so metres away on the headland above the cliffs, is a cluster of buildings surrounded by tall, whitewashed walls. The look is geometric and from here the only thing I can see is what looks like white boxes, the side profile showing the angular shape at the front. They all look out over the sea and, cleverly, with all the windows front-facing, when you are inside it must give the impression of having no one and nothing around you.

'This is a beautiful view, Reid. Where are we?'

'Carcavelos. This neighbourhood is called Sassoeiros. There are eight villas here and they were all designed by the same architect.' He releases me, letting his hand stray down to catch mine. 'We'll head back to the car. You grab the bunch of keys and I'll carry the shopping. We can come back for our bags in a minute.'

He parked in front of a triple garage to the rear of the first property. Rescuing the padded envelope from the side pocket of the passenger door, I turn to follow him. As we approach the tall wooden gate, he hangs back, instructing me to press the fob against the electronic pad. It swings back with ease. The path follows the line of the building, which runs off at an angle. When we reach the end of it and I turn the corner, the path opens out into a fan-shaped area and for the first time I glimpse the front of the property.

'Oh, my goodness. What a clever design. This is not at all what I was expecting.'

Reid juggles the two large shopping bags, so he can stand a little closer to me as we gaze out to sea. The view is, as expected, unobstructed, but immediately in front of us there is an infinity pool, surrounded by a wooden deck. Either side of that, the lawned areas are a luscious, mani-cured green. Instinctively, I turn to walk along the dusky-pink swathe of terracotta tiles forming a wide patio that spans the entire width of the property.

We walk past a pair of wide, glass doors and this part of the building is a cube, set at a slight angle, and next to it another pair of similar doors are at a right angle to them. Both look out onto two of the boundary walls forming a courtyard to the side. One is covered in a leafy green climber, the other is a profusion of vibrant pink blossom, which tumbles down in a cascade of colour like a waterfall.

As we turn slightly to the right, we approach the main part of the building and a set of triple sliding glass doors. Glancing inside, I see that it's a spacious sitting room. Overhead, a huge angular box rises up, forming the first floor and an overhang, giving some welcome shade. Beyond that, the straight wall to our right continues on for another three metres and the second set of triple glass doors is the kitchen and dining room. This part of the house is single-storey again. An oversized solid oak table and chairs stands directly in front of the doors, over which there is an open metal structure made up of square posts. Glancing up, there are hooks for sails to give some shade.

Reid hangs back, watching me with interest. I walk a few paces towards the edge of the inviting pool and turn to capture the full effect.

The centrally placed, huge, angular box that sits on top of the extended ground-floor accommodation is imposing and impressive. The front slopes back quite sharply when you look at it from this angle and the concrete base rather cleverly forms the overhang to the patio below. Running the entire width of the box structure is a balcony. There is no handrail, merely simple, clear-glass panels that don't obstruct the view. The flat roof of the box juts out far enough to keep it nicely shaded from the sun. Beyond that are bifold glass doors to what I assume is the master bedroom.

'Do you approve of our little summer retreat?' Reid asks, his eyes not moving from my face.

'It's beyond perfect. Whoever designed this little complex had a vision. It's so private, that feeling that we are all alone here. This is unbelievable.'

I walk back to Reid, leaning in to kiss him on the lips and he groans as we linger for a few seconds.

'And it was the right thing to do?'

It would be unfair of me to misinterpret this as merely down to trying to make an impression. 'It was and it's going to be so easy to relax here, Reid. It's like another world, isn't it? The person who owns this place must surely feel this is the perfect holiday location.'

'He does, but he rarely stays here, it's merely an investment. My father was the architect and he was also project manager throughout the build. They sold off-plan to people looking for second, or third, homes. It's always peaceful here and I knew you'd love it. We'd better get this food in the fridge before it spoils, the front door is straight on, then take a right turn. It's the large grey door at the end of the covered walkway.'

I wasn't looking forward to my birthday, I mean hitting thirty was bad, but hitting thirty-one simply makes me realise how fast time flies. But now I'm going to be spending the whole weekend with Reid. Suddenly I don't care about anything else going on around me as I'm going to treasure every single moment that we're together.

15

SUN, SEA AND SECLUSION

After a perfect night, the air conditioning keeping us cool as we laid in each other's arms, it felt to me as if I'd stepped into an alternative reality. What if there is more than one plane to life, a bit like in the film *Sliding Doors*. Gwyneth Paltrow and John Hannah's characters could so easily have missed each other, and they did on screen. Then they get a chance to replay the same scene again and the second time around it's a different outcome. What if this is my different outcome?

'You've gone quiet. I didn't realise chopping up strawberries required so much concentration.' Reid glances at me across the kitchen island, as he continues to lay out a breakfast platter of cooked meats and cheeses.

'I want to make them bite-size. I'm a perfectionist,' I reply, shrugging my shoulders at him, nonchalantly, as he grins back at me.

'Don't give me that, I can almost hear your mind churning. Care to share a few of your thoughts with me?'

I scoop the pieces off the chopping board and into the dish and we load up the tray. Grabbing the plates and cutlery, I follow Reid out onto the tiled patio area. He has already erected the sails above the wooden table, even though the sun is still low in the sky, but they gently flap in the breeze and it's a calming sound.

'It wouldn't feel like real life, living here permanently, would it?' I remark as I sit down, organising our place settings while Reid pops back in through the open doors to grab the orange juice and glasses.

'It wouldn't?'

'This is the fantasy you see between the pages of a glossy magazine, but it's not a lifestyle I imagine for myself. A holiday of a lifetime, or a special anniversary, sure, and memories that would never be forgotten. But I've always found that going back to the same place, it's rarely as good the second time around.'

'Even going back to the same place with the same person?'

'Yes. It's a case of right time, right place, right ambience and, obviously, someone whose company you actually enjoy. But is it possible to recreate that perfect minute, hour, day – whichever – again and again and again?'

'You're asking the wrong person. Moments of pure happiness have been fleeting in my life, but I suspect that's my own fault. I want you to come back here as often as possible this summer. Preferably with me, of course, but I meant it when I said there are no strings attached.'

'The thought of a stunning place like this lying unused and unappreciated for long periods of time is a waste. Money might buy a wealthy person anything they want, but if they don't have the time to enjoy it then what's the point?'

'I agree. And if you want to bring your friends, that's fine as I'm hoping to spend some quality time with Ana at the house over the next couple of months.'

'Why don't you consider bringing her here?'

Reid's loading his plate, twisting a wafer-thin slice of cured ham around the serving fork. I watch as he expertly twizzles it into what appears to be a rose.

'That's clever.'

He leans forward, placing it on my plate, and I smile gratefully. 'I have many skills you have yet to discover,' he replies, enigmatically.

'So why don't you bring Ana here?'

He shrugs his shoulders as I pop a strawberry into my mouth and sit back to savour the sweetness of it.

'Because we aren't at that stage where we could sit for prolonged periods in silence, with ease. It's better to take her out for a meal or, like last weekend, entertain her at the house, where she has Vitor and Gisela to chat to, and then invite her friends along.'

'Recent events have helped to start up a proper dialogue, though, haven't they?'

'It's been nice to talk one-on-one, for sure. When Ana was young, she kept me going when my paintings weren't selling, and things were tough. Just a hug, or one of her special drawings where I always had one eye higher than the other, would make me smile and count my blessings. It's been reassuring to see that we still get moments when she's prepared to lower her guard. It made me realise I need to make that happen more often, because she's at that age where what happens next will set the pattern for the future.'

I know he's referring to Beatriz and the fact that if he isn't present then he has no voice, no way of influencing the way Ana is guided through those tough teen years.

'Ana must be bilingual, then, if she spent the first however many years of her life living in London? But when you are together, do you talk in English or Portuguese?'

I pop a slice of cheese into my mouth and see that Reid is watching my every move. I chew quickly.

'Sorry, I'm starving.'

'No, it's lovely to see you have an appetite. We converse in Portuguese whenever family are around, but English if it's just the two of us. Ana can speak French fluently, too. She finds languages easy and she has inherited that from her mother.'

I did notice that Beatriz's English was almost flawless. Having lived in London, and with Reid and Tomas spending so much time there, I wasn't at all surprised.

'Are you in Lisbon for the whole summer, now?' I enquire, just making idle chatter really.

'Yes. I've decided to sell the place in London. There's little point in having two studios. I'm here until the autumn, after which I'll have a few trips back and forth to Paris for the exhibition there. I've decided to give some serious thought to setting up the art gallery at Casa da Floresta. It might not be feasible, but it's time to explore the possibilities rather than just talk about it. And Tomas is keen to organise an artists' retreat, maybe as early as next spring, just to see what level of interest it attracts.'

Is Reid planning on spending more time in Lisbon because of me? I wonder. Like the scenes from a film, it plays out in my head, but it isn't me I see sitting with Reid in the courtyard of his country house. It's yet another alternative reality that feels alien to me.

'But that's all irrelevant for now. This weekend is about celebrating your birthday and getting away from it all. Do you want to read for a bit after breakfast and then maybe we can take a walk along the beach a little later? We could then come back and have a dip in the pool.'

'Sounds perfect.' And he's right. It's time to switch off my thoughts, in the same way that we switched off the mobile phones. A getaway means just that.

* * *

I can tell that Reid's sketching me, even though he's pretending that he isn't. But even as I try to focus on reading, I can't seem to stop my eyes from straying in his direction. Whenever I catch a glimpse of him out of the corner of my eye, he's looking directly at me. I wonder what he's thinking. I don't really do *glam*, unless it's work-related. And that's different, it comes with the job and I accept that.

When I moved to Portugal, I put several boxes of clothes in storage as there was too much to bring with me. I think longingly of the items I wish I'd found space for, but I'm happy enough with what I managed to pick up on a little spree one lunchtime this week. Sunbathing isn't my thing, so I'm lazing on a lounger in the shade of the overhang beneath the balcony. I found the cutest floppy straw hat and the little bikini I'm wearing is quite modest. I'm not a thong person and the matching wrap doubles as a short, strapless dress or an ankle-length skirt.

I put the e-reader down and slide my feet over the side of the lounger, thinking it's time I stretched my legs.

'Would you like a cold drink?' I call across to Reid.

'Please. A bottle of water would be very welcome, thank you.'

It's an excuse to take a peek at what he's doing really, but I don't want him to know that as I return with an icy cold bottle in each hand. Yet, as I draw closer, he shuffles the little pile of cartridge paper together and places it inside a stout-looking portfolio case.

'Are you bored of reading?' he asks, taking the bottle from me.

'No, not really, although I miss holding a real book in my hands. I mainly use the e-reader at night, but my holiday treat is usually a pile of paperbacks, so it feels like something is missing.'

'You are a curious creature of habit, Seren.'

'Did you just wink at me?'

'I did. By the end of this weekend, I'm going to know a whole lot more about you. Everything you do is an insight into who you are. Would it be wrong to say how gorgeous you look in that?' He's treading carefully around me, and he shouldn't feel that way after planning such a wonderful surprise.

'This little outfit I picked up at one of those market stalls. You don't think the hat is a bit too big?'

'It's very you. But then you'd make anything look good. The clothes don't make the person, it's what inside that counts.'

He stands, taking the water bottle out of my hand and places it on the table. Then he wraps his arms around me and the heat of his body filtering through the crispness of his pale blue cotton shirt sets my skin tingling.

'I'm not as shallow as you think I am,' he murmurs. 'I, too, can reject the things that don't mean anything to me, while embracing them when it's the right thing to do. I'm beginning to understand a little more about what makes you tick. Come on, let's head off to the beach.'

We lock up and he's happy to walk along hand in hand.

'You aren't concerned anyone you know will spot us?'

'People who live here value their privacy and they've paid a premium for it. Sadly, there are things that only money can buy, as you well know.'

As we make our way down to the small cove, past the layer of rocks and cobble, we stop to slip off our shoes.

'The cove here is private, for residents only,' Reid explains. 'There's no access to the main beach at Carcavelos, which runs for about a kilometre and half in that direction,' he points beyond the cliff edge to our right. 'It's a busy beach, but big enough to cope with the vast numbers of tourists and locals it attracts.'

'The water looks inviting,' I comment as we head towards the wet sand.

'The pool is better, trust me. It's clean here and suitable for swimming and surfing, but the temperature of the sea is always cold as it flows from the Atlantic Ocean. Today it's probably eighteen degrees, so it will be a real shock to the system when you first get in,' he warns.

As we draw to a halt to watch the screeching seagulls as they circle overhead, Reid turns to look at me. 'Tell me a little more about your childhood and your relationship with your father.'

That's the very least he deserves, and I try to explain why I'm so determined to stick to my master plan.

'A plan you made before our paths crossed,' he points out.

I nod in agreement. 'Yes.'

'You have this way of looking at things which makes everything sound so achievable, so easy and so perfect, Seren.' He sounds wistful.

'I made a pact with my best friend, Judi, on my thirtieth birthday. We were both moaning about life and it hit me that we could either continue on as we were, hoping things would improve, or we could start being proactive and take control. The goal I set myself is to have enough saved within the next five years to buy a modest little home and then live a simpler life. I'll get a part-time job, anything at all really, to keep the bills paid and then I'll spend my free time making sculptures. It's a lifestyle choice. We're constantly striving to meet the often impossible demands we place upon ourselves. Or worse, to please others who do that to us without any sense of guilt. There is an alternative – I plan to draw a line and step back.'

'What if you never sell a sculpture? Would it break your heart?'

'No,' I answer truthfully. 'In fact, I wonder if I will ever be able to part with anything I make, if it comes to that anyway. It hurt to pack up my collection in the UK and put them in storage. But at least I know they are there waiting, and I can claim them when I finally find my forever home.'

'And you're serious when you say that you'll turn your hand to anything? Your job is high profile and you're already attracting attention. You really can see yourself walking away from that level of success, when I'm sure that Filipe would do anything to keep you?'

'I know how it sounds, but yes. I woke up one day and began to see everything in a totally different light.'

'I didn't fully appreciate how important your plan is to you. And yet here we are, two people unexpectedly thrown together and wondering what's going to happen next, because I sure as hell didn't see this coming.'

We turn to face each other, the ebbing water quickly returning, making me squeal and jump back, as Reid catches my hand. He's right, it's freezing cold.

'Neither did I, but I'm not sorry our paths have crossed,' I reply.

'Promises mean nothing, Seren, I know that. You are taking a risk being with me, but my life is changing in ways I never anticipated. It's too soon to say how it will play out because it's like a tower of bricks and they have to be taken down in the right order. If they fall, there will be nothing left and lots of people will get hurt. But I'm trying and you've made me see that feeling trapped is simply an opportunity to turn things around. It's up to me to do something about my situation, though. In the meantime, let's grab whatever time we can together, but if your feelings change, I understand. I'm not a man who promises something he can't deliver and right now I'm a work in progress.'

I stand on tiptoe to kiss him softly on the mouth. When we pull away, he looks down at me and I can't read his face, the emotions are too raw.

'I want what's best for you, too, Reid. You deserve not only happiness but peace in your life. If there's a way we can carve out time for each other, then that's a bonus.'

'My plans may end up changing, but, sadly, there are elements of that which aren't entirely in my control. You make me happy and if destiny is kind, peace will come.' It's good to hear him sounding mellow as we begin our leisurely stroll along the full length of the cove. We stop for a while to investigate the little rock pools at the base of the cliffs and then he reaches out to grab my hand.

'Are you ready to head back?' It's obvious he's had enough and I suspect he's eager to do a little more drawing.

'Are you bored?' I level at him in an accusing tone of voice.

'No, I just can't stand wet sand on my feet.'

'Wet sand? What a wuss,' I throw at him as I run back towards the cobbles.

When he catches up, we're both laughing and as he hugs me, the embrace is full of so much more than simply passion. Reid thought the good times in his life were all in the past and that was beginning to destroy him. I hope this happy little interlude is opening his eyes to the possibilities.

'We've both jumped through hoops for other people, people who don't care about anyone but themselves. Let's move forward with honesty and see if fate is on our side, Reid.'

He leans his forehead against mine and his breath tickles my nose. 'You give me hope, Seren, not just for us but for everything. I don't want Ana to settle for anything other than what makes her heart leap out of her chest. The best way to ensure that is to set an example, isn't it?'

My eyes are full of tears and when I open my mouth to speak, all I hear is silence. In a perfect world, love would be enough and everything else would fall into place. But life isn't like that, is it? Or maybe it is when two people are totally in synch, and the truth is that our paths were only ever meant to cross, not to merge. That thought is truly heart-breaking and I'm tempted to ask the universe what's the point if there is no hope.

16

BIRTHDAY BLUES

'You look happy this morning. How was your weekend?'

Carolina and I exit the ferry terminal and increase our pace, knowing that this is going to be the start of a busy and crucial week. The sooner we get to our desks the sooner we can make a start.

'Good, thank you. Relaxing. How about you? Did you see Antero?'

She tosses her head to clear the strands of hair that the breeze whisks across her face, so she can look at me. I do the same and we exchange a quick smile as I pull at a stray hair that is sticking to my lipstick. Often the sea breeze is welcome, today it's simply annoying.

'We have two choices and I'm leaving the decision with him,' she replies, heaving a little sigh while trying to sound positive.

As we hurry away from the busy exodus of people heading off to work, we begin the walk along the wide, waterside promenade. It's impossible not to let my eyes drift to the left, mesmerised by the way the breeze whips up the surface of the river as I stare across at the opposite bank and Almalda.

'That's a step in the right direction, though, isn't it?' I don't like to ask her outright what she means, because even though we are good friends now, I figure she'll tell me if she wants to.

'Perhaps. One is a waiting game and the other could cause problems.'

'For whom?'

'Antero has the most to lose.'

'Ah. Because he isn't an employee, but a contractor.'

She nods her head, glancing at me nervously. 'Yes, but while his duties are extended, he is a representative of the gallery. I know it is not a problem for you, Seren, but the directors would view it differently.'

'And the two options?'

'We can wait until his temporary contract is over and Antero is, once again, a freelancer, called upon when required. Or he informs Senhor Ferreira, as directed by the terms of the company's code of practice. But Antero is worried that it would jeopardise any chance of being considered as a permanent employee in the future.'

'I'm sorry it's so complicated, Carolina. But you did get to spend some time alone together?'

'We did,' she smiles at me, unable to hide her happiness. 'And I have a message from Miguel. He said to remind you that he's a good tour guide. He isn't going to give up, Seren. Would it hurt to meet up with him? Miguel is good company, he always makes me laugh and you shouldn't spend every weekend hidden away in your workshop.'

Not telling her the truth is getting awkward, now.

'I have a friend I see occasionally,' I reply, trying my best to keep my tone low-key.

Her gaze now is one of surprise. 'You are dating? That's good. Why did you not say? Antero will break the news to Miguel, but he will be sad.'

'I'd rather it wasn't common knowledge, Carolina. Perhaps it's best to imply that I don't have time to see anyone as my full attention is on work. I, too, am in a difficult situation.'

Her eyes spring open wide as she stares at me, her jaw dropping a little. 'Oh, Seren. That is not easy. I understand.'

As we walk through the doors to the gallery and say good morning to the woman on the reception desk, I have no idea if Carolina can guess who I'm talking about. But judging from her reaction my stomach is starting to churn, because when she said 'I understand', the tone of her voice told me my problem is much bigger than hers.

We head off in opposite directions and as I walk my phone pings.

Good morning and happy birthday. I wish it could be the weekend all over again. Expect an email shortly about your present. I was wondering if you were free on Saturday and up for a little sightseeing. We could blend in with the tourists, what do you think?

I've just unsettled myself talking to Carolina and yet here I am, unable to resist temptation.

I think you are up to mischief and we need to be careful. But I'll wear flat shoes.

I add a smiley face and a thumbs-up, before popping the phone back into my bag. It's time to get Reid Henderson out of my head, as I have a video meeting with the hair and make-up people who will be turning our novice models into the real thing. As a fashion show is all new to me, it's important to get a feel for the size of the team we are going to require and how many trailers will need to be accommodated. Space is at a premium around the periphery of the site and this is the next hurdle to jump.

* * *

'Seren, thank you for making time for me at such short notice, but this is important. I'm sorry to interrupt your morning and I hope your meeting went well?' Filipe indicates for me to take the seat opposite him.

'Very well, indeed. I can now give Carolina the information she requires to complete the parking plans for the evening photo shoot. It will be tight, and the models will be required to walk a little further than we had hoped, but their enthusiasm is such that I don't think it will be a problem.'

'Good. Would you like a cup of coffee before we begin?'

My nerves begin to jangle. Unscheduled meetings are usually brief. 'I'm fine, really.'

'And anxious to get back to your desk. We will get straight into it, then. As you are aware, I have been in discussion with Tomas, Beatriz and Bernadette to see about formalising a longer-term partnership. Initially, the intention was merely to extend the floor area of the gift shop temporarily during our major summer exhibition. Selling small prints, postcards and items from current exhibitors was a token, something visitors expect. However, expanding the area to accommodate the marvellous collaboration featuring Reid's designs has opened-up an exciting opportunity. Everyone is keen to expand the range and the gallery, naturally, is more than happy to become a partner in this initiative.'

I can tell he is pleased with the way things are developing.

'It's a great business opportunity, Filipe, and I'm delighted for all parties involved.'

'And I'm sure you will be pleased to hear that Beatriz has offered to take over the work you've been doing to set up the toiletries range. It will be one thing less for you to concern yourself with and she already has links with the company.' He looks at me expectantly.

'Oh, um,' I pause, momentarily lost for words. 'Thank you.'

I'm stunned. It's not my business to question the decision, but a part of me can't help wondering if Reid and Tomas are aware of what's happening. I try my best to shake off the uneasy feeling I seem to get every time Beatriz's name is mentioned now. Perhaps I'm wrong and Filipe wouldn't rely solely on her direction. Anyway, it does lessen my workload and I'm not even sure Reid is that interested in merchandising, full-stop. But I think Tomas sees it as a great opportunity and, obviously, Beatriz and Filipe do, too.

'And Senhora Veloso will be stepping in on a full-time basis until everything is up and running at this end. It will mean some structural alterations and we intend for the work to be done at night, with minimum disruption. She will also handle the contract negotiations, as that is her background. The gallery will commit to a three-year deal to be the main outlet. If it is successful, then we will be considering options to sell online through the gallery's website, further strengthening our links.'

The opportunities are clear and it's no wonder he's excited about the project, though I can feel a *but* coming.

'However, Senhora Veloso will require some help. Your time is fully committed until the middle of June, after your return from holiday. Then you will be focusing on the setting up of the exhibitions planned for the autumn, which will also involve Carolina on the advertising side. However, we have been impressed by Antero. What do you consider to be his main strengths?'

'He is very IT literate, a problem-solver, too. But his organisational skills are exceptional. He currently has sole charge of everything to do with the setting up of the catwalk, which involves liaising with Rafael's assistant, the sound and lighting people. I handed him the task and he reports back once a week to update me on progress. That is tailing off now, so he's been helping Carolina by keeping the Gantt charts up to date to ensure nothing falls behind.'

'Impressive. Once the new and improved shop is set up, we will be looking to take someone on to control the ordering, on-site storage and stock movement. I would value your opinion as to whether you think Antero is capable of handling that.'

My moment of nervousness subsides as this is exactly what Antero was hoping for, the chance of gaining permanent employment for a securer future. 'I think he would do an excellent job and be an asset to the gallery. If it would help for Antero to be freed up for a part of the week to assist Senhora Veloso in the short-term, I'm sure we can accommodate that.'

'That is most generous of you, Seren. And thank you for your evaluation. However, I do have one small concern. I think it would be best if Antero and Carolina did not work so closely together. This proposed change would help to facilitate that, of course. If you could ensure that in future their duties are kept separate, it would resolve any potential issues going forward.'

'Issues?' My response is instinctive, but I can see he's uncomfortable, even a little embarrassed, about raising this with me.

'Beatriz asked me to ensure there is no conflict of interest internally as we take the new initiative forward. It is commercially sensitive, naturally, and she stressed how important it is that our employees understand that, as I know you are also aware.'

Filipe is avoiding all eye contact and that is not his style. Is this really about Antero and Carolina, or has Beatriz confided in him about how close Reid and I are becoming?

I swallow, awkwardly, trying my best to remain composed and, seemingly, unruffled. Now is the time to speak honestly out of respect for myself, as well as my team, as no one has done anything wrong. 'I can assure you that we all take our professional responsibilities very seriously indeed. If I had any concerns, whatsoever, I would have addressed the issue immediately. From this point forward, there really is no need for any overlap between Carolina and Antero, until the week of the fashion shoot. It would be unfair of me to give them the impression that they are not free to socialise outside of work, though.'

Filipe is clearly surprised by my forceful response, but quickly recovers his composure. 'Of course, we are not here to restrict anyone's freedom, and as long as it does not affect our professional standing, I am content. I will reassure Beatriz that she has no need for concern.'

As he looks directly at me for a few moments, what I see is a fleeting look of relief before he resumes talking.

'Senhora Veloso will be delighted, as she holds Antero in high regard and this is a great solution all round. She's very excited to take this on, and it's going to help her enormously to have an assistant who is familiar with the day-to-day workings of the gallery.'

As I go to leave, I know that wasn't an easy topic for Filipe to raise and it definitely wasn't easy for me to hear. But I'm not really sure where it leaves me, other than to be cautious about what I say to Reid about work, whenever we're together.

As I pass Antero's office, I can see he's alone and as I tap lightly on the door, he raises his head, jumping to his feet as I step inside.

'*Olá*, Seren. How can I help?'

'In strictest confidence, Senhor Ferreira is going to ask you to assist Senhora Veloso on a task she's going to be taking forward. She will need support and your name has been suggested. How do you feel about that?'

His shoulders immediately go back, and I can see by his body language that he's interested. 'How will it affect the work I'm doing now?'

'As long as you can continue in your role as interpreter for our meetings and are happy to take the lead for any operational and technical issues on the day of the fashion shoot, we'll manage. It will mean a split in our team with immediate effect. I'm going to suggest to Senhora Veloso that you continue to work two days a week for me, but the hours can be flexible, as and when required. Do you think that will work?'

'If you are happy, then I am happy. I appreciate that, Seren.'

'It could lead to a job offer, but it's not for me to discuss that with you. When you get the call, I want you to go in prepared, because this is a great opportunity, Antero. Senhora Veloso will require you to pull together a timetable and liaise with contractors who will be working on site outside of normal hours of business.'

He takes a moment, his eyes scanning his desk while he evaluates the orderly piles of paperwork. 'I don't foresee any problems with that.'

'Good. If you can prepare a formal handover of anything you have outstanding, you should be ready to make an immediate start when you get the call. You've more than earnt a chance to raise your profile even further, Antero.'

'Thank you, Seren. That means a lot to hear you say that.'

'Right, I'm off to get some fresh air and grab a sandwich. See you later and well done.'

Today I brought a little cool bag from home, the contents of which were not made by me, but by lovely Maria. She had no idea it's my birthday today, but this is such a treat and I'm grateful to her. Her version of *pastéis de bacalhau* is among the fluffiest and tastiest I have sampled. Small pieces of salt cod, potato, onion and garlic, with a few herbs thrown in, are as tasty cold as they are fresh from the fryer. I added a little tub of mayonnaise as a treat and a carton of mango Compal Clássico, my favourite Portuguese soft drink.

Heading outside, the sun has disappeared for a few moments behind fluffy white clouds that drift aimlessly across the sky. I saunter along to my favourite seating area on the promenade. One of the benches is empty and I settle myself down, as my stomach rumbles in eager anticipation. After the morning I've had, a little fresh air is most welcome.

Stretching out my legs, I pop the lids and dip one of the bullet-shaped cod fritters into the silky-smooth mayonnaise. It's a veritable taste explosion inside my mouth and, before I know it, they are all gone. It's time for some people-watching, a pursuit I find curiously relaxing. There is always a steady stream of tourists and at lunchtime, workers, eager to stretch their legs.

I never tire of staring out across the river to the opposite bank, my eyes becoming more familiar with the landmarks. Or simply to watch the ferries going back and forth between the terminals. And yachts heading out from their moorings at the marina further along the riverbank, their sails billowing. Today there are two large cruise liners on the river, but it's so vast a span that they look like mere toys slowly making their way from right to left.

'Seren! How are you?'

The sun has reappeared, and I squint as I look up.

'Miguel.' I can't hide my surprise as I sit upright, gathering together the items on the bench next to me.

'I hope I'm not disturbing you?'

'No, of course not. I've finished my lunch and it's almost time to head back to work. It's a lovely spot, one of my favourite places to sit and relax.'

He slides into the space, which is a little tight now as there's one man sitting about two feet away eating a sandwich and another young man the other side of him. Miguel half-turns in his seat, holding up a little box in front of me and smiling. 'I hear you are a fan. Can I tempt you?'

It's a box of *pastéis de nata* from the little shop in Belém.

'Don't be cross, I asked Antero what would impress you. I was thinking flowers, but this was his suggestion.' He looks at me, hopefully, then shrugs his shoulders as he flips open the end of the box.

I can see he means well, so I accept and hold out my hand as he tilts the cardboard opening towards me. 'Thank you, Miguel, that's kind of you.' And awkward.

'I'm glad I caught you. I wondered if you fancied going for a drink sometime. It would be fun.'

I don't spend every lunch break relaxing out here and the thought that fleetingly enters my mind is how often has Miguel wandered along here looking for me? I shrug it off, knowing he's a close friend of Antero's.

We sit for a few moments eating and laughing as flaky shards of pastry fall down onto our laps. It doesn't take long for the box to be empty and we both end up stuffing the remainder of the last partly eaten tarts into our mouths.

'Delicious, no?' he asks, beaming at me.

'Delicious,' I agree.

A few seconds elapse and he eases himself back, stretching his long legs out in front of him as he relaxes.

'It's just a drink,' he says, inclining his head to look at me.

'I'm sorry, Miguel. But it would be wrong of me not to be honest with you. My job is demanding and being new here I have a lot still to prove.'

He purses his lips. 'But you have a little spare time?'

'And a hobby I enjoy doing, which is my passion. There isn't room in my life for much else at the moment.'

His eyes search my face and I can see he's hurt.

'That's sad for me,' he replies.

'Bad timing, I'm afraid. I'd... um, better make a move. Are you meeting up with Antero?'

'No. Not today.'

'Well, enjoy the views. And thank you for the kind thought. Sorry it had to be a no.'

'Maybe another day the timing will be better,' he calls out as I walk off.

My legs can't carry me away fast enough. What else could I say? My first job when I arrive back at the office is to have a quick word with Antero. Miguel is a great guy and I don't want to hurt him, so maybe Antero will come to my aid by letting his friend know that he's wasting his time.

When my phone pings, it makes me jump and I glance down to see it's a text from Mum.

Happy birthday, Seren. Missing you. I'll ring this evening for a chat, my darling. There is some news, and your father has no idea about timing, but he's instructed a solicitor. I didn't want you hearing it from Judi. I'm not bothered, and I don't want you to worry, either. Wish I was there and hope you took time out for a special lunch. x

None of the cards, or packages that have arrived are from my father. I guess my name has been struck from his electronic diary. Out of sight, out of mind.

* * *

Shortly after I arrive home at the end of the day, my phone kicks into life.

'Happy birthday, my lovely friend. We should be getting ready to go out on the town to celebrate, sob. Still, only two months to go until Claire and I will be busy packing our bags and heading to the airport!' Judi's voice trills down the phone, the excitement raising her pitch and making me wince.

I ease the phone away from my ear.

'Thanks, I had a little celebration at the weekend, but today was all about work. Your trip will be here before you know it, though.'

I can't wait to welcome my visitors, but today I'm living in the shadow of a perfect weekend and feeling sorry for myself. Not because I chose not to tell anyone here that it was my birthday, but because I won't be seeing Reid again until Saturday.

'Sorry, that was a little tactless of me, wasn't it?' Judi continues. 'You won't be in holiday mode until after the fashion shoot and the party at the gallery is over. But then it's relaxation time. Claire and I were wondering whether you wanted us to do some research and come up with an itinerary, given that you're rushed off your feet. Transport is quite easy there, I gather?'

'It's not a problem, I'll have a car by then. When we head into Lisbon, we'll take the ferry, anyway, as it's quick and easy. Your hotel is this side of the river and only about a ten-minute walk from my place. Aside from that, I thought you might enjoy a couple of days at the beach.'

'Perfect! I thought you said you weren't going to buy a car as you didn't want to put a dent in that savings fund. I'm surprised you find time to go on trips. Your kestrel must be finished.'

'No, he's coming along though. I do a bit of travelling connected with work to a location just outside of Lisbon. Besides, once things calm down, I'll enjoy exploring the wider area.'

'What are you getting?'

This is embarrassing. She'll think I've lost my mind if I tell her I'm getting a brand-new car. When the email from the dealership came through shortly after Reid's text this morning, I couldn't believe it. He's arranged everything and the car will be delivered on Friday.

'A Mini convertible.'

'You bought a convertible? You hate getting your hair blown about. That salesman saw you coming. A deal you couldn't refuse, was it?' She laughs, then immediately continues, 'What colour is it? Not some outlandish, car showroom, spotlight colour?'

'No. It's pepper white.' To me, a car is simply a means of transport and who cares what the colour is, or the model? It just has to be easy to drive but, Judi is right, I doubt I'll ever put the top down. Reid wasn't to know that, of course, and he meant well.

'Aren't they a bit small, though. Will the three of us fit, given we'll all have luggage?'

'I'm sure we'll manage,' I reply, never having sat in one and with no idea what the current models are like.

She's chuckling away. 'You'll be shopping for a headscarf then, like Grace Kelly. The beach sounds great. Oh, Seren, I really need this break. I bet you will, too, by the time we get there. We'll go shares on the cost of the place at the beach, of course.'

'A friend is lending it to us for a few days,' I reply, awkwardly.

'Goodness, some friend you have there.'

'It was an offer I couldn't refuse. How is life back at home?' I ask, desperate to change the subject.

'Ticking over. Have you heard the latest from your mum?'

'She's working full-time for Fi, now and loving every minute of it. But I assume you're talking about the divorce?'

'Ah, I'm glad she warned you. How do you feel about it?' With Judi, our conversations can sometimes feel like a full-on inquisition. But I know it's just her bubbly nature.

'If she's not worried, then neither am I. If the marriage is over, then they both have to move on. Mum seems to have embraced that already.'

'Did your father remember your birthday?'

'No. There's been no contact.'

'That's sad. And you're not panicking about work, it's all coming together nicely?'

'I have a good team, and everyone is totally focused on fulfilling the part they have to play. Any panicking will probably centre around the live fashion shoot, so I'll apologise in advance as it will be a quick hello from me when you arrive. I will arrange for someone to collect you both, drop you off at the hotel and pick you up two hours later to drive you to the Cristo Rei monument.'

'Seriously, this is going to be awesome. Neither Claire, nor I, have been to a fashion show, or seen anything being filmed before. And we promise not to be a distraction, but we're so excited about it all. It's a step up from the last event you invited me to – the building and construction industry exhibition, if I remember correctly,' she giggles.

'I seem to remember you spending a fair bit of time chatting to that rather handsome guy trying to sell you a conservatory.'

'He was plying me with free snacks and coffee. I think he was equally as bored as I was. Are you still *sort of seeing* that client of yours?'

I've dodged Judi's questions lately, as too much has happened and it's not easy to explain.

'It's casual, that's all.'

'And as for the birthday celebrations, I presume you had a good time at the weekend?'

At last, a question I can answer with enthusiasm in my voice. 'It was monumental.'

I'm not about to enlighten her about my romantic weekend with Reid, of course, but she's still not wrong in her assumptions. And I'm sure the party atmosphere of the fashion shoot won't disappoint.

17

ABSENCE MAKES THE HEART GROW FONDER

Every day I travel to and from work by ferry I still feel like pinching myself to check my new life is real. It took a while to get everything set up, but I now have a *cartão de residencia*, which allows me to live and work here for the next five years. The fact that I have a local bank account and pay my taxes here means it really is time to think about selling my house in the UK. Stupidly, I hadn't realised that I'd have to pay tax on anything I earn back there too, as rent is income. Moving abroad isn't easy and it's the things you don't know which cause problems, not the masses of information that is easily gleaned.

And now I also have a shiny new car parked up on the hill a few metres away from the house. Maria was a little surprised when it was delivered, given that transport in Lisbon is such an easy alternative. But I told her that I intend to take a few road trips. When exactly I'll have time for that, I have no idea, but I have taken it out for a couple of test runs and it drives like a dream. I still feel uncomfortable about accepting a gift like this from Reid. It feels wrong, even though it was a kind gesture.

In the autumn, I will begin taking classes to learn Portuguese and I wish there had been time to set that up from day one. I know there are protocols, but so much is lost in translation, things that go over my head.

Reid is more aware of those than I am, but after that chat with Filipe, I'm so glad that we're being careful.

The tough part for me is that I can't confide in any one person. I would hate to upset Maria, or offend her in anyway, given her religious beliefs. She has a crucifix hung up in her dining room and, as the Roman Catholic Church does not recognise divorce, my involvement with Reid is best kept hidden. Carolina and Antero are my friends, but in this instance the less they know about my private life, the better. Having reorganised our little team, I was upfront about Filipe's concerns. I could see that they were both relieved that they would no longer be working side by side, which was another good thing to come out of the changes.

The other option is to share everything with Judi, or Mum, but they wouldn't understand that different rules apply here. And where would I start to explain the mess I find myself in? For now, I have no choice but to take it one day at a time and see what happens, because I don't want to distance myself from Reid.

Even though it's been warm and sunny so far this week, I've spent the entire time wishing the days away, consumed with the thought of being with Reid again. I'm also nervous, as we've had little contact and I have no idea whether Beatriz is causing him problems. But today the rain clouds appeared and, late on a Friday afternoon, all I want to do is to hurry home. It is a real pity I can't use the car, but parking is limited close to the gallery and, ironically, the ferry is much quicker than queuing in the rush hour traffic. It's the reason I didn't buy one in the first place, but once I can take some time off to go further afield, I'll be making the most of it.

Carolina had the day off to go and visit her parents for a long weekend and I miss her company on the journey back to Almada.

Tonight, I'll eat, shower and crawl into bed to read. If the sun comes out again tomorrow, then I'll take that as a sign that the gods are shining down on me and I have their approval. It's been another full-on week, but I can manage just as long as I have something to look forward to that lifts my spirits and fills my heart with love.

* * *

'It's Saturday, relax,' Reid chides me, grabbing my hand and pulling me towards him. We don't kiss, that would be too risky given the throng of people exiting the ferry terminal, but he firmly grasps my hand in his and I let him lead me forward. 'Most of the people who work in Lisbon will be heading in the opposite direction. It's foreign tourists and those who live further afield, who flock here at weekends. We'll be swallowed up amongst the general crowds, so there's nothing at all to worry about.'

Reid's words are reassuring, and I follow half a pace behind, as he's eager to get started.

Once the crowd thins out a little, he slows his pace.

'I'm glad to see you've worn sensible shoes. Are you content to wander? It's just over a kilometre before we have a rather steep climb ahead of us and you have a choice. We can queue for a packed tram, or we can walk. What do you think?'

I love the colourful, vintage trams that are so much a part of Lisbon, but time with Reid is special. 'Let's walk,' I reply, giving his hand a gentle squeeze.

He stops for a moment, spinning me around to face him and then leans down to kiss me gently on the lips. 'Sorry, I couldn't resist that, but I promise I'll behave now.'

I smile up at him, savouring the moment. It's nice to feel like a normal couple, doing normal things for a change, even if my eyes are constantly scanning around in case I spot a familiar face.

I watch an electric tuk-tuk as it passes by and these often brightly coloured vehicles are virtually silent. This one has a gold livery, with star bursts of purple and lavender-coloured seats. A family of four sit facing each other and the two young children wave as they go past. Reid and I wave back; it puts a smile on our faces.

'Where are we heading?' I ask.

'Alfama. It's a labyrinth of alleyways, stone steps and hidden gardens that makes it feel like a village. There's a little shop I know you'll appreciate. It's like comfort food for people who are touchy-feely. But we're stopping off somewhere else first. The old streets are tightly packed and it's easy to get lost, or miss a little gem, if you don't have your bearings.'

I look at him as if he's totally mad, shaking my head, but I can see he's excited to show me around. As we begin the uphill climb, a bright red tram slowly edges up the hill past us. It shakes and rattles as it wends its way up, almost as if it's moaning about the heavy load it's carrying.

The pavements are steep but not slippery. There are people walking in both directions and it's narrow in places. Both sides of the street are lined with little shops, which is handy as it's an excuse to take a break. Most carry the usual gifts: printed tote bags with scenes of Lisbon, fridge magnets, postcards, small replica azulejo tiles to use as coasters, soaps, little toys and jewellery.

One shop we linger in for a while sells canned fish in vintage tins. Tuna, sardines and even squid, in a variety of sauces. I love the decorative and colourful, ceramic sardines and chickens. The white china is painted with either gaily coloured stripes, the traditional Portuguese designs that remind me of blue Delft pottery, or random hand-painted flowers. Lisbon is full of colour, everywhere you look you turn a corner to find a painted mural in the most unexpected of places.

Aside from the trams, the streets here are virtually car-free, but with sections of the pavement being so narrow, we end up walking single file, weaving in and out of the constant throng of people as we begin to wilt in the heat. The cobbled pavements are uneven, but not so much that it's bothersome when wearing comfortable, flat shoes. It's only the steep slope that begins to take a toll on my calf muscles.

Up ahead, I spot a shady bench beneath a tree, set back in a little nook. I make a beeline for it, hoping to get there before anyone else claims it. An elderly man is sitting in the middle and, as I approach, Reid two paces behind me, the man very accommodatingly edges along to one end. I give him a smile, and he nods his head, waving one hand in the air in acknowledgment.

Lowering myself down with a slight groan of relief, Reid sits next to me and engages the man in conversation. From what I can make out, they're talking about the weather, as the old guy points his hand to the sky, and it's lovely to listen to them chattering away. I wish I could join in, but I know the day will come and I am already able to pick up on the odd phrase here and there.

It's a delight to sit and look around. Set on seven hills, the streets of

Lisbon wind their way up and up. There's always another corner to turn and another stretch to climb. Every single tram that has passed by so far is full and I'm glad we decided to walk. But the shade here is welcome and I pull a bottle of water from my bag.

The man bids us goodbye and Reid slides his arm around the back of the bench, resting a hand on my shoulder.

'It's a long time since I did this walk,' he reflects nostalgically.

'Where does it lead?'

'To one of my favourite viewpoints, Miradouro de Santa Luzia. I wanted to be the one to bring you up here.' There's such a warm, genuine tone to his voice that I can tell he's happy that we're together today.

'There's still so much to discover and I can't wait to see it all,' I remark.

'You will, if you're here to stay, that is. You didn't make it clear when you told me about your plan, where you wanted to put down those roots.'

I turn my head to look directly at him and I can see it is a question, but one he felt he couldn't ask until now.

'Shortly after I arrived here, I realised that Lisbon, or Portugal at least, is my forever home. This is where I'm meant to be. It's not easy to explain, Reid, but here I can simply be myself and it's a different version of me. One that is free to be whomsoever I choose.'

He catches my hand in his, staring down at it. 'Your words resonate with me more than you can appreciate, Seren. I only feel truly free when I'm in my studio and I shut the door on the world outside. The moment I reappear it starts all over again. People wanting something, the manipulation, the hoops I jump through to keep everything going, because what's the alternative?'

'You step off the path and you realise your world doesn't come crashing down. It's not easy, but you can take back control.'

Staring deep into my eyes, the smile he gives me is unconvinced. 'I'm at the stage where every step I take in a different direction feels like I'm slamming myself up against a brick wall. What's surprising is that I'm beginning to see people in a whole new light. Anyway, enough of this depressing talk, it's time to get going. Did you know that this quarter has Moorish influences and that it dates back to the Romans? But even they weren't the first settlers here.'

Reid pulls me to my feet, and I can see that he wants to kiss me, but there are too many people around, so we set off again. The pavement gets even narrower and for a while we walk in the road as it's so busy, but Reid doesn't let go of my hand. He's talking to me the whole time, my own personal tour guide, although it's hard to stop my thoughts from whirling around inside my head.

I think about the problems surrounding him and his life and heave a sigh. Even from the little he told me while we were together at the beach, I can't help but be worried for him. What if he isn't over Beatriz and they have that toxic but addictive sort of relationship where you can't live with someone, but you can't live without them either?

Selling the property in Sintra would allow Reid to cut all financial ties with Beatriz and I know he said that he would lose money, but at least he'd be free. I realise that it represents everything he's worked towards, but the consequence of not selling it is a huge price to pay in order to realise a dream. It could be years before he's able to buy his freedom. How sad, especially as Beatriz is now making her presence felt. My intuition is telling me that Reid knows what's happening, but whether he has an issue with that, I have absolutely no idea at all.

We are at two opposite ends of the spectrum when it comes to what we want out of life and yet I wouldn't change one single second of the precious time we spend together.

I'm so engrossed in my own thoughts that I'm surprised when we reach a flat, balustraded garden, with a vine-clad pergola, known as a loggia. It runs along the entire length of a terrace to our right. Straight ahead of us, in the far corner, a courtyard is formed by the walls of a church. We walk past a rectangular pond, to a pretty, circular feature with a stone bust set on a plinth in the centre of it. Around it, is an arrangement of small shrubs and the pathway is formed in two-tone, limestone cobbles in a stone colour and dark grey. The attention to detail in these beautifully formed paths is so typical of Lisbon. It must take hours to place the cobbles so tightly together that they form perfect curves as the dark grey runs around the edges like a border of ribbon.

Behind us, I glance back at two men with guitars, setting up ready to begin playing, but Reid pulls me forward, steering us towards the garden area set within the courtyard beyond. Huge swathes of bougainvillea have taken over the walls and the pop of colour is magnificent.

'It's enchanting,' I say, as Reid pulls my arm into him, giving it an affectionate squeeze.

'That's the church of Santa Luzia. The best bit is yet to come, but let's wander and we can take a few photos with the climbers behind us.'

We wait while a group of people stroll along the small path bordering the garden and then it's our turn to take the obligatory selfies. But this is a first for us. We laugh, as Reid extends his arm and we look up at the screen, my head resting up against his chest as we smile. We could be a real couple on holiday together, spending a romantic day enjoying the sights. A part of me wishes it could be as simple as that, but then we'd be different people, wouldn't we?

But it's fun to pretend and Reid is full of energy, determined to show me everything. He leads me over to look at two large panels on the church walls. Made out of azulejo tiles, they depict two very dramatic scenes.

'This is Lisbon's waterfront, Praça do Comércio, before it was flattened by the Great Earthquake. It's beautiful, isn't it?'

In the traditional blue and white colouring, the detail is amazing. Either side of the panel is an angel set against a curtain that has been drawn back, as if it is exposing the scene. It looks a little like a stage setting, with a beautifully curved scrollwork emblem at the top of the frame. The faces peer back at us and their almost cherub-like features are so finely done that the panel is museum quality. Reid connects with the skill of the artist and his eyes seek out every little detail, revelling in it.

'No matter how many times I look at this frieze, every single time I spot something I haven't noticed before. As a painting, it would be a real achievement, but as a picture painted on tiles, it's a masterpiece. The other one depicts the Christians attacking the Castelo de São Jorge.'

The scene is one of chaos, with knights brandishing their swords and shields, bodies lying at their feet. In the background, ships bearing more Christians approach as the battle continues. It's a perfect snapshot of history and a bloody one, at that.

We walk on past a group of men sitting around a small table playing cards, as the musicians begin playing. There's a vendor selling bottles of water from an ice cart and he's doing a brisk trade. There are dozens of people milling around, even though the sun is now almost directly overhead. We approach the long terrace, which is divided from the garden area by a waist-height wall which supports a long run of stone pillars. All I can see in the distance is the mesmerising topaz-blue sky and a thin sliver of water glinting on the horizon. The closer we get, the more the view begins to open up. As we stand beneath the loggia, around which various climbers have formed a natural canopy to help cast some shade, the view is unreal. I can feel Reid's eyes studying me and he's amused by my reaction.

'Not quite what you were expecting?'

'I've ventured into some of the winding streets in and around Belém and Almada, obviously, but up here you are right – it has a village-like feel to it.'

As I stand looking down over Alfama, the beautiful white buildings topped with the warm colour of the roof tiles and the silvery-blue shimmer of the sea as a backdrop, I'm staring at two luxurious cruise liners. Beyond them, like matchsticks floating on the water, two tankers going in opposite directions serve to give depth to the scene.

'It's breath-taking. Can we stay here for a while?'

'We can if you like. The day is all ours.'

Reid nods and we lean against the wall. The vista is captivating and there's simply too much to take in. It's yet another view of the river Tagus that is totally different from the one I'm used to looking out onto. One of the cruise ships is enormous. It must have ten or twelve decks at least. The length of it, I can't even begin to estimate, but between us and the ships is a church with a bell tower either side of it and it's a sizeable building, but the ship is probably five times its length.

'Oh, there are three ships anchored up.' I crane my neck to the left and see a smaller version of the big ship. In between them is a sleek-looking liner which is only half the size. But it's a long quay to house all three at the same time and it disappears out of view.

Reid is more intent on watching me than he is the picture in front of us.

'That haunting music in the background is one of the traditional Portuguese songs, although a more modern version of the *fado* style. It's about a fisherman who is lost at sea and every day his wife scans the horizon in the hope that he will return,' he explains.

'On a day like this the water looks so tranquil and harmless. I can't imagine what it must be like to be on the ocean when the sea is angry, and the waves are crashing all round.'

I could happily stand here gazing out for hours, but I'm hot and thirsty, my water long gone.

'Thank you for bringing me here, Reid. It is incredible and I feel I'm standing in the heart of old Lisbon. Shall we grab a cold drink before we head off?'

'Two waters coming up, I won't be a minute and then it's on to our next little treasure.'

Turning back around, I glance down once more at the scene and the tightly packed buildings on the slopes leading down to the dockside area. The buildings run off at different angles and taking up the whole side of one four-storey property is the painting of a woman with flowers in her hair, releasing a dove. It's an enchanting scene, despite the lack of uniformity, because all the colours are either white, pale yellow, or natural stone.

'Here you go,' Reid hands me the cold bottle and I hold it against my forehead for a few seconds. 'Come on, it's shadier where we're heading next. And after that we'll find a little place in one of the side streets to sit and enjoy a late lunch. It'll be quieter and we can rest our legs.'

Reid is right, it is all downhill now, and after crossing over the road, we disappear into a network of narrow alleyways. At every twist and turn, there are little openings, beyond which clusters of terraced buildings are arranged around delightful, cobbled squares. The sound of some children playing football close by echoes around us. These must be private dwellings as I catch glimpses of washing, hung from metal balconies.

The road steepens and Reid offers me his hand. 'Come on, it's not much further until we reach the steps. Just be careful here on the slope.'

My shoes are flat, but they don't have much grip, so I'm glad to cling onto him. The way his hand clasps mine is so comforting. A rush of sadness washes over me, momentarily taking my breath away. This connection between Reid and me isn't a conscious thing, it just happened. It's scary not being able to rein in my emotions when my head is telling me to put up my guard.

We take a left turn and all I can see is a long run of wide, cobbled steps that spiral down and disappear out of view as they bear to the right.

'This is lovely and quaint,' I remark, forcing myself to shake off the negative thoughts.

I let go of his hand and hold onto the handrail as we begin our descent. The high wall to our right is clearly a house and the lower wall to our left has an old wooden gate set into it, behind which is more than likely a garden. We are looking down onto the roof of a property, as the land slopes away. At the bottom of this alleyway is a three-storey block of apartments, the mustard yellow walls peeling a little and the weathered wooden sills making it no less attractive. Shabby chic here has a charm of its own and every windowsill and metal balcony is stuffed full of colourful flowerpots.

We keep on going, turning the corner to see yet more steps. This time they are deeper and narrower, leading down onto a flat area in front of a marvellous old building. It's painted a soft cream colour, with stonework around the windows and an impressive oak doorway painted in a faded white. Standing three storeys high, it's very grand. In the centre of the top floor is a pair of oversized French doors with a stone platform extending out and intricately worked, bow-fronted wrought ironwork forming a balconette. Either side of that, the windows add to the overall aesthetic as I gaze up at it.

Reid stands behind me, snaking his arms around my waist. 'There's a surprise at every turn, isn't there?'

'Beautiful, truly beautiful. It's charming, authentic and atmospheric. I love the way the buildings all cling to the side of a hill so gracefully. It's amazing. How many people have climbed these steps over the years? I wonder.'

'You really feel the history, don't you?'

'Yes. I can't imagine anyone not being overwhelmed by it.'

We stroll along and a few minutes later there is another steep corridor of steps and these are even older. It's much narrower here and the walls either side are broken only by single doorways every couple of metres. Stone-framed, the old wooden doors are all at least three metres high and colourful. One is a pale blue, with the inset panels painted a bright yellow; the next one is a tired, dusty-grey, and this time the inset panels are metal filigree.

There's a turn, and the steps become harder to negotiate, but I hear a voice, talking quite loudly as we round the corner. We stop and Reid catches my hand as we make our way down onto a series of wide, sloping cobbled terraces, separated by three deep steps the width of the alleyway. There are at least fifty people sitting here, listening to the speaker.

The man stands on the lower level and Reid indicates for us to sit on one of the narrow stone ledges abutting the flat area in front of us. It's like an outdoor theatre with an arena, as we look down over the crowd.

Reid whispers into my ear, 'He's a poet and a storyteller. Are you happy to sit here for five minutes to soak up the ambience?'

I nod, smiling at him gratefully.

The young guy talks way too fast for me to understand what's being said, but there's no general chatter as he has the full attention of his audience.

Gazing upwards, the reason the acoustics here are so good is that either side of this terraced meeting place the buildings rise high above us. From what I can see, it's all apartments, but only a couple of them have small, Juliet balconies, even though most have at least one set of double French doors. It makes me shudder, though, to see full-length glass doors with no restrictions as the drop is unnerving. But the light it must bring into those rooms must surely make a huge difference.

Looking on past the speaker, whose hands seem to be constantly painting a picture in the air as his voice rises and falls lyrically, a building juts out at an angle. Spanning the width of the alleyway, it forms a bridge at first-floor level, below which another set of narrow steps disappear into the tunnel it forms. I glance back up and catch sight of a woman standing at one of the partially opened windows, listening.

When the narrator finishes, he turns to pick up a book off a small pile lying next to a backpack at his feet and waves it in the air. Everyone begins clapping and Reid offers me a hand to pull me up, indicating that it's time to go.

We make our way carefully down through the assembly of people and into the tunnel beneath the building. As we negotiate the uneven steps, when we get to the bottom we turn left, and the path widens out again as the incline isn't as steep.

'And here we are,' Reid indicates to the doorway in front of us.

Set into the thick stone wall is a set of double brown doors and one of them is open. Either side of the doorway, hung on the walls, are cabinets full of old books. My eyes light up and Reid begins to laugh.

'I figured you'd enjoy a little trip here when you said you were missing your paperbacks. I mean, books all end up smelling the same, don't they?'

Smiling, I shake my head at him and, realising we are alone in this little alleyway, I stand on tiptoe to plant a grateful kiss on his cheek.

'This is so sweet of you. I love it!' Then I turn and head inside.

It's like a cave, bookcases extending from floor to ceiling and only a very narrow gangway, wide enough for one person to walk through at a time. Every shelf is crammed full and there are books jammed in horizontally here and there to use every single inch of space. I can't stop myself from trailing my fingers very lightly along one section of old books with cracked leather spines. The air is filled with that slightly musty, dusty smell and it's heavenly.

The aisles extend back into what must be a significantly sized building, of which only one room appears to have been turned into a bookshop. We seem to be the only people in here, but it's hard to tell as it's like a rabbit's warren of narrow walkways. I can't even see Reid any longer, as I've wandered off down an aisle and squeezed myself along a little space at the end. There is a single bookcase in front of me blocking the way and turning it into a dead end.

At eye level, I spot a shelf of books all with a pale, creamy-yellow binding. I slip out one which has *Monet* printed on the spine and nothing else. It's in beautiful condition and in my hands, it has the feel of a notebook, with a slightly silky, grained texture. It's no more than half-an inch thick and slightly larger than my hand if I hold it out flat. Close up, there's a hint of a pattern on the cover, but it's so subtle it almost looks like tiny hairs strewn across it and it makes you want to brush them off. I realise, on closer inspection, it's the outline of tiny rose heads. Flipping the hardback cover open, there's an inscription. *A notre chère fille Catherine. Noël 1953.*

It's in French and as I flick through the pages, to my delight, three-quarters of the book is taken up with prints of Monet's paintings. Some are in colour and the weight of the paper is sufficient to make them usable to frame if someone didn't mind destroying the book. As I flick through, I discover four smaller pages set within the binding which are of a similar quality to tracing paper. It's a copy of a handwritten letter from Monet himself, dated 23 November 1889, together with what looks like a shopping list of art materials. I'd need a dictionary to translate the letter, and the handwriting, while clear, is of a style that isn't easy to read. But what a find!

Instinctively, I hold it up to my nose and it smells a little dusty, but it's been stored in a dry place. I notice that the top edge of the pages are a pleasing rose colour, which is a nice touch, considering the book isn't that old.

'I see something has caught your eye,' Reid calls out, sneaking up behind me.

'Yes. Although it's in French.'

He waves an intriguing little softcover book in front of me. 'Well, I've found you something that will help you when you start those language classes.'

Reid hands it to me, looking pleased with himself.

The ageing cover is printed in a pale terracotta design, which was once probably a more vibrant colour.

'Fontes Medievais Da História de Portugal. Volume I,' I muse, as I carefully open the front cover.

The pages within are printed on what must be handmade paper, the edges so roughly cut that they are all irregular sizes. The bottom and side edges are relatively straight, but as I try to flick through, the tops of the pages seem to have been cut in batches with a rather blunt tool.

'It's never been read. Look at this, the cutting hasn't perforated it all the way through and it was printed four pages to one sheet,' I laugh, surprised.

'I thought that might amuse you. It's one of three thousand reprints according to the fly sheet. You'll be able to practice what you learn and find out all about medieval Portugal.'

Reid steps towards me and I hold out my arms, a book in each hand, so he can home in for a kiss. What a perfect day this has been and as our lips touch, so softly, the tenderness is exquisite.

'I did good, then? This time I haven't unwittingly put my foot it in?'

'You did good.'

It makes my heart leap to see how hard Reid is trying to figure me out. It's the little things that turn a moment into something special and I can see he gets that, now. The incredible views out over Alfama and the river, listening to the poet whose words flowed straight from his heart, and the delights of this little book cave. This means more to me than the shiny car parked up at home.

'It's time to head for the beach,' he whispers into my ear.

PART IV
JUNE

18

THE PRESSURE IS ON

We had the lull before the storm and now it's the frenzy of activity and preparation before the tornado hits, or in our case, the weekend we hope Lisbon will never forget. It's Tuesday; Carolina and Antero are holed-up in my office to run through everything in fine detail for the last time.

'Tomorrow we have our final video meeting with Reid, Rafael and Bernadette,' I confirm. 'On Thursday, Bernadette and her assistant head to Lisbon. Senhora Veloso will wine and dine them, after showing them around the gallery while we're up at the site. Carolina, can you just remind us of the arrangements.'

'Of course.' She taps away on her laptop, calling up the itinerary for Thursday. 'We will be meeting with the site manager and the attendants we've hired to control the parking facilities. Then we'll be briefing the security people, who will direct the ticket holders on the night and make sure that no one sneaks in.'

'Good. And, Antero, you'll be on site for the entire day to address any problems?'

'Yes, I'll hang around until closing time. The temporary signs will be put in place last thing. The trailers won't start arriving until the evening, but we don't want any of them misinterpreting the plans they've been sent and parking outside the main gates, as that would disturb the locals.'

'And, Carolina, can you do a quick run-through of the plan of action for Friday morning, please.'

'The site manager will give us access an hour before the gates open to the public. You are meeting with the models to walk the promenade and they can have a little practice. We can't mark up the runway until after the monument closes at six o'clock, but I'll make sure there are a couple of temporary markers in place as a guide. The trailers we're using as changing facilities, and for hair and make-up, will already be in situ, so you can then head straight over to show them where they need to go.'

'Perfect. How about the catering vehicles?'

'They will be allowed into a cordoned-off area of the on-site car park first thing. Antero will be marking up the pitches for the marquees on the large grassy area towards the rear of the site. The crew will be allowed to begin erecting them in situ at four o'clock.'

My head is so full that it feels like it might burst, but even though every single detail is charted and is on one of a dozen last-minute check-lists, I fear something will be overlooked. There's this constant, nagging little worry that won't go away.

'And is everything in place for the VIPs?'

'Yes. I believe that Tomas has arranged for one party to be picked up from Reid's house in Sintra and a second group from the gallery. The drivers have been given their instructions and we have allocated parking spaces at the rear entrance, as it's quieter and closer to the marquee. The people on the gate have a sheet of names and I've also printed out photos of our VIPs in case anyone wanders off.'

'Well done, Carolina. Senhor Ferreira will be pleased to think that his guests will be greeted properly. They will be escorted to the bar area, where you will be waiting for them?'

'All arranged,' she confirms.

'Good. Antero, will you require any additional help? I'm a little concerned that you can't be in several places at once if there's a problem with either the models, the lighting people, or Rafael. There's always a chance I might get pulled away at a moment's notice, but I will try to hover in the vicinity if at all possible.'

'Carolina's assistant, Inês, will escort the models back and forth to the trailers and will contact me via walkie-talkie if she needs help. But I agree, it would be wise to have someone spare we can call upon.'

'How about Vicente, our security guard here?'

Antero nods his head in agreement, 'Great idea. I'll get onto it.'

'And Yolanda Abreu's team?'

He gives me a thumbs-up. 'All in hand. I'm in touch with them and they will arrive at four o'clock to erect their booth. I did have a separate meeting with the site manager to discuss it, as obviously it will be more visible than the marquees. The booth will be at the end of the designated runway. His only concern is that they don't do their soundchecks until after the gates close and that they'll be mindful that the monument will still be open and that there are no trip hazards.'

'I'm sorry to have sprung that on you, Antero. My thanks for getting it sorted.' Without Antero's help, my workload would have been impossible. He is a gem, I just wish Miguel wouldn't keep popping up, as I don't want to offend either of them. Antero and I have spoken about it and he's embarrassed. Miguel turned up again at lunchtime yesterday, pretending he was passing by and he brought me a little box of *rissóis de camarão*, shrimp turnovers, this time. I didn't have the heart to tell Antero as he would have been mortified and it's hardly his fault his friend can't get the message.

Carolina's phone bleeps and she scans the screen, then looks up excitedly. 'The programmes have arrived,' she declares.

I love it when a plan comes together. The only thing making me nervous now, is that Reid flew to London three weeks ago and I've only had a few brief texts from him since he left. He was apologetic, without explaining what was happening, but Tomas went with him, so I know it was something business-related. Fingers crossed he'll be back today, or at the very latest tomorrow morning, in readiness for the final briefing in the afternoon.

* * *

On the uphill walk home, I decide it's ridiculous trying to second-guess what's going on and I make the call that's been on my mind all day.

'Leonor, I'm sorry to bother you, but the final video meeting is tomorrow and I wondered if Reid will be back in time to take part?'

After a period when she was being a bit cool with me and unhelpful, things between us seem to be back to normal. I don't feel I can quiz her too closely, but I'm hoping she'll at least be able to give me an update on when Reid is likely to return.

'I was about to ring you, Seren, my apologies. I have just put the phone down after speaking to Reid for the first time in five days. He is flying back via Paris, as one of the crates of paintings for the exhibition is being held by customs. It seems it has been damaged in transit. Reid is required to carry out an inspection, together with a representative from the insurance company, and confirm what, if anything, is missing or damaged. Tomas will be back in Lisbon tomorrow, so he will step in for him and report back.'

'Oh, my goodness! What a nightmare. I'm so sorry to hear that, Leonor.'

'It is bad news. Reid is most upset about it and asked me to update you.'

Well, it's not what I was hoping to hear, but it explains why I've heard nothing from him for a while.

'Are you coming along to the fashion shoot on Friday evening?' I ask, casually, thinking it was remiss of me not to ask before.

'The tickets were all sold when I went to the website and by the time I heard that the second batch had gone on sale, they were gone, too!'

'Oh, Leonor, I'm sorry. If you would like to come along with a friend, then I'll make a special arrangement for you.'

'Ah, that would be marvellous, thank you, Seren. I would really love that.'

'I don't know if you'll come across on the ferry, I know a lot of the ticket holders will, as the parking is limited. But if you head for the main gate, ask for me by name and the attendant will let me know when you arrive. *Tchau*, Leonor.' I have no idea whether she has a boyfriend or if she'll bring a friend as her plus-one, but I'm so glad I thought to ask. I'm surprised neither Tomas, nor Reid, thought about it.

The last stretch home is always the hardest and my legs are now complaining. I'm tired, hot and ready for a cold drink. When I turn into the courtyard, my stomach turns over. Maria is in conversation with Miguel, who has in his hands a bouquet of flowers.

'Ah, here she is!' Maria calls out and I try not to grimace at the sight of my unexpected visitor. 'I was just about to make your guest a cup of coffee,' she informs me.

'We're interrupting your dinner preparations, Maria. Please, do not stop on our account. I arrived back just in time.'

She smiles, shrugging her shoulders and I can see that she's not sure what to make of Miguel, or the flowers in his hands. But she wanders off and disappears back into her kitchen.

'Miguel,' I say, trying my best not to sound cross. 'How are you?'

'Good. But Antero is angry with me and I wanted to apologise. These are to say sorry. And to assure you that I meant no offence. I can't help that I like you.'

Agh! Just when I was about to get angry, he disarms me yet again, as he passes me a ridiculously large bouquet of hand-tied roses.

'Forgive me, I need a long cold drink and a sit-down,' I reply. I take the flowers from him and tuck them unceremoniously under my arm.

Inserting the key into the lock, I swing open the door. This conversation isn't going to be easy and it's best done out of sight of any curious onlookers.

'I'll show you through to the rear garden and then I will grab some drinks, okay?'

Miguel certainly isn't complaining, and instead, to my dismay, he looks delighted.

I place the flowers on the coffee table in the sitting room and walk him through the bedroom, sliding open the patio doors indicating for him to take a seat on the bench.

'I'll be five minutes,' I say, leaving him to it.

Heading back to the kitchen, I stuff the, admittedly gorgeous-smelling, roses into a glass vase and make up a jug of mango juice and carbonated water. Grabbing two glasses and placing everything on a tray, I compose myself and go out to join him. But he's nowhere to be seen and then I notice the shed door is open and I am unable to suppress a heavy sigh. I decide to sit and wait for him, while I pour myself a refreshingly cold drink. It hits the spot and I close my eyes, too tired to care about what my intruder is doing.

'Antero did not say you were so skilled!' Miguel's voice disturbs my few moments of peace and quiet. 'Why do you work in the gallery when you could be exhibiting?'

'Sit down, Miguel. We need to have a frank talk.' If I encourage him by making polite conversation, he'll probably take that as a positive sign. It's kinder to leave him in no doubt at all that he's wasting his time.

He shrugs his shoulders. 'I know, I crossed the line. But how often does one meet someone as interesting as you? If I give up without trying, then I will hate myself forever.'

I pour Miguel a glass of fruit juice and pass it to him as he sits down next to me.

'I'm seeing someone.'

'Oh. A serious someone?' he asks, frowning.

How do I answer that?

'It could be serious, but I can't commit to a long-term relationship right now. As I told you, work is my life, while I establish myself here in Lisbon. And if I'm not working, I'm creating. Please listen to what I'm saying, Miguel. Following me around isn't going to change anything between us. We can only be friends.'

'But if it isn't going to happen with this *serious* someone, then there is still a chance for me?'

'No, you're missing the point entirely.' I raise my eyes to the heavens and he can see that I'm beginning to lose my patience with him.

'Is that a firm *no*, or a no as in *not now*?'

'It's a firm no, I'm afraid.'

He leans back against the bench, the glass in his hands untouched. 'You break my heart, you know that? You likely break his heart, too. Am I banned from coming to the event on Friday evening? I have a ticket.'

'I can't ban you, but for me it's a work event, Miguel. I'm there in a professional capacity and I hope you will respect that.'

'I understand, Seren. And the flowers are a real apology, not simply a reason to grab your attention. But you can't blame me for trying one last time, can you?'

I guess I can't.

'I am flattered, Miguel. But there's no point in giving you false hope. Persistence isn't going to change my answer. I've come to Lisbon to realise a dream and I can't let anything get in the way of that.' It's not strictly true, I suppose, as Reid is a temptation which I'm failing to ignore, but could I let myself get dragged off course?

'Having seen your work, I can understand what you are saying. You should be creating art, not promoting it. But if there's ever anything I can help with, just as a friend, Antero has my number.'

Miguel didn't need to say that, and it's a kind gesture. He is a good guy, it's just a pity he's... what? At times, he feels too young for me, but then I realise that we're probably of a similar age. And then I remember that Reid once said that he's too old for me, but age is just a number when two people have a strong connection.

'That's most kind of you, Miguel.'

'I hope you find what you are looking for, Seren. Having lived in London, I know how different things are and how strange it can be at first. You know, until you get settled and get to know a few people outside of work. Maybe that's the reason why I find it easy talking to you. But you seem to feel at home here and I can see the change in you each time our paths cross. I would like to go back to London to visit sometime. I would have stayed, but a broken heart prevented that, and I had no choice but to accept that, without her, this is where I belong.'

'I'm sorry to hear that, Miguel. Time is a great healer and the right person will come along.'

Miguel finishes his drink and I see him to the door. I can't help feeling his disappointment is partly my fault for not making my situation crystal clear that day we first met at the Time Out market.

'Do you need a lift back?'

'No. I drove here. It's not easy to jump on the ferry carrying flowers,' he grins at me and I believe we can be simply friends.

As I watch him walk away, it occurs to me that it's true when they say home is where the heart is. I have no idea why my heart feels it belongs here, but it does.

The vibration from my phone on the kitchen worktop filters through and I rush back inside to grab it.

'Hi, Judi. How's the packing going?'

'Everything is on hangers until the last minute, you know me. I don't do creases. We do have a problem, though. Claire has had an ear infection which has now affected her sinuses and the doctor has advised her not to fly. She's already been off work with it for three days and now they've doubled her antibiotics.'

What a blow. I was so looking forward to the three of us having some time together as, after the party on Saturday, I'm off work for an entire week.

'Technically, the tickets we bought are non-refundable, but I'll find out if ill health is a get-out clause. The other option is to ask around and see if anyone else is free and up for a break at short notice, what do you think?'

'I'm just glad of the company and I'd hate to see Claire lose out financially. Aside from that, how are things?'

'Good.'

'You sound happy.'

'I'm steering clear of the family as there's another row brewing. My nan warned me, luckily, so I hope it blows over by the time I'm back in the UK. How about you? I bet it's crazy there.'

'I'm nervous but excited, too. Honestly, if anything goes wrong, it's down to bad luck, not bad planning. My team and I have all the details nailed, but my fingers are crossed.'

Reid will make it back in time, I know it. He wouldn't let me down, as he's the person everyone will want to talk to, while Rafael puts on a spectacular show.

'It's going to be so good to see you again and have a real heart-to-heart.'

I know what she means. So much has happened here and it must be the same at her end. She hasn't said much about Alex, but I know she was disappointed to have to walk away from her feelings for him.

'Guess we'll have a few late nights then. Please tell Claire I'm sorry to hear her news and I hope she gets well really soon.' I unsuccessfully stifle a yawn. 'Sorry, I'm dog-tired and I need to fall into bed.'

'Two days and, what, fourteen hours? But who's counting,' she chuckles down the phone line. 'Sleep well, lovely!'

After a quick shower, I slide between the cool cotton sheets, only to find that sleep doesn't come. My head is too busy processing information. When my phone pings, I try to ignore it, as it must be almost midnight and I need to get at least a couple of hours' sleep. But a second ping, shortly afterwards, has me reaching out. I sit bolt upright. Both messages are from Reid.

Are you awake?

Reid's second text has a ring of disappointment to it.

Guess not. Sleep well and I'll call you tomorrow, I promise.

I immediately press the phone icon and the seconds pass, agonisingly. When Reid picks up, he sounds slightly breathless.

'Why aren't you asleep?'

'Why are you checking? My mind won't shut off. You're not exercising, are you?'

He laughs. 'No. I've just run up an entire flight of stairs in about three seconds to grab my phone and it winded me.'

'There was no need to rush, I would have hung on a bit longer.'

'I know, but the thought of hearing your voice took over. I impressed myself, though, as I took the stairs three at a time. See what effect you have on me.'

I tut at him. 'You know I'd have answered the phone to you at any time of the day, or night.'

'I didn't want to be an unnecessary distraction, as I realise how hectic it must be at your end with the weekend fast approaching. It's been a crazy time with all sorts of unexpected things happening here. I'm sorry you had to chase Leonor to find out what was going on, but every time I was about to phone you, something else cropped up. I've only just arrived back at the house where I'm staying, hence my desperate text.'

'Leonor said you will be flying back via Paris.'

'Yes. There was an accident and it sounds as if a couple of the paintings we sent over in preparation for the exhibition in the autumn are badly damaged. I won't know for sure until the morning. I'll be flying back later in the afternoon, which is why Tomas flew straight back to Lisbon, to take my place. So, don't worry, he'll relay everything to me.'

'Don't concern yourself about it. We can catch up when you're back and rested.'

There's a rustling of papers and the sound of movement. Then a soft sigh, and I imagine Reid sinking down onto a sofa, or the bed.

'I signed the contract on the apartment in London, yesterday.'

'You've sold it already?'

'Yes, to friends. Mark and Philippa live in the same building and contacted me the moment they heard it was going up for sale. They've been looking for something bigger and intend to rent out their old apartment. That's why I flew over with Beatriz, as there was a lot to sort out.'

'Beatriz has been with you?' My heart sinks in my chest, but I'm also annoyed at myself for questioning him.

'Only for a week. I was intending to sell the flat fully furnished, but when I told Beatriz about my plans, she said there were some items she'd like to have shipped over to Lisbon. It was easier to let Philippa and Beatriz sort that out between them.'

I can't help feeling winded. Were there cosy little dinners, two couples talking over old times? Why does he continue to let Beatriz back in?

'I've also given up the lease on the studio. That was tough. Crating everything up ready to be shipped back to Lisbon with the furniture Beatriz wanted from the apartment marked a real ending.'

He sounds perturbed, rather than excited.

'You're having regrets?'

'No,' he states, emphatically. 'But I can't deny that there are a lot of good memories, of course. It was Ana's first home. But for the last few years it's been the only place I could return to, to get away from it all. You know, away from the rows and the pressure. The move had to be done at some point, although I kept putting it off. This trip might not have come at the best time, and the other complications I could cheerfully have done without, but it's a major turning point.'

It's taken a toll on him, though, I can hear it in his voice. He might have divorced himself from his links to London, but are the memories of their happy days together another reason to begin questioning his divorce from Beatriz?

'You sound exhausted. Get some sleep. Travel safe and you know where I am if you need me.'

My heart is hurting as I disconnect, too dejected to stay on the line any longer.

For all my bravado about being able to handle a casual relationship, I've backed myself into an impossible situation. I see now that a part of me is more fragile than I could have imagined. It was impossible from the start and there was only one way it could end. Someone was going to get hurt and it was always going to be me.

19

THE BIG DAY HAS ARRIVED

I'm awake before the alarm on my phone goes off and I reach out to check for any messages. There's one from Judi and it's an animation. Clover leaves fall like rain, cascading down onto a growing pile that explodes to reveal the words *good luck*. It makes me laugh. And there's one from Reid, asking me to text him as soon as I'm awake. It was sent over an hour ago, but I turned the volume of my phone off as it was the only way I was going to get any sleep.

Hope you slept well, Seren.

I tap in a quick response.

Morning, Reid. I managed a couple of hours, but I've been awake on and off since dawn.

Throwing on a pair of jeans and a top, it's time to head into the kitchen to make a coffee and sit outside to enjoy it.

What time will you be heading up to the site?

They're opening the gates an hour earlier for us, so about eight-fifteen. Why?

I'm parked up around the corner and I have the key you gave me to the back gate. Can I pop in for coffee if I'm really quiet?

My face instantly breaks out into a smile.

Of course. The kettle is on.

As I jump up and grab my mug, Maria opens her kitchen door and waves out to me.

'Do you have time for another coffee?' she asks, her voice hushed, but I shake my head sadly.

'There are things I need to do before I leave for the monument.'

'I understand. It's a big day for you.'

Hurrying inside in case Reid suddenly appears to see where I am reminds me that creeping around like this is no way to live your life. And when I sneak out through the patio doors and see him walking towards me, I put a finger to my lips. As soon as he steps inside, I shut the doors.

'My neighbour, Maria, is up. Let's go into the kitchen.'

His face lit up the moment he saw me and yet I feel guarded today. Whether it's the result of nerves making my stomach flutter because of the day ahead, or because there are some things I need to say to him – I don't know. But they are words I can't pull together right now.

As I make his drink, he comes up behind me and his hug is gentle. He rests his chin on the top of my head, and we stand for a few moments without moving. When I turn back around, I can see how much he's missed me.

'Come on, sit down. You look like you need this.'

He takes the mug, looking timorous. 'I know I shouldn't be disturbing you, but I couldn't help myself.'

'I'm glad you did,' I reply, making a monumental effort to sound light-hearted. 'I have a favour to ask.'

As we sit opposite each other, his eyes don't move from my face. 'Any-thing, anything at all.'

'Carolina's father bought one of your prints for her mother for their thirtieth wedding anniversary. She'd dearly love to be able to give them a signed copy of the official exhibition programme and I just happen to have one here.'

'If only all requests were that easy.'

'I know, I don't ask for much, do I?' I reply and his smile fades. I'm quoting him, of course, and he remembers.

'That's true and I wonder why.'

Say it, Seren. It's always going to be an awkward moment and there never will be a right time.

'Because – ultimately – what we each want out of life means that we aren't even on the same page, Reid. We're fooling ourselves, aren't we, by brushing aside the obvious.'

'I know it seems impossible right—'

I can't bear to see the look on his face, so I put up a hand to stop him.

'Please don't feel you need to explain, Reid, it's just the way it is. I'll... um... go and grab that programme.'

Feeling like the bottom is about to fall out of my world, I head into the sitting room to find the brochure and a pen. Facing the inevitable is tough and I didn't imagine it happening like this, but I tell myself that fate presented me with this moment for a reason. And who am I to question the wisdom of that?

'Here you go. Carolina has written their names on a piece of paper, it's inside the folder. I'm just popping out to my workshop to fetch something. I won't be a moment.'

When I return, the brochure is tucked away inside the folder, the pen placed on top of it and Reid is cradling his mug in both hands, pensively.

He jumps up to help me manoeuvre the bird of prey onto a chair. Hovering above his square metal base, the bird's beady eyes seem to stare back at me with a sense of melancholy. Our journey together ends here, today, and my emotions are raw.

'He's not heavy, just an armful,' I explain, my voice barely a whisper and I cough to clear my throat. 'The box is hollow and it will need cementing in as he's top-heavy.' Letting go isn't easy, but I need to pull myself together.

Reid stares at the kestrel, then reaches out to run his fingers over the intricately constructed feathers. 'It's beautiful.'

'The piece is called: 'Freedom in Flight'. I made it for you.'

Reid looks at me questioningly. 'Did I do something wrong?' he asks, his voice husky.

'It's not about right or wrong, Reid.'

The seconds pass as he stares at me, without moving a muscle, or even a blink of his eye.

'But what does that mean?'

'It's a present. I hoped you'd like it.'

'Of course I do,' he says, glancing down at it appreciatively. 'It's an outstanding piece and it must make you realise how talented you are. It touches my heart for you to give this to me, but why do I feel as if it's a parting gift?'

'How do I begin to explain what—'

A loud tap on the front door startles us both and, once again, I raise a finger to my lips.

'It's probably Maria,' I mouth. 'You'd better go. Please, please, don't make a noise.' I put up a hand, gesturing him to wait a moment. I hurry out to the tiny alcove to fetch an old blanket from the cupboard. 'Here,' I thrust it at Reid, 'Wrap him in this, please hurry.'

He looks at me, his expression one of confusion and urgency, as he can see that I'm panicking.

There's another slightly louder tap on the door. Lifting the statue and holding it tight against his body, Reid follows me back through to the bedroom. As I let him out through the patio doors, I can't meet his eyes.

'Coming,' I call out over my shoulder, as Reid strides across the garden.

I take a moment to pull myself together before retracing my steps back through the sitting room to open the door.

'I hope I did not disturb you, Seren, but I meant to give you this, it is for good luck – *boa sorte*. Is old, made by my grandfather. Carry it with you and everything will be fine.'

Taking the little package from Maria's outstretched hand, I give her a grateful smile. Did she hear us talking? I wonder. She might have assumed I was on the phone, but then the door is solid oak and the walls are thick, so it could simply be a case of bad timing. Guilt is a terrible thing and it can play tricks on you.

'Thank you, Maria, I will treasure it.'

'Is only small, but I felt... well, I may be a foolish old woman who should mind her own business, but I know you will forgive me.'

She turns and walks away without looking back, leaving me puzzled.

I take the gift into the bedroom, sitting down on the bed to open the package and inside is a little ceramic swallow in a black glaze, with a bright red beak. His wings are outstretched, and I'm touched by the gesture. I had no idea swallows represented good luck, although you see them everywhere in the gift shops here. I lay it down next to me and sit for a moment bent over, holding my face in my hands.

I'm feeling overwhelmed by life in general. It isn't just this weekend, Reid, my job, my parents' divorce... it's everything. I set off a chain reaction leaving my old life behind and whatever I do next will have just as much impact. I need to be mindful of that fact.

My original intention was to give Reid his present the next time we were alone together at the villa, by the beach. Was I subconsciously sending out a message that we have no future together, while still struggling to accept that fact myself?

I feel numb, emotional and wrung out. Anxiety claws at my chest, making it hard to breathe and I focus on keeping myself calm. Reaching out for the swallow, I hold it in my hand, closing my fingers around it.

'It's not luck I need,' I whisper out loud, 'it's direction. And the strength to get through the next two days.'

Going to pieces is not an option; I'm made of stronger stuff than that and now is the time to prove it. There are too many people counting on me today and I'm not going to fail them, they've all worked too hard on this for it not to be a dazzling success.

* * *

I leave half an hour early to take a leisurely walk up to the monument. Packing everything I need for this morning's meetings into a small tote bag, I head off. Several years' ago, when my life was hellish at times, I developed a coping technique for when things began to overwhelm me. Ironically, I have my father to thank for that and without it I know that I would be useless today. I call it *parking*. I visualise myself stretching out my arms to scoop up all my worries and concerns, the things not on today's agenda but which are crowding my thoughts, and I place them in an imaginary box. I picture myself sealing it with tape and placing it in the corner of my workshop. I know that once the weekend is over and my visitors have flown back, I can dust it off and address the problems, one by one.

Logic tells me that if my focus wanders, everything will fall apart. Nothing else matters until this is done. Times when my father wanted me to fail, when his constant fault-finding and interrogation had me doubting myself, I couldn't allow myself to make a mistake. He hated that I was able to keep my cool at times like that, because the power was firmly back in my hands. And it's a tool I can use now.

I love this walk. The minute I step out of the courtyard onto the steep pavement and look up, way above the rooflines at the top of the incline is the back of the Cristo Rei statue. The plinth it sits on is so tall that he appears to rise up out of the roof of one of the houses and, if I squint, I could hold the statue of Christ the King in my hands. With his arms outstretched, it's as if he's embracing the entire world, wanting to give comfort to all. And I'm in need of comfort and reassurance.

Walking past a run of terraced houses, *casas geminadas*, as Maria has taught me, the second one is painted a very pale pink, which always makes me think of strawberry ice cream. When I reach the top of the first stretch, a wall mural on the side of a house advertises the restaurant Rampa do Pragal, which is on my to-do list, but I have no idea where it's located. The artwork, though, is amazing. An image of the Cristo Rei looks towards the Ponte 25 de Abril, the background perfectly capturing that mesmerising blue Lisbon sky with a smattering of tiny, fluffy clouds and the twinkling water beneath it. What I love is that, peeking over the top of the wall, the bushes in the garden on the other side of it have grown about a foot higher, so they now form a natural frame.

I always pause for a moment to stare at the face of Christ, it's a kindly face with a hint of a smile that reminds me of the Mona Lisa. Enigmatic. A smile that says, *don't give up, I can't answer every single prayer, but I'm listening*. I smile back, then move on.

There is a run of thick bamboo abutting the pavement now, forming a hedge to the side of what might be a grand property, but nothing at all is visible from the road.

In contrast, on the opposite side of the hill, a rough-rendered block wall is broken only by a pair of faded green, battered metal doors. One is pinned open, although there is a waist-height, metal grille across the opening. In front of it is a sign, propped up by a small planter, and there's a message scrawled across it in chalk. It looks like the sort of place that might sell car parts, or garden supplies, maybe.

Turning the corner, I step off the pavement onto what I refer to as *the square,* but it's really a roundabout that has a cast-iron water pump in the middle of it. It's surrounded by a sweeping curve of dark grey, cobbled limestone. There are three trees which cast shade over a solitary bench and cars are parked at varying angles around the perimeter. The buildings are an eclectic collection of old properties with the usual charmingly peeling walls and paintwork, and a small café with two, sun-bleached canopies shading some tables and chairs which are set out on the narrow pavement. There are doorways, some with windows next to them, and I know from experience that you can't tell the size of the property behind an innocuous-looking entrance. It could simply be the gateway to an unexpected treasure hidden beyond. Even a tiny opening can lead into a large orchard and the high walls don't allow glimpses of what might be tucked away out of sight.

I suspect that a couple of the properties that sit on the very edge of the pavement are empty, and some may well have holes in the roofs, not visible at street level as I glance up. The only clue is the odd gutter full of sprouting plants and grass, and occasionally I spot a window that has been boarded up.

In between, there is often a newly built property. The old and new sit side by side, and if a property is beyond repair, at some point in time the plot will be redeveloped, and life begins all over again.

And just like that my mind is calm, my focus is back, and I accept that

I cannot control everything around me. I can only be responsible for my own actions. Today my job is to have eyes and ears everywhere. And if a problem occurs, to be ready to jump on it.

As I cross the road and walk towards the gates of the Santuário Nacional do Cristo Rei, there is already a large group of people assembled in front of them, and in the middle of the wide road, a long line of vehicles are parked up.

I wave to Carolina and Antero, but they are deep in conversation with a group of burly-looking guys.

'*Bom dia*,' I call out as I walk briskly up to them and everyone turns to look at me.

Several people begin talking at the same time and I put up my hands to stop them.

'Antero, can we please gather everyone together in little groups. The catering people over there, anyone connected to the fashion show itself here in the middle and anyone involved with the marquees and trailers on the right.'

Antero barks out the orders and people gather into little groups.

'Carolina, as soon as the gates are open, can you show the caterers exactly where we want them to park up.'

She nods and then turns to pull her little group together to explain what is happening in a rush of Portuguese.

'Antero, is there a problem? Some of the guys seem a little agitated.'

'Yes. They arrived late last night and have all parked up in the designated area. They're saying there isn't enough room and four of them have had to park further down. I haven't been over to look yet, but I'm sure it's a case of leaving too much space between each trailer. In fairness, they did arrive in the dark and I'm sure we can move them around to fit everyone into the space we've been allocated. The café is opening for us shortly, so I will encourage them to grab a little breakfast while I sort out the marquee people first. I'll get them to unload their vans and stack everything up ready for later. Everything is in hand.'

'Good. Carolina has the plans confirming the pitches, but I have copies in my bag if you need extras.'

The group in the middle are all tall, willowy young women. They are being bossed around by a diminutive, older woman who is trying to call together several stragglers who are sitting on a low wall to one side, chatting.

'Senhora Vala? *Me chamo* Senhorita Maddison. Seren.' I thrust out my hand as she steps forward to shake it.

'Ah, Seren. Please to say Danielle. English not so good, *desculpe*.'

Well, I think it's good enough for me and I know that *desculpe* means sorry, so I hold out my hands in an appreciative gesture and she inclines her head. We are going to do just fine. I'm sure some of the girls will speak a little English, anyway.

Quickly checking that Carolina and Antero have everything they need, we head off in different directions the moment the big gates swing back.

'Danielle, can you explain to the girls that we have an hour before the public are admitted. You understand?' I turn my wrist, tapping my watch, and she nods.

Her briefing to the girls goes on for several minutes, which is a little worrying, but judging by her demeanour and the way she is waving her index finger around, she is telling them to listen, observe and not waste time by wandering off. In fairness, since I arrived, they've settled down and the exuberance is pure excitement, that much is obvious. They will all have practised walking the runway at modelling school, but I'm not sure if any of them will have performed live in front of an audience of two hundred people before.

The path leading across to the promenade leads us past the café and the gift shop, to the Pius XII walkway, which is a paved area with eight brick-pillared loggias. We walk in the shadow of Cristo Rei, which towers way above us, and without warning, goosebumps begin to run up and down my arms, making me shiver involuntarily.

'Is exciting, yes?' Danielle remarks, as we approach the promenade.

Drawing to a halt, the models all crowd around, but everyone's eyes are on the silky-looking surface of the vast expanse of water as it flows with eddying currents beneath the mighty bridge. This morning, the steelwork looks salmon pink as the early light catches it.

Everyone is quiet, waiting in anticipation for me to begin, and I take a moment to glance around at their eager faces, then it's time. Pulling the large folder from my tote bag, I give Danielle a pile of printed sheets to hand out.

A guy appears, placing a cone over by the edge of the path and then he walks off into the distance, a second cone in his hand. Bless Carolina, she said she would get me a marker to indicate the length of tonight's fashion runway.

'Thank you all for coming and I hope this is going to be a most wonderful experience. As time is limited this morning and the monument will be opening in forty-five minutes, let's begin by taking a walk along what will, tonight, be our catwalk.' I raise my voice slightly, competing with the constant drone of the pounding traffic as commuters head across the bridge into Lisbon.

The group of twenty-two girls close around Danielle, as she translates. I peer down at the sheet in my hands, skimming the text which is printed in Portuguese on one side and English on the other.

'Your photographer, Rafael Osorio,' I stop for a second as a little buzz of excitement ripples like a wave around me, 'will direct each of you in turn this evening, before you do your first walk. Remember, this is a video shoot that won't be done in one take and he will also be taking still photographs in between. Rafael wants this to be a fun experience and it's important that you enjoy yourselves as you will become living canvases.'

Watching Danielle as she speaks, the words coming out her mouth sound like serious instructions and I do wish she'd smile occasionally. I hope it doesn't put the girls off.

'Can I ask for a volunteer?'

Hands go up and Danielle points to a dark-haired girl dressed in shorts. She steps forward and she's at least five inches taller than I am. In fact, they are all taller than me and I can see already that the gowns are going to look amazing on them.

'Thank you...'

'Andreia,' she confirms, giving me a nervous look.

I point up at Cristo Rei as he smiles benevolently down on us. 'Isn't he magnificent?' I ask and she nods. 'The gowns you will be wearing will fall to just below your ankles and when your arms are extended,' I strike the pose, 'your silhouettes against the evening sky will mirror his outline.'

I have their full attention as I wait for Danielle to finish translating.

'Andreia.' I indicate for her to move further forward.

With her back towards her peers, she faces the long, gentle curve of the promenade and I can see she's nervous, so I stand a pace or two in front of her, in line with the first marker.

Turning my head to look at her, I spread my arms wide, indicating that they should be kept straight, and she follows my lead.

'When you hold out your arms like this, the designs printed on the gowns will be on display and our artist, Reid Henderson, has captured the natural beauty of the banks of the river Tagus. Smile as you walk forward and then, after a few paces, stop and turn full circle. You will be wearing flat pumps, so simply turn on the balls of your feet.'

I demonstrate while Danielle explains.

Turning back around and lowering my arms, I nod my head, indicating for Andreia to give it a go. Her movements are a little clunky because she's wearing wedges and she starts laughing as she begins to topple. I glance around and spot one of the other girls who is wearing flat shoes and beckon her forward.

At least they all seem relaxed and we watch as the girl takes three steps forward and executes a perfect, three-hundred-and-sixty-degree turn with ease. I clap my hands, delighted, and they all join in.

'You cannot keep your arms outstretched like this for long. So, you will walk for twenty paces, extend your arms and slowly twirl around. Rafael's assistant will tell you when you can go, and make sure there is an even space between each of you. The runway will be marked out properly tonight, as it will not be the entire length of the promenade. But you can see where the two cones are and that's where it will start and finish.'

As Danielle repeats my instructions, I scan their eager faces. They are all beautiful girls and it's wonderful to be able to offer them this opportunity. I can see that getting them to smile tonight is not going to be a problem. This isn't about catwalk attitude, but a celebration of what nature has created and, for those who believe, what Christ has bestowed.

'Right, you have twenty minutes to have a little practice and then we'll

head over to the changing rooms for a dress rehearsal, to check everything fits properly.'

Once Danielle has said her piece, we both stand back and watch as
they walk and twirl, effortlessly, looking like graceful ballerinas with their
arms outstretched. Rafael said he wanted it to be a spectacle, like the
carnival in Rio de Janeiro. Vibrant, happy and with our wonderful models
looking like elegant mannequins when they spin around and suddenly
each scene is revealed for a few seconds, before they move on. I glance at
Danielle.

'*As meninas ficarão maravilhosas!*'

Any sentence with marvellous in it works for me and Rafael is going
to be delighted.

My phone pings and I excuse myself to rescue it from my bag, then
saunter off in the opposite direction.

I'm sorry about this morning. I shouldn't have just turned up like that. The
kestrel is a work of art, Seren. I love him, almost as much as I love you.

My heart misses a beat and my legs feel wobbly. Leaning up against
the stout, wooden ranch fencing, my body sags as I read his words. I so
want to believe that but waving aside the problems is just pushing them
away temporarily, until the day there is no choice other than to face the
facts. The first part of my life involved living a lie because I wasn't being
true to myself and I won't put myself in that position again. I can wear
beautiful clothes and engage in cocktail party conversation, but my heart
isn't in it. I'm no Beatriz and I don't want that lifestyle. If you truly love
someone then you want what's best for them, even if it means letting
them go. Reid has worked hard, and I believe he will realise his dream,
but I can't be a part of it. And I understand why he can't be a part of my
dream, because he has an exceptional talent.

The girls are still twirling, their voices becoming more distant the
further away they get. I can hear Danielle booming out instructions as
she trots behind them, gesticulating and encouraging them to keep an
even distance from each other. She is a professional coach, whereas I'm
just a... woman who wants to spend her day turning inanimate bits of

metal into something that comes alive. How can I get Reid to understand that the side of me that he's seeing now isn't the person I want to be forever, it's simply a means to an end?

The breeze is light and refreshing, as I stare down at the narrow strip of shrubby ground beyond the fence. My gaze is drawn to the backdrop of shimmering blue water as I look across at the coastline opposite. It's easy to ignore the fact that the land falls away quite sharply, but the edge of the cliff is invisible from this position, hidden by the greenery. It's merely a few feet away from where I'm standing, and yet I'm oblivious to it and the potential danger.

In a way, it's a little like the situation I have with Reid. He can't comprehend the simple life I'm dreaming about because it's so far removed from his reality, it's unimaginable. Wouldn't it be worse to be together, full of love and hope for the future, and gradually the connection between us begins to die because we disappoint each other? It happens all the time. It's the differences that divide you, not the things you instantly have in common.

My fingers begin tapping away, as if I don't respond he'll get anxious.

Well, our fabulous models are going to make the audience fall in love with your wonderful artwork tonight. We'll speak later, I promise.

* * *

It's been a hectic morning and I make my way to the café when Carolina texts to let me know that she's grabbed a table and Antero is ordering us some lunch.

Walking past the chapel, I linger for a moment, stopping to listen to the haunting voices of the monks singing. I know it's only a tape, but it's easy to imagine them inside on bended knees, raising their voices to the heavens.

I turn, heading for the covered terrace and spot Antero carrying a tray on his way back from the café.

'Seren,' he calls out, 'over here.' He tilts his head and I crane my neck, unable to see Carolina at first, as I make my way towards him. She's managed to bag a table that is completely in the shade and I sit down gratefully, feeling extremely hot and bothered.

'How was your session with the models?' she asks and they both train their eyes on me.

'Wonderful. They have it nailed, and they are going to be amazing. They immediately got the fun vibe we're aiming for, and when they tried on the gowns, well, you'd think they were wedding dresses. With the undergarment, the dresses are heavier than I thought they would be, but I can see that it's necessary to keep the fabric straight if the wind whips up. But everything is looking good and the show is going to be phenomenal.'

They turn to look at each other, eyebrows raised, and I watch as they relax back into their seats.

'This calls for a toast,' Carolina declares, raising her coffee cup and beaming.

The look that Antero gives her makes me want to sigh; he can't help smiling as his eyes sweep over her face.

'To a great team. The best!' I say, as we touch cups.

'And to a boss who knows what she's doing,' Antero chimes in. 'It's all about the hard work to get it to this stage and tying down every little detail. Success is never down to luck, is it?'

I laugh, dipping into my tote bag to retrieve the little black swallow. 'Talking of luck, my neighbour gave me this just before I left this morning. I don't know what the symbolism stands for, but a little luck might come in useful, as we don't want the wind to pick up at the tail end of the day.'

Antero stares down at the swallow lying on my open palm. 'Portuguese sailors used to have tattoos of swallows on their arms. They viewed the birds as a symbol of good luck because swallows always return home. It was also believed that if a sailor drowned at sea, a swallow would carry his soul to heaven.'

Carolina reaches out and I pass the little bird to her.

'This isn't one of the new ones you see in the gifts shops. It's lovely and obviously handmade, rather than mass-produced. My grandmother always said that swallows are symbols of love and loyalty, but also of home and family values, which is at the heart of the Portuguese culture. Swallows keep a single partner during their entire lifetime and as a keepsake it represents faithfulness and loyalty.'

'Maria told me that her grandfather made it. I think both her father and brother made traditional *azulejo* tiles, too, including the ones in the house I rent. It was very kind of her, and I was very touched.'

Antero is already tucking into his *bifana* roll.

The pork isn't just grilled and sliced, but it has been marinated first and then simmered in a rich stock. I can taste the paprika as soon as I bite into the soft roll and then the mustard and chilli hit my tongue. My stomach rumbles, appreciatively. I couldn't face breakfast this morning, but I quickly push those thoughts aside.

'Can I assume, by the way you both seem so relaxed, that everything went to plan this morning?'

Antero gives me a thumbs-up as his mouth is full and Carolina, nods her head, wiping her mouth with a napkin.

'After lunch I'll check that the site manager is happy and that we haven't caused any unnecessary disruption so far, then I'll head into the office to update the directors. After that I will pop home to change and I'll be back here about four o'clock.'

'Sounds good to me,' Carolina replies. 'I've brought a change of clothes with me and will get ready shortly before Bernadette is due to arrive on site. I'll give her and her assistant a hand preparing the gowns. I'm sure I can operate a garment steamer if required.'

'And I'll be on site the whole time, too, doing the rounds. So, if you need any errands run and things are going smoothly elsewhere, you can call on me.' Antero winks at Carolina but doesn't realise I caught it and I have to bite my lip to stop myself from smiling.

Maybe swallows do bring good luck, because so far the plan is playing out item by item as we move down the tick list. Then my phone starts ringing. It's a number I don't recognise, so I excuse myself, hurrying off to find a quieter area.

'Seren Maddison,' I reply cordially.

'Seren, it's Beatriz Esteves. Can you hear me?'

I increase my pace, walking away from the noisy café area and across to the grassy expanse the other side of the loggias. 'Sorry, I'm walking to get away from the background noise. How can I help, Beatriz?'

'I'm calling to thank you for kindly extending an invitation to my niece, Leonor, and a friend, to tonight's exciting event. As my daughter is here, too, Leonor asked me to check if you are happy that Ana comes along as her guest?'

'Of course, that's wonderful.'

'We will all travel together, so is it all right if we arrive at the rear entrance as planned and then they can wander off together? They are so excited to see Rafael Osorio in action, and the models up close, of course.'

Beatriz's enthusiasm throws me a little.

'Perfect. I will arrange for someone to show them around so that they can get their bearings and then leave them to enjoy the show.'

'Thank you, Seren. We are all looking forward to this evening. I'm sorry if I didn't fully appreciate how much work you have put into this project. Filipe talks of nothing else and he's not an easy man to impress. Reid and I are most grateful, Seren. I won't hold you up any longer as I know you will have much to do. *Tchau.*'

Beatriz sounded friendly and an uneasy fluttering begins to stir in the pit of my stomach. About a week ago, I woke up in the middle of the night, my brow covered in sweat. I couldn't shake off a bad dream that stayed with me. Everyone was here, at the monument and the show was in full swing, and then I heard my name being called. Beatriz walked towards me, her eyes blazing as she shouted out, 'There is the woman who is having an affair with my husband,' and every head turned my way. I wanted to run and hide. The cold, grim light of the early hours didn't help to dispel my mortification. Or the fact that it wasn't real, or even that Reid isn't her husband any longer. It is my worst nightmare, the thought of being called out like that, publicly. It could damage my professional credibility. It would embarrass the directors, Reid and my team. Would anyone give a damn that Reid's free to do what he wants? Here, family, and well-known families, in particular, have a code of conduct.

I wander back, my mind racing. Antero and Carolina are standing next to the chapel, waiting for me. Carolina has my bag in her hand and holds it out to me.

'Thanks. Carolina, can you walk with me to the gates as I'm a bit short for time now. That phone call was Beatriz with a request.'

Antero bids us goodbye and the two of us set off.

'Problems?'

I do my best to hide my unease. 'No. But Reid's assistant, Leonor, and his daughter, Ana, are coming as special guests. They will arrive with Beatriz and when we whisk her off to the VIP tent, could you organise for someone to show the two girls around? I will, of course, look out for them both and if I spot an opportunity, introduce them to Rafael.'

She laughs. 'No problem and all eyes are going to be on him, so they'd love that. I'm sure quite a few of the tickets will have been snapped up by his fans.'

'Oh, before I forget.' I slip the tote bag off my shoulder and pull out the folder. 'Here's the signed programme I promised you for your parents.' It's neatly tied together by a silver grey ribbon and I can see she's delighted.

'Bless you, Seren, when you are so busy. This will mean so much to them, I can't thank you enough!'

'On another, more personal note, and please don't read anything into this, but I'm just covering all bases.'

Carolina turns her head, her eyes searching my face.

'If anything unexpected happens tonight, and I disappear for whatever reason, you can have total trust that Danielle Vala will keep the models on their toes. And I'm sure she can take any of Rafael's demands in her stride. But I'd be grateful if you could step in for me, keeping a general eye out to ensure our special guests are never left unattended. I have no doubt that the directors will be doing their bit, too.'

'Where would you go?' she asks, incredulously.

I shrug my shoulders dismissively. 'I like to have a contingency plan in place should an emergency arise. Just in case.'

The scene playing out in my head makes me feel a little queasy, as I picture Beatriz and Reid together. The perfect couple reunited as one happy family. It's not easy to dismiss the image.

'Seren, you make me laugh. We are all here to make sure any little problems are quickly smoothed over and, besides,' she does a half-turn, pointing her index finger up towards Cristo Rei, 'we can always say a little prayer if we are in need. Now go, do what you have to do, and grab a little quiet time before you return. You deserve it.' With that, she leans in to give me a hug.

Then it hits me full on like an unexpected slap in the face. I draw back, my hand instinctively covering my mouth as my jaw drops open.

'What?'

'My visitors are in the air as we speak and I was supposed to arrange for someone to pick them up at the airport to take them to their hotel. And then bring them here for seven-thirty. I totally for—'

Carolina raises her hand, palm facing me to stop me talking. 'It's not a problem. Leave it with me and I will sort it. Text me the details of the flight, their names and the hotel. Now go. It's one small detail that is easily fixed.'

As I step out through the gates, I take a few deep breaths. Given the circumstances, something was bound to fall between the cracks, but if anything could convince me that I'm in need of a break, it's this.

Crisis avoided, but only just. Let's hope that's the only one.

20

THE VISION BECOMES REALITY

When you draft out an idea on paper and begin breaking it down into individual elements, virtually anything seems achievable. It becomes merely a list of action points, the steps involved turning it into reality. As the minutes tick by until the gates are opened, the nervous excitement everywhere around me is tangible. And my own stomach is churning.

My job now is to circulate, thank the hardworking crews who are doing their final adjustments and exude confidence as a representative of the gallery. If I look nervous, then it will make everyone else nervous, so I stand tall, smoothing down my magenta Dolce and Gabbana fluted crepe midi dress, knowing that it was worth every single penny. Tonight, I will be hovering and keeping a watchful eye over everything; calm, professional and able to step in and step up, if necessary. Like any good host, I am only here to facilitate because this evening is all about our guests.

There's an hour to go until the gates open at seven o'clock. Striding down the avenue of palm trees, past the catering marquees where the waiting staff are busy getting their final instructions, the walkie-talkie in my hand kicks into life.

'Seren, can you hear me, over?'

There's a little static, but Carolina's voice is loud and clear.

'Yes, I'm here.'

'Heads-up. Yolanda Abreu and her father have just arrived. They are at the VIP entrance and Senhor Ferreira is heading over there now. Were we expecting them?'

'No, but Senhor Ferreira probably extended a personal invitation and forgot to mention it. It's a little early and the music isn't due to start playing until seven-thirty. However, I'm on it. I'll head over to the booth now and see if they are ready to kick off. Over.'

I take a short cut, wending my way between the spiky, pineapple-like palm trees and, up ahead, there are three guys clustered around a pop-up, open-fronted tent that looks like a mini studio.

'*Olá*,' I call out as I approach. '*Fala inglês?*'

I hold up my official badge and smile.

One of them stops what he's doing, nods his head and smiles back at me. 'Is there a problem? he asks.

'Yolanda Abreu has just arrived, so I wondered if you were able to start playing the music as soon as possible.'

The moment I mention Yolanda's name, all three of the guys turn to look at me and give a thumbs-up.

'*Obrigada!*' Well, that was easy enough.

Turning around, I spot Danielle and one of the models as they take the same shortcut I did, on their way to the catwalk. I head in their direction.

Danielle introduces me to the young woman, whose name is Lili, and we hurry across to where Rafael and his assistant are stooped over, looking at a small monitor. He glances up and there's an exchange in Portuguese between Danielle and Rafael, but his eyes are firmly on Lili. He turns to me and we shake hands.

Antero appears, carrying two cups of coffee for Rafael and his assistant, who take them gratefully. After a short conversation, Antero explains that they are going to film Lili doing a test walk, so they can make the final adjustments to the lighting.

'Can you let Rafael know that I'm on hand if he needs me. The gates open in just under an hour, so once the test is finished if they have time before the shoot begins at seven-thirty, they might like to walk over to the VIP marquee to grab something to eat. I know you have it all in hand, anyway. Also, can you pass on my sincere thanks. In the UK we'd say break a leg, instead of good luck, so if there's an equivalent Portuguese saying, please add that, too.'

Rafael is watching us closely and I turn to look at him, smiling appreciatively.

'Break a leg,' he repeats. 'That I know. Thank you.'

Well, well. Carolina said once that Rafael understood some English and I wonder now just how much.

He smiles at me, courteously, just as the sound of Yolanda Abreu's voice wafts over our heads. His smile grows exponentially.

'An angel,' he says, and I nod in agreement before leaving him to get back to work.

Next stop is to check on how the models are doing. It's a fair walk across the site, out through the rear gates and along part of the perimeter the other side of the fencing. It's a wide, quiet road, with low, limestone-cobbled pavements and we have permission to park along a section of this stretch for two nights. Even from here, I can see a large group of people standing around.

As I get closer, I wave at Inês, Carolina's assistant, who is talking to Vicente.

'Olá, Seren,' she says, as they both hurry towards me and away from the throng of people.

'Lovely to see you, Inês and Vicente. I hope everything is all right?'

'Is good,' Inês confirms.

'I'll just pop in to say hello to everyone and make sure they are running to schedule. When will you begin escorting the models over to the promenade?'

Vicente, looking every inch a security guard and wearing his uniform with an air of gravity, checks his watch. 'Twenty-three minutes and Inês will take the first twelve ladies across. As soon as the others are ready, I will walk them over.'

'Will we need any security here?'

'No. I make arrangement. Four people here at all times, Seren. Staff can come and go. Get refreshments and take a look at the show. Everyone happy, but safety first,' Vicente confirms.

'Excellent. Thank you, both. I will see you later.'

There are eleven vehicles in total parked up. Three of them are massive units on the back of cabs. These are smart trailers, with a flight of metal steps and a handrail leading up into office-style accommodation. Two of them are changing rooms and the other one houses the hair and make-up team.

Beyond that are a variety of other vehicles belonging to the various contractors on site.

A group of models are clustered around the steps to the first luxury unit and they turn to say hello as I walk towards them.

'*Olá!*' I say as I approach. 'Hair?'

'Yes. We are waiting our turn,' one of the girls replies.

I notice several of them are ready and they look amazing. One does a quick twirl for me and I give her a thumbs-up before I head up the steps.

Popping my head inside, it's pleasantly cool as the air-con blasts out, which is just as well, as there are five workstations. Two for make-up and three for the hairdressers, who are all working flat out. Everyone looks up and I'm greeted with a mass of hellos in both English and Portuguese.

'All good?'

Heads nod. Judging by the smiling faces, no one is panicking and the girls sitting in the hot seats are probably anxious to finish up and slip into their gowns.

'Good luck!' I call out, giving a wave as I head out through the door.

Inside the second of the two trailers where the girls are changing, I finally catch up with Bernadette. She feels like a friend now, as we've spent hours talking, albeit with Antero helping us to communicate and fill in the gaps.

'*Bonsoir*, Seren. *Nous sommes enfin là et les modèles sont magnifiques!*'

We air-kiss, as we are both wearing full make-up.

'*Totalement magnifiques!*' I confirm, because the models do look wonderful, even better than I think any of us could have anticipated. 'You are well? Is there anything you need?'

'More time, but we will do it and all is good. Carolina was *merveilleuse*, helping to get the gowns ready. *Asseyez-vous.*'

Bernadette indicates for me to take a seat and walks along to one of the three curtained cubicles, popping her head around it. She disappears inside, and a minute or two later the curtain sweeps back. She indicates for the model to walk forward and under the bright lights I get my first up-close look of one of the gowns as it will appear on the catwalk.

As the young woman extends her arms and does a slow twirl, the dress falls perfectly. There's no rippling, or folds to hide the artwork. Along the hemline is a frieze of delicate strands of wild grasses, the sort you see along the banks of the river. They extend upwards and the palest hint of blue wraps around like a ribbon, representing the river, and then a hint of pale yellow, where the sandpipers are pecking away in search of insects. Above that, from chest-height up, the graduating blue of the sky is decorated with a few wispy little dots of cloud and a flock of seagulls in a pale, off-white, with the merest stroke of grey defining their feathers, glint with a touch of silver as if the sun is catching the tips of their wings.

'Perfect, simply perfect.' The words slip from my mouth without any need to think. Job done.

* * *

I'm probably slightly out of range, as Carolina's voice is breaking up.

'Say again?'

'Executive coaches h... ar... VIPs an... wait...' Her voice disappears and I increase my pace as I head in through the back gates and across the rear car park. '... prob... come...'

'I can't hear. You are breaking up. I'm on my way. Over.'

By the time I draw alongside the Mercedes minibuses, our guests have already been offloaded and as I scan around, they are nowhere in sight.

My walkie-talkie kicks into life once more. 'Seren, it's Antero.'

Thank goodness we have a good signal.

'Carolina is in the VIP tent settling our guests. I've alerted the directors who are heading straight over. There's a problem, but Carolina needs to explain what's happening. As soon as Senhor Ferreira arrives to take over, she'll meet you behind the music booth.'

'Any clues about what it might be?' I ask, my heart suddenly missing a beat.

'No. She was brief, and I could hear lots of voices around her. From what I've seen, everything is fine. Rafael is taking some still photos and the models are all lined up awaiting their turn. The video shoot begins in about thirty-five minutes. When you catch up with her, shout if there's anything I can do. Over.'

The last thing I need now is for someone to stop me en route, so I take the slightly longer path, skirting around the edge of the grassy area. I can hear general sounds, above which a song floats on the breeze, which has definitely picked up a little, but not enough to worry me – yet. Reid was right, *fado* music has a haunting quality. Yolanda sings from the heart and even though I can't understand the words, I can feel the emotion. Whatever scene is playing out in the lyrics, she's living it completely.

Stepping out of the shelter of the trees and onto the very end of the promenade, the sound booth is about fifty metres in front of me and, beyond that, the lights are now on as the models pose and a crowd is starting to gather.

'Seren, Seren!'

The second I hear my name, I turn around and a tear forms in the corner of my eyes as I spot Judi and my mum rushing towards me.

'We've been looking everywhere for you!'

'Mum, what are you doing here?'

We throw our arms around each other and I almost drop the walkie-talkie.

'Long story. We don't want to interrupt, we just wanted to let you know we're here and it's wonderful, truly wonderful. Now, go do your thing and we'll catch up when the evening is done.'

As we step back, I can see that Carolina is waiting for me.

'You have no idea how good it is to see you both. I'm sorry to hug and run. I'm so glad you arrived safe and sound.'

I lean in to give Judi, then Mum, a lingering hug before hurrying away.

'Carolina, what's up?'

'One of the three reporters we invited to the event has disappeared.'

'Hmm, that's annoying. We need as much coverage as we can get.'

'Oh, I think we will get coverage, all right, but not quite what we were expecting. Senhora Veloso came to me to say that after chatting with Yolanda, they walked across to spend a little time with Rafael. Leonor and Ana were hovering, so she introduced them and then escorted them back to get a drink. When she returned, to her surprise, Yolanda and Rafael had disappeared. They had stepped away from the catwalk and were standing under cover of the trees holding hands and kissing, apparently. Yolanda's agent had already spotted them and was hurrying over to escort Yolanda back to the VIP tent, but not before a photographer appeared and managed to snap a whole series of shots. Senhora Veloso witnessed it and chased after him but was unable to catch up. Yolanda's agent wants to talk to you in private. I said I would find you and we'd meet him by over by the gift shop.'

My face freezes. 'And the photographer has left the site?'

We set off, walking quickly. 'It seems so. No one has seen him since.'

Which means they've been keeping their relationship a secret and now he has the scoop.

'Oh dear. Are Yolanda and Rafael aware of what was going on?'

'I'm not sure.'

'Have you seen Reid?' I enquire, trying not to sound irritated. When he first suggested I contact Yolanda's publicist, he said she was well-known to Rafael. I didn't interpret that as them being in a relationship. If I'd realised just how sensitive the situation was, this could have been avoided. I can't control the press, but I would most certainly have made sure someone kept an eye on Rafael at all times to step in if necessary.

'Yes, he arrived with Beatriz, Tomas, Leonor and his daughter, Ana. They were all in high spirits and I had no idea Reid and his ex-wife were back together again.'

Her words make my heart miss a beat for a second and I swallow hard.

'I wasn't aware of that,' I reply and, to my horror, my voice wavers a little.

'Oh, maybe I'm wrong, then. It was something Ana said about how happy she was to have her father back in her life, so maybe it's not officially out there yet. Anyway, the girls are fine and happy to do their own thing. They won't stray far away from the catwalk; they are captivated by Rafael. Senhora Veloso has been wonderful and she suggested that she take over chaperoning our VIPs around this evening and is more than happy to do so. It takes off a little pressure, yes?'

'I'll remember to express my gratitude to her. And Reid is looking after Beatriz?'

'No. Reid is with Senhor Ferreira, at the moment. They are doing general introductions as everyone wants to talk to him. Beatriz is busy talking to a group of business acquaintances. I think they will both struggle to get away from the VIP section. Have you had time to sample any of the food?'

I shake my head as food is the last thing on my mind right now. 'How about you?'

'No. Agony, isn't it? Ah, here we are. *Senhor Sequeira, esta é a Senhorita Maddison.*'

We shake hands, cordially, but I can see by his frown that he's not happy.

'Carolina, can you please express my apologies to Senhor Sequeira that someone should have taken photos without permission and I am anxious to address his concerns.'

Senhor Sequeira begins a lengthy conversation with Carolina, whose brow is now furrowed. It's a couple of minutes before the exchange comes to an abrupt halt and she turns to face me, looking grave.

'He says that Yolanda and Rafael are close, but that there must be no announcement, or leak to the press, ahead of the release of her next album. He says it is a very delicate matter and that it would be in breach of one of the clauses in her recording contract.'

My heart sinks to the floor. We've been all about seeking publicity, but I have no idea how to go about applying pressure to suppress something.

'I'm afraid it might already be too late. Clearly the reporter knew the value of what he'd managed to snap and that's exactly why he left when he did.' I shake my head sadly, acknowledging the gravity of the situation.

Carolina delivers the news and his face is grim. Thinking on my feet, I seriously doubt we can stop this from getting out, it's a reporter's dream, but what if we *manage* it?

'Carolina, ask Senhor Sequeira if he can get hold of anyone from the record company tonight? I have an idea. I suggest we keep this to ourselves for the moment. There's no point unsettling Rafael, or Yolanda, until we can tell them exactly what is going to happen and when.'

If Rafael finds out, he's so fiery he might even walk off in disgust, feeling that, somehow, it's our fault. This is a problem I couldn't possibly have anticipated, but it's imperative to regain control of the situation before it escalates.

21

BASKING IN THE LIMELIGHT

'Here, you deserve this,' Reid's voice startles me. He hands me a champagne flute. 'I've been looking for you all evening to say thank you and congratulations. Here's to a resounding success!'

I take the glass, accepting his toast and we clink. I find myself wondering if the real reason he sought me out is to break the news about getting back together with Beatriz. However, he's standing there staring at me and I can see how tired he is, having been constantly in demand since the moment he arrived.

'I was hiding, tucking myself away out of sight to grab a quiet moment.' It's hard to sound upbeat.

'Carolina told me where to find you.'

We're at the far end of the site, there's no lighting here, on a small patch of rough ground that is awaiting development.

'Few get a chance to see this,' I murmur, a little overwhelmed as we stare out across the darkening sky. The stars are out, and some are clearly visible, despite the bright lights of the catwalk in the background and the light pollution from the city on the opposite bank of the river.

In the fading light of day when the monument is usually closed, we are privileged to see this enchanting view out across the river. As dusk settles the city begins to twinkle like Christmas lights on a tree.

'Everyone else is looking in the other direction at what's going on behind us,' Reid points out. 'But I knew that your eyes would be elsewhere. It's all a little too intense to cope with, isn't it?'

Accepting the inevitable is tough, I can't lie, but I also can't bear to hear him say the words. And maybe he can't bring himself to utter them.

'Yes,' I reply softly. However, Reid is a client too, so I should probably be reassuring him. 'It's wonderful when all the hard work pays off, though, and the reaction tonight has been amazing. Have you spoken to Bernadette? She's so excited about the project going forward.'

'I'm not involved in that. Tomas was in on the negotiations, but Beatriz is taking over from him now, as he's heading back to London the day after tomorrow. He has decided to move his operations back to Lisbon, so he won't be around for a while until it's all sorted. You delivered everything and more, Seren, you must be on a high tonight.'

The way he so casually slips in the reference to Beatriz leaves me feeling hollow inside. I'm on the verge of saying something I know I will regret, so I glance down at my watch.

'I need to head back,' I reply apologetically. I don't know what he's expecting me to say. *Yes, it was a success and I'm so happy?* 'It's time for Rafael to dismiss the models. They will be shattered after all that twirling.'

We lock eyes, so many unspoken words lie between us like a barrier, but the night is not yet over and there is still work to be done. Besides, this is no place for what is going to be a harrowing conversation, at best.

'You look stunning tonight,' he blurts out, unexpectedly shattering the silence around us. 'You make a fabulous dress look out of this world and you've been turning heads. Your name is on everyone's lips. I've hated every minute of this evening, not having you by my side,' Reid's tone is full of regret as he turns and walks away from me.

Shoulders slumped, he disappears into the growing darkness, leaving me feeling desolate. I can't bear to think of him feeling as sad and alone as I am right now. Everyone around him is celebrating an artist who has no real idea how talented he is, and tonight's event wowed everyone. Standing here, feeling like this while I hold a glass of expensive champagne in my hand, it's a stark reminder of why this isn't the life for me.

I'm sure Beatriz is very happy indeed with what she's achieved tonight but it's blatantly obvious that she is no longer in love with Reid.

Why couldn't I simply bring myself to wish Reid well and put an end to this unnecessary suffering? I draw in a deep breath as I empty the contents of the glass onto the ground next to me. It's harrowing to see Reid giving up the fight and sounding so defeated. After tomorrow's party at the gallery any involvement we have comes to an end and my heart aches for us both.

* * *

'Rafael that was an amazing spectacle.' I place my hand on my heart, realising he probably didn't understand what I said. '*Obrigada.*' Although a mere thank you isn't enough. He turned those models into superstars tonight. The crowd was enthralled, and the girls all shone brightly, but, more importantly, in the image of Cristo Rei, they became the living artwork that celebrates Lisbon.

Rafael takes a step forward and I get ready to shake hands, but instead he bestows a swift kiss on my cheek, and I turn to let him kiss the other one.

The panic in his eyes, when Carolina and I approached him to tell him what had happened earlier in the evening, is still etched on my mind. He wasn't worried for himself, but for Yolanda. When we quickly ran through the solution we came up with, together with Yolanda's record producers and publicist, he simply nodded his agreement. The reality is that when they wake up in the morning, photos of them will appear along with headlines that one of the songs from Yolanda's new album will be the backing track to Reid Henderson's voice-over of the fashion shoot. There is also an exclusive interview scheduled with the happy couple for the same week that the album is released. I suspect, by then, Yolanda will be wearing a sparkly new engagement ring, so everyone wins in the end.

Senhor Sequeira seemed happy, Tomas thought it was an advantageous collaboration and Rafael realised a secret like that will always trip you up if you lower your guard for one single moment.

'How you say... uh... win-win tomorrow? I hope.' He shrugs his shoulders and we exchange fleeting smiles. It's been a long day, but while the general public are beginning to head for home, the VIP marquee is still buzzing. How much business will have been conducted under that canopy this evening? I wonder how many old friends were called upon to do favours. And Beatriz, thanks to an appeal from Senhora Veloso, made one, short phone call and called in a favour for me to put a spin on the story that will break tomorrow. I haven't had a chance to thank Beatriz yet and it would be unprofessional of me not to do so, but I'm dreading it.

I wish I could go straight home, but I can't simply disappear. First I need to find Judi and Mum. There are still groups of people scattered around the site, chatting and laughing after having had a couple of drinks and some excellent food, that looked and smelt divine. It's getting darker by the moment and even the sturdy lights erected around the catwalk and the catering marquees make it hard to identify people from a distance.

My feet are aching and eventually I end up wending my way back to the VIP area. I immediately spot Reid, who is over in the far corner talking to two men I don't know. He doesn't look my way and as I walk towards the bar, Beatriz calls me over to the little group she's with.

'Seren, we were just about to leave. I'm so glad we caught you, you must meet Ana, my darling daughter. What a great success tonight has been.'

I can see Ana is rather shy, so I give her a very British little wave, like the Queen and, to my relief, she waves back, laughing.

'I'm so sorry I got caught up. Did you have a good time?' I include Leonor in my question and it's plain to see they've had a wonderful time.

'Rafael was amazing, wasn't he?' Ana replies, unable to hide her excitement, her eyes shining.

'He took some photos of us and he's going to email them to Dad,' Leonor adds. 'It was such fun. And we took some selfies with him.'

I glance at Beatriz and she seems delighted with how things have gone, and she has every right to feel that way.

As she begins preparing the girls to leave, I beckon to Vicente, who is standing guard. Whispering into his ear to take Leonor and Ana over to Reid to say goodnight, I turn to Beatriz.

'Beatriz, thank you for your help earlier on. It was unfortunate we were unable to stop the photographer leaving the site. But it was very good of you to make the call and come to my assistance.'

'It was not a problem. These things happen, Seren.' A momentary look of pure satisfaction flashes over her face.

Ironically, we both glance in Reid's direction, watching as he throws his arms around Ana and they hug. He looks so happy and so does Ana.

'It upset me to find out that Reid was seeing someone. It was hard for me not having a role in his life even though he could not understand that. His career was my life for so long and that will continue.'

'Oh, I... I am sorry if I...'

'There is no need for you to explain Reid's questionable behaviour and his total disregard for my feelings,' she snaps. 'As difficult as it has been to witness this little crisis he's been going through, the one good thing to come out of it is that this project has given him back his motivation. I am grateful for that, believe me. And now it's time for you to move on. I'm sure you understand that and there will be no need for me to raise the subject with Filipe.'

I'm dumbstruck at the way she's trying to put me down, as if I tried to steal her husband. They aren't even married, but she acts as if that's not the case. Before I can assemble my thoughts, Leonor and Ana appear, eager to head off home.

'I... um, Vicente will escort you to the minibus. Thank you all for coming this evening,' I say, trying my best to maintain my composure, despite the fact that I'm trembling all over.

'Our pleasure,' Beatriz throws over her shoulder as they all follow Vicente.

Behind me, Carolina calls my name and I turn around, still in a daze.

'Seren, look who I found.'

She's ushering Judi and Mum towards me. Both look happy, but tired, and then I spot Miguel, bringing up the rear.

It takes a lot of determination to compose myself and act normally, but my pride won't allow me to make a spectacle of myself.

'I've walked the entire site looking for you two. I thought you'd gone back to the hotel.' My eyes feel heavy and I steel myself, refusing to let Beatriz's scathing comments get to me.

'Miguel's been waiting to take us back, but we didn't want to leave without saying goodnight. We're too tired to stay any longer, I'm afraid. I feel like I've walked for miles, but it's been amazing, Seren. What an introduction to Lisbon. And Miguel just took us on a tour of the site, so we'll know our way around when we come back to see it all in daylight,' Mum explains.

He looks at me, a little embarrassed.

'Miguel, I can't thank you enough for looking after Mum and my best friend, tonight. It was so kind of you.' I didn't give it a thought that Carolina would phone Miguel to come to my rescue, but I am grateful. In the midst of my gut-wrenching sadness, I have true friends around me. They might have no idea what I'm going through, or how I value every little act of kindness. Rubbing shoulders with affluent people only serves to remind me how easy it is to become detached from the real world, because like attracts like.

'It was not a problem. And I was coming tonight anyway. I've enjoyed the company.' I can see that he has, and I can also see that both Mum and Judi are flagging.

Mum throws her arms around me, whispering in my ear: 'I'm so proud of you, Seren. Your father would be too if he wasn't such a stubborn, lost soul.'

When I turn to Judi, she looks at me, eyes wide. 'What a result, Seren, you did it! You upped the bar and some.'

'Ah, it's just so good to have you both here,' I reply, swiping away a solitary tear as I try my best to sound jolly. 'One more day then it's kick-back time and I can show you the sights. But, first, a few days at the beach I think to relax.'

'You bet,' she says, relinquishing me.

That leaves Miguel. Poor Miguel. I can't leave him out. As I lean in to give him a brief, but heart-felt hug, I find myself staring over his shoulder at Judi and plotting. What if you put together a rash, kind-hearted musician and a woman who organises every little aspect of her life to the nth degree? Would she become mellower and would he become more in control of his life? I realise this hug is going on and on, and as I draw back, I look at Miguel for a second or two, measuring him up and thinking *this might work*. I give him a genuinely grateful smile and then turn back to Mum and Judi.

'I'll text you tomorrow. It might not be that early, but I'll fetch you late morning and bring you back to the house for lunch. Sleep well.'

As I watch them walk away, they have no idea how much it means to me to have them here right now when I'm at my lowest ebb. I can get through this, I tell myself, the end is in sight.

There are only four small groups of people still gathered inside the marquee as I express my thanks to Carolina for everything she's done.

'Where's Antero?'

'He's helping some of the guys carry their equipment back to the trailers. It's strange, but I feel a bit sad that it's all over. I know we have the party tomorrow evening, but we've spent so much time working on this—'

Filipe appears at my side. 'Seren, I'm glad I caught you.' He steps aside, raising a hand in the air. 'Ladies and gentlemen, can we all gather around for a moment?'

People drift towards us and, as if by magic, waiters appear to top up everyone's glasses. I glance at my boss nervously.

When we had that awkward talk in his office, I have no doubt at all that Beatriz would have been very circumspect about what she said, while dropping hints to try to undermine my position. Filipe did his duty by raising her concerns, but did the fact that he didn't issue me an ultimatum mean he, too, believes she's overstepping the mark? And with hindsight, I'm beginning to wonder whether Beatriz purposely rowed with Ana just before the party at Reid's house. She knew he would have no choice but to drop everything as soon as he got the call. If Beatriz had been really concerned about her daughter, she wouldn't have left him to it just to play hostess. No, she knew Ana would go to a friend's house and that's why she wouldn't let Reid call the police. Now it's all beginning to make sense. But that doesn't alter the fact that Reid is caught in the middle and I'm the only one who can see that.

'It feels wrong to end the night without a toast to the team, Seren's team, who pulled this together so perfectly tonight. Every single member involved, and at a rough guess I'd say that's in excess of a hundred people, has executed their role diligently. On behalf of the directors, I would like to propose a toast to acknowledge the sheer dedication that has paid off so handsomely. Seren, please pass on our grateful thanks to everyone involved. Bottoms up!'

That raises a genuine smile – where on earth did Filipe hear that expression?

It's only polite to stay a little longer, but after half an hour, I just want to escape as my nerves are in shreds. Antero is giving Carolina a lift back and we walk out together, leaving Vicente and the site manager sitting drinking coffee. It's likely it will still be a few hours before the catering staff are ready to leave.

'You're not walking back, are you?' Carolina asks as we hug goodbye.

'No, I offered to give Seren a lift home.' Reid's voice appears out of nowhere.

'You look exhausted, so don't hang around,' she whispers into my ear before drawing back. 'Make sure you have a lie-in tomorrow, and we'll see you late afternoon at the gallery, then. Sleep well.'

'You, too, my friend.'

Carolina's eyes scan my face to see if I'm comfortable accepting a lift from Reid. She thinks we'll end up talking about work, but I give her a reassuring nod.

When they are out of earshot, I turn to look at him. 'You don't have to take me home, it's not far.'

'I have no intention of letting you walk, Seren,' he replies and I can tell there's no point in protesting.

'I didn't realise you drove here, I assumed you came in the minibus with Beatriz, Ana and Leonor.'

'Tomas and I wanted to chat through a couple of things in private, so I gave him a lift. He's travelling back with Beatriz and the girls. When I drove past your place earlier and saw the car parked up, I guessed you had walked.'

Why did Reid take the detour in the first place? Those little streets are narrow, so it meant going out of his way. He planned this; he was keeping an eye on me while we were in the marquee, I could feel it, but every time I turned my head to look his way, his eyes were elsewhere. I fall in line with him, too dispirited to make polite conversation for the sake of it.

Several of the contractors' vehicles have been driven around to the main car park and Antero is one of the men helping to pack up the equipment. He waves and I wave back, but he's too far away to wander over and say goodnight. I know he'll understand. Reid and I walk over to his car, keeping a distance between us and it's awkward.

'You're very subdued,' he remarks.

'Just exhausted. Are the problems with the container sorted now?' I ask, as he opens the passenger door for me, and I settle myself into the seat.

I wait anxiously as he walks around the car, nervously fiddling with the bag on my lap. My fear is that he'll want to talk about this morning, but I just don't have the energy. It won't have been an easy day for him, but I've had the day from hell, too, and this is about self-preservation.

'Pretty much. It's a pity about the damage to the paintings, as they will have to be substituted. But it could have been worse.'

My stomach is in knots, but they begin to ease as it dawns on me that Reid is as tired as I am and unlikely to want to enter into a heavy conversation.

As the car pulls out onto the road, Reid starts speaking. 'Ana and Leonor had a great time. Thank you for thinking of them, Seren, it was an oversight on my part.'

'You've been busy, so I'm sure they understood. I had a last-minute panic getting my friend and my mum collected from the airport.'

'It wasn't on one of your tick lists?' he teases.

'I guess we both messed up a little.'

'You didn't tell me that your mum was flying over, too. I saw the likeness immediately and it was obvious from your reaction who it was. Will I get to meet them, or were you purposely keeping us apart?'

I close my eyes for a moment, not quite sure what to say to him.

'I didn't know she was coming. We have a lot planned. They're coming to my place for lunch tomorrow before I head off to the gallery to oversee the final preparations for the party.'

'And after that?'

'Two nights at the villa, thanks to you, and then some sightseeing. I get to be a tour guide and I will be taking them to that little bookshop.'

'And the guy you were hugging? Was that a surprise, too?'

His tone has changed and it catches me unaware.

'What do you mean, a surprise?'

'You were expecting him, then.' Is that jealousy I hear in his voice?

'No. When I realised I'd forgotten to arrange a lift for them, Carolina said she'd sort something out. Miguel was doing me a favour.'

'But you know him, that was obvious.'

'Reid, he's just a friend who stepped in to do me a favour. Why are you quizzing me?'

'Have you been seeing him while I was away? Has he been to your house?'

'What business is it of yours?' I demand, angrily.

He pulls the car into a space a few metres away from the entrance to the courtyard. I notice that there's still a light on in Maria's kitchen.

'Because when I saw you two together, I wondered if that is what this morning was all about.'

I push my head back against the headrest, expelling a sigh that comes from deep within me. 'Reid, I'm tired and I can't do this right now.'

'But he's been here?' he asks, turning to face me and watching for my reaction.

'Once, yes, briefly but I didn't invite him.'

'And yet he came,' he replies, sounding angry now.

I'm speechless. It sounds like an accusation. Does that make Reid feel better about his decision to reconcile with Beatriz? Is this a way of appeasing his conscience?

Then a horrible thought pops into my head. Does Reid think he can live a sham of a life with Beatriz and turn to me for comfort and support whenever he needs it? I'm in danger of saying something I'll regret if I don't stop this now.

'Reid, thank you for the lift, but forgive me, I'm very tired and you must be, too.' With that, I open the car door and ease myself out. 'I'll see you at the gallery tomorrow, goodnight.'

Walking away from him, I don't look back. But even when I reach the front door and slide the key into the lock, Reid still hasn't started the engine. It's so quiet, so peaceful, and yet I've never felt so jaded and on edge. After the mistake with the car, this is another step in the wrong direction. I'm no one's property and I can't be bought, but I didn't for one moment think Reid was that kind of man. Did he think I'd settle for whatever attention he was willing to give me?

Two minutes later, there's a light tap on the door and I pause for a second to steel myself, before swinging it open. But it isn't Reid, it's Maria, carrying a little casserole dish, wrapped in a thick cloth.

'I've been listening out for you. I made some of your favourite *pastéis de bacalhau* in case you were hungry.'

'Come in and thank you, Maria, that was so thoughtful of you.'

She follows me into the kitchen and places the casserole dish on the chopping board. It's obvious that I'm upset and in no mood to eat.

'Can I ask how it went tonight?' she asks, hesitantly.

'Everyone enjoyed it, so yes, it went well,' I say, indicating for her to take a seat.

'And yet you are not happy?'

I shrug my shoulders, too dejected to speak.

'Was there an upset? Or is this something to do with your visitor this morning?' she enquires, gently.

It's out of character for Maria to probe, but how can I talk to her about this given the delicacy of the situation?

'Not really. I'm not involved with two men, Maria, but I know how it looks. Miguel is the friend of a friend, no more than that. He's lonely, looking for something to fill his life because he's a little lost at the moment.'

'And the other man?'

I can't look her in the eyes. 'He's not married. He was, but he's divorced.'

Her brow lifts a little. 'It happens. It is sad.'

Well, that wasn't the reaction I was expecting.

'But he and his ex-wife have a daughter, and even though they no longer love each other, it's never really over is it? The connection might not be the same, but they fit together, and I can see that.'

'But if two people make each other unhappy, what good does it serve living a lie? How do you mean "fit together", I do not understand?'

'She has family connections that help him in his work.'

'Ah, business. That is a different type of partnership. Do not confuse the heart with the head, Seren. It is not a sin to grab happiness. If no one gets hurt, then surely the world is a better place, yes? There is too much hate. It's what I believe.'

She leans on the table to pull herself up from the chair.

'But what if two people want different things?' I look up at her, frowning.

'If both hearts say it is right, then they will find a way.'

I stand to follow her out and she stops, turning around to face me.

'When my son told me that he had fallen in love with someone, I was thrilled. Then he explained that she was not of the Catholic faith and she had been married before. It was not what I had expected for him. They had a simple wedding and before he was taken from us, she made him truly happy. Would I change anything? No. And I have Luis, who grows more like him every day. And a daughter-in-law who is also my best friend. That is what matters and I am grateful to God for the blessings he has bestowed upon me. Decide what is right for you, Seren, then make peace with your decision.'

* * *

'Are we all set? Everything looks good, including us,' I laugh, as Antero, Carolina and I stand nervously awaiting the first arrivals. It's party time, but I will be glad when tonight is over.

Antero is looking very smart indeed and Carolina, who has the height and the figure of a model, is wearing a gorgeous, floral print dress in muted shades of green and lemon.

Feeling a little self-conscious, I smooth my hands down over the seams of my figure-hugging, burnt orange halter-top dress and wonder if I should have gone for something simpler. Cascading down from the clasp at my hairline, a line of ruffles end at the hem, which is mid-calf length and is more dramatic than I'm used to. When I bought it, I thought it would boost my confidence, but tonight I'm not sure I can carry it off after what happened yesterday. Then, having spent a couple of hours with Mum and Judi this morning, it was hard to switch back into work mode. And the truth is that I'm dreading seeing Reid. My emotions are all over the place still, but somehow I must put my feelings to one side because it's supposed to be a celebration.

'Tonight the gallery will really come alive,' Antero remarks, unable to take his eyes off Carolina. It's wonderful to finally see them a little more relaxed around each other in public. It also marks the official end of our team venture, as well as any direct contact between Reid and myself.

'Were we expecting so many photographers to be outside?' I ask Carolina.

'The news about Rafael and Yolanda has created a lot of interest. Is she coming tonight?'

'Not as far as I'm aware,' I reply. 'But who knows?'

My phone rings and it's Filipe, asking if I can join him in the board-room, and I hurry over to the lift.

The moment I walk into the room Filipe looks up, smiling.

'Seren,' he hurries towards me and, to my surprise when I hold out my hand to shake, he grabs it in both of his, taking a moment to look me directly in the eye. 'We were just talking about the media coverage today. A crisis was averted and we all agree that you managed the situation perfectly.'

Behind him, Senhora Veloso, Senhor Portela, Reid and Bernadette are gathered around a laptop set at the end of the conference table.

'Come and have a look at a preview Rafael sent through of the still shots.'

'He isn't here yet?' I query, thinking that he's cutting it fine.

'Senhor Sequeira has confirmed that they are running late, but that Yolanda Abreu will be accompanying them.'

'Well, I'm sure the press outside will be delighted,' I reply, hoping the gossip doesn't steal the limelight from Rafael. 'These shots are amazing. It's hard to believe the models are still trainees. I can't wait to see the footage.'

'Has the date been set for Reid to do the voice-over?' Senhor Portela asks.

'Yes. The studio is booked, and we will have the full thing ready for the VIP premiere showing on Friday.'

'But aren't you on holiday next week?' he replies.

'Yes, but I'm leaving it in capable hands. Carolina will ensure that everything runs smoothly.' I'm purposely avoiding looking in Reid's direction and he's ominously quiet.

'Ah, yes, and that reminds me,' Senhora Veloso joins in. 'Filipe, it is time we offered Antero a permanent contract. His help has been invaluable, and as his work on this project is now complete, we need to get that sorted.'

If Antero were in the room, he would have to restrain himself from fist-pumping the air. His hard work isn't going to go unrewarded and I'm thrilled for him, but I won't spoil the surprise as I think Filipe will want to be the one to break the news.

Reid walks around the table, to stand next to me. 'And I hear that the soundtrack in the background while I'm doing the narrative, will be one of Yolanda's new recordings?'

If this is an attempt to get my attention, then it won't work. I give him the briefest of glances before looking away.

'Yes. Her music is wonderful. Thank you for suggesting it in the first place, Reid.'

I feel it's only right everyone is aware it was his idea, but I'm conscious that all eyes are on us.

'And Bernadette,' I add, taking the focus in another direction, 'what a triumph. The models' gowns were such a brilliant representation of Reid's incredible artwork.'

All eyes are back on the computer screen once more, as Filipe scrolls through the photos. Everyone seems content. That just leaves Rafael. But as it's obvious that he's madly in love with Yolanda, I'm not expecting any problems.

22

FEELING OVERWHELMED

'Seren,' Tomas waves out and I make my way across to him. The gallery is buzzing and the party is in full flow.

'Hello, Tomas. I hope you are having a good time.' He leans in to kiss my cheek, giving me a broad smile.

'We are. Let me introduce you to my wife, Marisa.'

The woman in front of me has a friendly demeanour and her eye contact is warm.

'Lovely to meet you, Marisa. I'm so glad you were able to come.'

For a brief second, I hesitate and am about to offer my hand when she steps forward and then throws her arms around me as if we are already friends. It's a pleasant surprise. Marisa is at least a foot shorter than Tomas and whereas he exudes a rather cool, professional vibe, she has a bubbly personality.

'I feel I already know you, Seren,' she exclaims. 'Leonor and Ana have talked about nothing else other than the fashion shoot since I arrived. It sounded amazing and I so regret I could not get away any earlier. Tomas springs things on me at the last moment and then he flies off, leaving me to it. And so I end up missing the event that everyone is talking about!'

Tomas begins to laugh, before bowing his head rather apologetically.

'It's all change for us now, but it will settle down my love, I promise. And when the video is ready, you'll be one of the first to see it.'

I feel like I'm interrupting a special moment between them, as he takes her hand and raises it to his mouth. He kisses her fingertips and it's rather touching that he doesn't care that we're surrounded by business acquaintances, as well as friends and family.

Marisa blushes, extracting her hand and giving him a knowing look.

'Seren,' she says, turning to look at me. 'Do you have time to escort me around the exhibition? I'm sure my darling husband has other things to attend to. Perhaps you could share with me your personal favourite in Reid's collection?'

'Of course. I'd be delighted, Marisa.'

She waves Tomas off and as soon as he steps away, she turns back to face me. 'He feels he can't leave my side, but I'm perfectly capable of doing my own thing. Besides, every two minutes someone calls out to him, which is frustrating as I'm here to see the exhibition, not listen to the endless chatter.'

As we wander off towards the stairs to the first floor, I lean in, conspiratorially. 'Well, I'm delighted to get away from the noise for a while,' I acknowledge. 'It's much quieter upstairs.'

'Tomas said you have not worked at the gallery for very long?' she enquires, sounding genuinely interested.

'A little over six months, now. The time has flown.'

'And you don't miss home?'

We stroll along the first-floor landing and then on into the main exhibition room. There are probably only about twenty people milling around as most are downstairs enjoying the buffet and refreshments.

'I did, at first, but my mum and my best friend are here for a week and it reminds me that they are only a plane ride away. Here you go, this is my favourite display, but I love them all, equally.'

Every piece features a bird and with more than thirty pieces of artwork, it's impossible to single out just one. From the intricate pencil drawings to the bold, colourful canvases where the brushstrokes seem quite crude up close, but as you step back you can appreciate the skill involved. The purple heron seems to draw Marisa's gaze.

'He's gorgeous, isn't he?'

She nods her head, as she takes a few moments to focus on the details. 'Have you ever seen Reid while he's working in his studio?' she asks.

It's funny how instinctively you know when someone is genuine and that you are going to get on with them. Marisa is one of those people.

'No. I caught him sketching once, but he wouldn't let me see what he was doing.'

She laughs and it's such a tinkling, happy sound. I wonder if that's why Tomas is so relaxed, because his home life keeps him grounded.

'He's very secretive. But when he's in the flow the ceiling could fall in and he probably wouldn't even glance up. Some things cannot be taught, they simply come from within.'

Before I have time to respond, Senhora Veloso approaches, waving to attract my attention.

'Ah, I should have guessed I would find you in here. Wonderful, isn't it, Marisa? Have you seen the main display and beautiful fabrics, yet?'

'No. This is our first stop.'

'I apologise for interrupting you then, but Filipe was hoping to have a quick word with Seren.'

'Of course. It was nice chatting, Seren. Hopefully, we can catch up later.'

'I do hope so, Marisa. Senhora Veloso, where will I find Filipe?'

'He is on the second floor looking at the plans for the extension to the shop. He promised he wouldn't keep you away from the party for very long,' Senhora Veloso smiles at me. 'And please, I keep forgetting to say you must call me Mara.'

As I walk off to find him, I'm rather touched by that gesture of friendship.

Sure enough, Filipe is tucked away behind the temporary screens that were erected to separate off the shop. A special display has been set up next door to showcase the fabrics and soft furnishings tied in with the exhibition. Surprisingly, there are more people up here than there are browsing around the artwork on the first floor.

He's poring over the architect's plans, his glass of wine on the makeshift table next to him, untouched.

'Ah, she found you! Marvellous. Please take a seat.'

Settling myself down opposite him, he seems very relaxed tonight.

'The directors and I have been talking with our investors and we have a little proposition to run past you, Seren. It seems that the general consensus is that the fashion shoot was an enormous success and one that people are already asking if we intend to repeat again in the future. What are your thoughts about that?'

I'm thrown, as that's the last thing I expected to hear. 'Hmm. Well, of course anything is doable, but it is a huge commitment in terms of man hours. And there's always the risk that if the tickets don't sell well, then it may not even be possible to recoup the costs, let alone make a profit. I think we were extremely lucky to attract three such prominent names, which undoubtedly drew the crowds.'

'Your concerns are duly noted, Seren. But we have been approached by a garment manufacturer here in Lisbon, who is prepared to underwrite the costs if we do something similar for them. That would entail a two-month-long exhibition, tied in with the photo shoot. It would be promoting a new, sustainable fashion label. Perhaps give this some thought, as the chances are that if we can repeat this success, our investors would consider making this an annual event. This would involve upscaling your team on a permanent basis, as together with the spring and winter exhibitions, you would be very busy indeed. Anyway, we can talk further about this after your holiday, but I wanted you to take some time to think it through at your leisure.'

'Thank you, Filipe. I will do that.'

'Success reaps many rewards, Seren. Continue on like this and I can see you joining our board of directors within a couple of years. Now, go and enjoy yourself, you've earnt it.'

As I walk away, I can't even begin to process this turn of events. This wasn't what I signed up for at all.

I hurry over to the lift when, to my horror, the doors slide open and out step Reid, Beatriz and three other people who are all chatting and laughing. I'm not even sure they spot me, as I veer to the left and begin descending the large, spiral staircase until I'm out of view. As I slow down, my heart is racing, and I stop to catch my breath and survey the party goers on the ground floor.

So many things could have gone wrong and yet here we are, all expectations have been exceeded. But it's never enough. Now it looks like we're going to do it again and every year I suspect it will be bigger and better. Why am I not feeling inspired by that thought?

I hear a cough behind me and I do a half-turn, to apologise for hogging the handrail, which is essential when you are wearing heels.

'Sorry,' I continue on down, but the man increases his pace to walk alongside me.

'It's Seren Maddison, isn't it? A fellow Brit, I hear,' he says, pointedly.

'Yes.'

'Congratulations. I was at the Cristo Rei last night. What an amazing evening. I don't know if you work exclusively for the gallery but, uh...' His hand disappears into his pocket and he withdraws a wallet, extracting a business card and handing it to me. 'I'd love to talk sometime. My name is Jeff. No strings attached, but maybe we could chat over dinner whenever you're free. Just give me a call.' He extends his hand and we shake, briefly.

'I'll bear that in mind.'

The moment we hit that last step I turn to him, smile politely to excuse myself and then hurry away in the opposite direction, only to see Reid striding towards me. I'm a little disconcerted, as he must have turned straight around to take the lift back down in order to waylay me. He greets me as anyone watching would expect, a brief kiss on each cheek, but he can see I'm uncomfortable.

'We haven't had a chance to talk and I'm sorry about that. I didn't want to intrude today as I know how special it is for you to spend time with your visitors. But I can't—'

'Reid, I'm just going to smile as I'm sure there are lots of people looking in our direction. I hope you're pleased with the way everything has turned out. I know I am.'

His eyes seem to bore into mine, as if he can't believe what he's hearing. 'Pleased? It's been a phenomenal success and you can see that for yourself. I don't think anyone expected how quickly this would take off, but it has. If Jeff is trying to snare you for his company, then there will be others, but you can trust Filipe. He's a man with principles and he isn't easily swayed. Don't get sucked into the hype people like Jeff will be bombarding you with.'

Does he think I'm that easily persuaded that this will go to my head and I'd leave the gallery?

'I will bear that in mind, thank you.'

'Why are you being so cold to me? Don't you know that it's agony for me being here and towing the line, when all I want to do is grab your hand and head for the door?'

'We both know that isn't possible, Reid.'

Before he has a chance to answer, I spot Tomas striding towards us with Beatriz in tow. They're engaged in conversation as they walk, and as I glance at Reid, I see a fleeting look of desperation in his eyes.

'We've been looking for you both. The speeches are about to begin,' Tomas calls out.

'We must talk, Seren, and soon,' Reid whispers, leaning in to me. Instinctively, he begins to reach out his right hand to touch my arm, then realises what he's doing and withdraws it quickly. Half-turning to face Beatriz as she closes in, I shuffle backwards, away from Reid as it's obvious she intends to step into the space between us. I don't let her see that I'm annoyed, instead I smile pleasantly at Tomas.

'Perhaps you can help Tomas look for Marisa, Seren. She finds business talk a little boring,' Beatriz remarks, without even looking at me. Her eyes are firmly on Reid.

I muster the biggest smile I can as I look up at Tomas, and as we walk away, he grins at me.

'Beatriz and Marisa don't get on,' he informs me, his voice low. 'Life is about to get very interesting.'

I have no idea at all what he means. 'My mother always says that life would be boring if we were all the same.'

He grimaces. 'Personally, I'd prefer a little less drama, but I know my place.'

'Me too,' I murmur, not realising it was loud enough for him to hear, until he starts laughing.

I glance behind me briefly and see that Beatriz has already dragged Reid away. As they head towards the podium on the other side of the hall, she appears to be talking at him, rather than to him. He looks totally disinterested, like a lost soul.

This isn't quite the ending I'd imagined for this journey Reid and I have taken together. I thought that maybe tonight we'd be stealing glances over the heads of other people, happy to think that the pressure would be off. Instead, this marks a parting of the ways.

23

THE END SIMPLY HERALDS A BRIGHT NEW BEGINNING

Mum and Judi look up in awe at the rear of the villa, admiring the angular architecture and it's clear this wasn't at all what they were expecting. Their reaction mirrors my own, the day Reid first brought me here. I unlock the gate and then lead them around the side of the property and out onto the patio at the front. They stand beside me, rendered speechless as they gaze out over the ocean.

But my eyes are elsewhere. I, too, am unable to speak because I'm in total shock as I stare at the kestrel, my kestrel. He sits off to one side, mounted on a stone plinth set in front of the courtyard wall, the bougainvillea cascading down behind him. It's a perfect setting, but I can't believe Reid gave him away to a friend. A favour for a favour? I wonder angrily.

'I don't think I have ever seen anything as spectacular as this, Seren,' Judi remarks, turning to look at me. 'What's wrong?'

The smile on Mum's face is instantly wiped off, as they both hurry over to me.

'The kestrel. It's... my sculpture.'

'Oh, how wonderful! You sold a piece?' Judi asks excitedly, as she links arms with Mum and they head over to look at it close up.

'Darling, this is amazing. Truly amazing!' Mum blurts out, a hand flying up to her face in delight.

'No. Not exactly a sale.'

They look at each other, puzzled, but how do I explain what this means? I can't, so I grit my teeth, raise a smile and tilt my head in the direction of the front door.

'The entrance is around here. You wait until you see inside. The master bedroom is upstairs and there are two guest bedrooms on the ground-floor. Come on, let's crack open a bottle of wine.'

My heart is in tatters. That little bird might be made of cold metal, but every tiny little piece of him was made with love. Did Reid think he was doing me a favour; hoping the guests of his rich friend would see it here and be inspired to think about commissioning a piece? Setting aside the emotional aspect, this creation was art for art's sake, not art for money. No one would be prepared to pay what it cost in time to make it and that was the whole point. Which Reid totally missed and that's what breaks my heart.

As I show Mum and Judi around, I'm on autopilot and do my best to hide just how upset I'm feeling. It wouldn't be fair to spoil their visit when it's the only thing helping to keep me going. My whole world is collapsing inwards and each breath I take is laboured, as my emotions threaten to take over.

'Your father and I have been lucky enough to stay in some wonderful villas around the world, but I can honestly say that this is amongst the most special, Seren. The attention to detail is phenomenal. Every view has been carefully positioned, every angle has a purpose. Contemporary properties sometimes feel slightly clinical to me. I know clean lines and shiny surfaces are popular, but you know me. I'm used to a sprawling farmhouse and I love a little history to a property. But this isn't space created just for the sake of making it luxurious, if you know what I mean. It was designed to be a home.'

I laugh, hoping she doesn't pick up on the jaded tone of my voice. 'It's just an investment property, Mum, like the other villas on this clifftop. They don't even rent it out, so it stands empty most of the year.'

'Oh,' Judi walks over to join Mum and me as we look out of the patio doors in the kitchen. 'That's a shame. But luckily for us, you know the owner.'

I shake my head. 'No. I know a friend of the owner.'

'Well, you are mixing in the right circles, girl. I wasn't expecting your life here to be so glamorous. I mean, from an exhibition centre in Wales where the most exciting thing to happen was the annual wedding fair, to this... mixing with the rich and famous.'

'You have rather been underselling your achievements, Seren,' Mum joins in and I note the worried look that is now dominating her expression. She knows something is very wrong.

'Okay, I can see how it looks, but, seriously, the work I'm doing over here is no different than it was for an exhibition selling bathrooms and kitchens. You've only witnessed the glitzy, over-the-top bit, as it was a special celebration. The partying is now behind us. The gallery attracts all sorts of visitors and most can't afford to buy even the least expensive pieces, but that doesn't stop them enjoying the exhibitions. This here, is just an example of what the privileged few enjoy.'

Mum and Judi exchange an awkward glance.

'Right, um... shall we bring in our bags and get settled before we open the wine?' Judi asks, diplomatically.

'Yes, let's do that,' Mum replies, holding her hand out for the keys. 'We'll leave you to get yourself sorted,' she adds.

Handing over the fob, they make a quick exit and seconds later I watch them strolling past the patio doors in front of me. They are so deep in conversation they don't even realise I'm watching them. This isn't the best start, but I'm determined not to slide any further into that bubble of self-pity and the 'why me?' syndrome.

I race upstairs, taking them two at a time and head straight into the en suite, next to the master bedroom. Once inside, I perch on the edge of the stone, egg-shaped bath and make the call.

'Seren, I wasn't expecting to hear from you today. Are you at the beach?'

'Yes, Reid. We're here at the villa.'

'Is everything okay?'

'Mum and Judi love it, and I wanted to say thank you.' It's harder than

I thought it would be to sound blasé and detached. My anger is so close to the surface that I have to choke it down. Ironically, Reid sounds happy this morning. And if that's the case, then I'm fine with it.

'Thank me for what? It's yours to use as you want for the summer.'

'When we leave, I'll pop the keys back through the door. Both sets. I'll leave the car parked up in the garage.'

'What's going on?' His words explode down the line, making me wince.

'I know you meant well, Reid. But it was wrong of me to go along with it all. I'm sorry if you can't understand the why, or the fact that loving someone doesn't mean everything will work itself out.'

'But I deserve to be given a chance, Seren. You can't walk away as if you don't care because I know that you do. I thought I explained that there was a lot to sort out and I'm doing just that. Some of the decisions are mine alone, but others aren't, and that requires negotiation. I'm doing everything for you.'

Now he's gone too far. Sorting out a cosy and quiet, family life with Beatriz is nothing to do with me.

'No, Reid. Don't try to make me feel guilty. Your life is where it is because of the decisions you made, and the ones you chose not to make in the past. I haven't asked you to do anything for me.'

The silence between us is deafening.

'Did you really just say that?' he bellows down the line. 'I'm simply trying to prove how much I love you by putting my life in order.'

And what, encouraging your friends to support an unknown sculptor because it's all about who you know? Does Reid think that if I become successful, I will be eternally grateful to him? Will he expect me to hover in the background while Beatriz is the woman on his arm at every cocktail party and event, supporting him? Then, whenever he can slink away, we grab those elicit moments together that make it all worthwhile. Well, that's not who I am and I'm shocked that it reflects his true nature, unfazed by the thought of living a fake life.

'This has all been a huge mistake, Reid, and I'm done with it.'

I press end call, my hands shaking. It takes me a while to compose myself and after splashing a little icy-cold water onto my face, I stare back at myself in the mirror.

'It would only hurt more, further down the line,' I say out loud. It's time to face facts and get over it. From the beginning, he was treating me more like a mistress, than a partner. Why didn't I see that?

Walking out onto the patio, Mum and Judi look up and I give them the warmest smile I can muster.

'Where's the wine?'

'Oh... we were waiting for you to join us. I'll sort that out now.' Judi jumps up, diplomatically heading back inside as Mum pats the seat next to her.

'What's going on, my darling? I can see that it's tearing you apart and you are barely holding it together.'

I slump down into the seat.

'Everything and nothing, Mum.' Where do I begin?

'Don't be cross, but Judi said there was a man you were seeing? I don't know any more than that, but whatever has happened has had a devastating effect.'

'Yes, there is... *was*, someone. We fell into a relationship, even though it was obvious from the start that it wasn't going to work. I couldn't sleep last night, and I found an article online written by a relationship expert. Did you know that women tend to go for a similar type of man as their father, even if they've had a bad father/daughter relationship?'

She raises her eyebrows in surprise. 'This man is like your father?' She sounds appalled.

'No. The differences between them are huge. He has a good heart. He's kind and generous, even though he is successful. And affluent. He works hard and... it's difficult to explain. I thought he was searching for a woman who would be by his side for the rest of his life. His ex-wife helped build his success, but the love isn't there. That doesn't stop him needing her more than me, but for all the wrong reasons.'

'He's in love with you and you're in love with him?'

'I thought so, but now I have my doubts whether any of it was real.'

Mum's eyes search my face, looking for clues. 'And what did this expert have to say?'

'That our gut instinct is to look for the traits we admire, then live in the hope that we can fix the man we choose to spend our lives with to make the relationship work. We are each in love with a person who doesn't exist because we want different things. But it's not just that. I'll never settle for anything less than total commitment; I'd rather end up alone than feeling betrayed.'

Mum reaches over to rest her hand on mine. 'Oh, my dear girl. You deserve a man who understands what it is to truly love someone. I couldn't bear for you to settle as I did, and end up miserable. I can see how painful this is, but I'm proud of the strong young woman you have become. It took me a long time to grab my freedom and it's liberating. You inspired that, my darling.'

I heave a weary sigh as Mum withdraws her hand.

'We all kid ourselves at times, don't we? But let's enjoy our two nights here. I guess I only saw what I wanted to see, but now it's time to face the truth. The villa is rented for the summer, but the car was a present for my birthday. I wasn't happy accepting it in the first place, but when you think you're in love with someone you don't listen to your head. I just rang him and said I'll be leaving the car here when we head back to Lisbon, I'll arrange for a rental car to be delivered and then it's over.'

'Seren, you poor thing. I can imagine how horrified you were when he gave you a car and how puzzled he must have been at your reaction to his gesture.'

'I felt he was trying to buy my love, Mum. I didn't want to believe he was like that. And that's what really hurts. He made a fool of me, of my feelings for him.'

'I can understand that, darling. Did it hit you suddenly, today, now that the pressure has lifted and you have time to relax?'

'No. It was the kestrel.'

'What?'

'It was my gift to Reid, but he just gave it to his investor friend to display it here. No doubt thinking people would see it and that it would generate some business for me.' My tone is bitter.

'Ah, now I understand. But the artist? Seren, did you not stop for one moment to consider what you were walking into? It represents everything you hated about your old life. Unless your own plans have changed? If that's the case, there's no need to be afraid of that if it's for the right reasons.'

We hear a noise of glasses tinkling together and turn to see Judi standing there with a tray in her hands. I have no idea what she heard, but I dash across to take it from her because she looks as if she might be about to drop it.

'R... Reid Henderson?' she stammers. 'Oh, Seren, what were you thinking?'

After a large glass of wine, everything seems a little less raw and Judi, being the staunch friend that she is, injects a little of her humour to lift our spirits. My pride is dented, but I will survive and it's time to draw a line under it all. This isn't the first big disappointment in my life, although I suspect that it is one that will take a while to get over and it's clear they can both see that.

'Well, leave me to tidy up these things,' Mum says. 'Afterwards I think I'll lie on the bed and have nap. What are you two going to do?'

'The pool is beckoning me,' Judi replies, tilting her head in my direction.

'Do you mind if I take a walk to clear my head? When I get back, I'll shower, change and wow you both with my culinary skills by preparing you an authentic Portuguese meal for this evening. I will return a new me, I promise.'

'Don't worry, lovely. We all make mistakes. It's how we bounce back that's important. Look at your mum, she's like a new woman.'

'I am, aren't I?' The little smile on Mum's face continues to grow. 'There's hope for us all,' she declares.

* * *

As I step down onto the sandy beach, I press the sun hat further down onto my head and bend to slip off my shoes. Instead of walking along the seashore, I turn to my right and the welcoming shade of the rocky cliffs towering above me. I'm wearing my favourite summery boho dress from Etsy which cost less than the price of a steak dinner. But I love it. It's a pale, turquoise blue maxi dress with a vintage floral fabric. The fitted, empire-line bodice has a paisley design and, below that, tiny white flowers run down to the hem, with pale green leaves and a touch of bright orange. This is the real me. And anyone who doesn't appreciate that, doesn't know who I am.

I find a little outcrop of low-level rocks and sit myself down to watch the water as it ebbs and flows. It's time to begin filling in the finer details of my five-year plan. What if I manage to achieve it earlier? That would be a bonus. Or should I hold out and increase my safety net?

Salaries are not as high in Lisbon as people might imagine, given the cost of living and that's one of the reasons why I opted to live in Almada, where the rent is cheaper. Each month I'm able to save some money, but not a huge amount. Perhaps I should consider producing smaller, more affordable sculptures and see if I can sell them. Is that something I even want to try? It's certainly an option if I want to fast-track my plan.

'You're hiding. I wasn't even sure it was you.' Reid's voice floats across on the breeze and I turn to look up at him.

'No. Just relaxing and being me.'

He's wearing jeans and a T-shirt, his feet are bare and I know how tortuous this is for him as he hates the way the damp sand sticks to his skin.

'Can I join you?'

'I don't own the rocks,' I reply quite casually.

'You knew I would come?'

'I hoped you wouldn't.'

'Am I destined always to disappoint you?'

'Do you want the polite response, or the truth?'

Reid stops to look at me for a moment and I chide myself for not jumping up and heading back to the villa. 'The truth, always.'

Now he's trying to score points, but it's too late for that.

'What I admire about my father is his strength and determination; what he's achieved coming from humble beginnings. What I loathe about him is that he thinks everyone can be bought. He bought my Mum a big house, thinking that was doing his bit to keep her happy. And she was miserable. What she wanted was his love and affection.'

'You compare me to him – someone you hate?'

I close my eyes, pushing my head back and my hat falls off. It skitters across the sand and Reid chases after it. When he brings it back to me, I look up at him, sadness overcoming me.

'We are who we are, Reid. Can't you see that?'

'Ask me to do anything and it's done. Anything at all.'

'Life doesn't work that way. You can't have it all, no matter how hard you try.'

'Just listen to me, please,' he holds up a hand in front of my face, his expression fixed. 'Beatriz and Tomas will run Reid Henderson Designs from the first of September. Tomas is moving his family back here and they will take charge of the house and, together with Beatriz, they will set up the art gallery and run an artists' retreat. Casa da Floresta will fulfil its true potential, at last.'

'Congratulations. If there is one thing that I wish for you, it's that. Your vision is about to come true, Reid.'

'I did it for us, Seren.'

Here we go again.

'No. You did it for you, Reid.'

'You think that walking away was easy?'

'From what?'

'From everything. I'm just one of the directors now. Tomas and Beatriz have an equal say and they're in charge of the business. They can over-rule me whenever they want.'

'What have you done?' My voice wavers, as our eyes meet.

'I've signed a contract. A maximum of twelve appearances a year at their request. All of my paintings are sold via the new company, including special commissions, but if, and when, I work is entirely up to me.'

'But if Tomas is going to be living at Sintra permanently, where will you live?' I ask, as I try to figure out what this means.

'Here, at the villa. I bought it for us, but I knew the moment I saw your reaction to the car that I couldn't tell you that. There were too many loose ends to tie up first. It was obvious that you were expecting something to go wrong. I knew that I had one chance to get it right and I didn't want to blow it.'

Getting back with Beatriz never was an option for Reid, I can see that quite clearly now. But maybe she hoped she could scare me away. For him, it was always more about his daughter and what was best for her, but my insecurities made me wonder whether he was still in love with Beatriz. I pushed him away because I was afraid of getting my heart broken, but now it's beating so fast it feels as if it's trying to leap out of my chest.

I bow my head a little as my emotions begin to overwhelm me. 'And that's why the kestrel is here,' I mumble.

'A little piece of your heart will always remain with me, no matter where you are. I was close to breaking down when you gave him to me, Seren. But I refused to give up hope, regardless of the cost. I knew it was from one of my drawings and I felt the love reflected in every little detail. It was then that I knew no price was too high, because my life would be nothing if you weren't in it. He represented the freedom I longed for; you were the one who spurred me on to make it happen.'

Turning my head, I look out to sea, as the enormity of what Reid has sacrificed for me makes my heart soar.

'The question is, Seren Maddison, what will you give up for me?' Reid reaches out to grab my hand and I turn to look at him, unable to speak. 'If you love me half as much as I love you, then you will hand in your notice at the gallery and come here, so we can make this our home. It's a huge compromise, I know. This isn't exactly the simple life and I can't pretend I'm walking away from the new arrangement a poor man. But if it was all about the money, then I'd have been mad to sign that contract. Is it enough to demonstrate that you are all I need in my life? I still want to be able to take care of you and money is only an evil if you put it before everything else.'

As the tears roll down my face, I realise that the relationship expert was wrong. And I was wrong, too. Reid represents all the good qualities of an honest man, trying to do his best for his ex-wife and daughter after his marriage fell apart. He lost his way and his inspiration, facing an unknown future, alone. If he had given the kestrel away, I could never have forgiven him, ever. But he didn't. He understood what it meant.

I stand and offer my hand to pull him to his feet.

'Promise me one thing,' I half-whisper as the birds overhead try their best to drown out my voice.

'Just name it.'

I swipe away the tears running down my cheeks, but they are quickly replaced, making me laugh. 'That every morning, you and I walk down here and take a few minutes to sit and reflect. No matter what life throws at us, this moment is the defining one. When the impossible happens. No one can change another person. People can only change themselves. You let go of your dream for me and I'll let go of my dream, for you. Together we'll create a new dream. I have no idea what that will be, Reid,' I smile at him. 'But it will be ours.'

He looks back at me, stepping in to touch my cheek and then plant his lips on mine, briefly. 'Who cares, as long as we're together?' he whispers, his voice touchingly hoarse. 'And we'll call our new home *A Vila dos Sonhos* – The Villa of Dreams.'

Reid wraps his arms around me, and we stand for a long time clinging onto each other. Then, reluctantly, he draws back to gaze down into my eyes.

'You rescued me from myself,' he whispers.

'We were two lost souls, Reid, and we rescued each other.'

As he smiles down at me, he tips his head back, takes a deep breath to fill his lungs with the salty air and then shouts out as loud as he can, 'I will love you forever, Seren Maddison.'

His words are caught up on the breeze and seem to echo around us both as we hug. And now I finally know what happiness means... *forever.*

ACKNOWLEDGMENTS

I'd like to give a virtual hug to my amazing editor and publishing director, Sarah Ritherdon, who is truly a pleasure to work with. You are a real inspiration!

Also, to my agent, Sara Keane – your support means the world to me.

And to the wider Boldwood team – a truly awesome group of inspiring women I can't thank enough for their amazing support and encouragement. The editing process is a long one and I'm eternally grateful to everyone who plays a part in polishing the manuscript to allow the story to sparkle.

As usual, no book is ever launched without there being an even longer list of people to thank for publicising it. The amazing kindness of my lovely author friends, readers and reviewers is truly humbling. You continue to delight, amaze and astound me with your generosity and support.

Without your kindness in spreading the word about my latest release and your wonderful reviews to entice people to click and download, I wouldn't be able to indulge myself in my guilty pleasure... writing.

Feeling blessed and sending much love to you all for your treasured support and friendship.

Lucy x

MORE FROM LUCY COLEMAN

We hope you enjoyed reading *The Villa of Dreams*. If you did, please leave a review.

If you'd like to gift a copy, this book is also available as an ebook, digital audio download and audiobook CD.

Sign up to Lucy Coleman's mailing list for news, competitions and updates on future books:

http://bit.ly/LucyColemanNewsletter

Explore more glorious escapist reads from Lucy Coleman.

ABOUT THE AUTHOR

Lucy Coleman is a #1 bestselling romance writer, whose recent novels include *Summer in Provence* and *A Springtime to Remember*. She also writes under the name Linn B. Halton. She won the 2013 UK Festival of Romance: Innovation in Romantic Fiction award and lives in the Welsh Valleys.

Visit Lucy's website: www.lucycolemanromance.com

Follow Lucy on social media:

facebook.com/LucyColemanAuthor
twitter.com/LucyColemanAuth
instagram.com/lucycolemanauthor
bookbub.com/authors/lucy-coleman

ABOUT BOLDWOOD BOOKS

Boldwood Books is a fiction publishing company seeking out the best stories from around the world.

Find out more at www.boldwoodbooks.com

Sign up to the Book and Tonic newsletter for news, offers and competitions from Boldwood Books!

http://www.bit.ly/bookandtonic

We'd love to hear from you, follow us on social media:

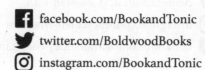

facebook.com/BookandTonic

twitter.com/BoldwoodBooks

instagram.com/BookandTonic

Lightning Source UK Ltd.
Milton Keynes UK
UKHW041807060223
416534UK00002B/125

9 781804 262221